I0820341

SAVING MACARTHUR

SAVING MACARTHUR

The Story of America's Most Daring Naval Rescue, and of the Men it Left Behind

RUDY TOMEDI

CASEMATE
Pennsylvania & Yorkshire

Published in the United States of America and Great Britain in 2025 by
CASEMATE PUBLISHERS
1950 Lawrence Road, Havertown, PA 19083, USA
and
47 Church Street, Barnsley, S70 2AS, UK

Hardcover Edition: ISBN 978-1-63624-562-1
Digital Edition: ISBN 978-1-63624-563-8

A CIP record for this book is available from the British Library

Printed and bound in the United States of America by Integrated Books International
Typeset in India by DiTech Publishing Services

For a complete list of Casemate titles, please contact:

CASEMATE PUBLISHERS (US)
Telephone (610) 853-9131
Fax (610) 853-9146
Email: casemate@casematepublishers.com
www.casematepublishers.com

CASEMATE PUBLISHERS (UK)
Telephone (0)1226 734350
Email: casemate@casemateuk.com
www.casemateuk.com

Cover image: A U.S. Navy PT boat patrolling off the coast of New Guinea, 1943. (U.S. Navy)

Contents

Author's Note

For invaluable assistance in locating source materials I would like to thank Allyson Bethune at the PT Boats Inc. museum and archives in Germantown, Tennessee; Rachel Barnett at the National Museum of the Pacific War in Fredericksburg, Texas; Candice Milburn of the Veterans History Project at the Library of Congress in Washington, D.C.; and Heather, Hilda, Phillip, and Cecilia, the extremely competent and ever cheerful staff at the Still Pictures Branch of the National Archives in College Park, Maryland.

Introduction

It was while I was researching an unrelated subject that the seeds were planted. I was looking through the June 10, 1942 issue of the *New York Times* when my attention was arrested by a full page of text and photos featuring a young naval lieutenant named John Bulkeley. Sitting with his wife in the back of an open touring car, Bulkeley was being treated to a New York ticker tape parade. Under confetti clouds, hundreds of thousands of people were cheering him in a display of unbridled adulation not seen since Charles Lindbergh returned from his solo flight across the Atlantic over a decade before.

The thirty-year-old Bulkeley was just back from the Philippines, where he had pulled off one of the most spectacular rescues in U.S. naval history by taking General Douglas MacArthur out of the besieged islands aboard a PT boat. MacArthur's escape from the Philippine death trap was front-page news not only in the U.S. but all over the world. America's most illustrious soldier had been a hair's breadth away from being killed or captured by the Japanese.

Hardly a week after reading the *Times* story, and quite by accident, I encountered John Bulkeley again, in Nigel Hamilton's biography of the young John F. Kennedy. In the book, Kennedy's former squadron commander is reminiscing about Kennedy's wartime service in PT boats when he abruptly starts talking about Bulkeley, whom he also knew well. "If MacArthur had traveled out of the Philippines by any other method," he told Hamilton, "you probably would never have heard of John Bulkeley. And that would have been a blessing. Bulkeley was really a joke to a lot of officers."

That jolted me. The most celebrated American hero since Charles Lindbergh, a joke?

I started poking around into archives and doing a few interviews and soon realized there was much more to the story of the "Great Escape" than the exploits of John Bulkeley. What I learned was that the story did not end with MacArthur's rescue. Seventy-one men of Motor Torpedo Boat Squadron 3 were left behind to endure the most incredible hardships, some as prisoners of war and others as guerrillas fighting in the Philippines, upholding America's honor in a land America had pledged and utterly failed to defend. For them, the rescue was not the end of something but only the beginning of a long night's journey into day. And as I soon found out, their story, at once inspiring and heartbreaking, was entirely lost to history.

I felt compelled to write about it. Especially after I realized that as a journalist I had already been to most of the places where the dramatic heart of the story unfolds—in the Philippines. That made it easy to visualize the action, and more importantly for me, to get a sense of history as lived experience—the actions, thoughts, and feelings of flesh and blood characters, people just as real and human as anyone you might meet on the street today.

A careful reading of numerous secondary sources showed them to be so consistently at odds with each other, in small details and large, that I have made a determined effort to use only primary sources—the letters, diaries, interviews, oral histories, and memoirs of the participants, as well as after-action reports and other official documents. Unfortunately, these too consistently contradict each other, often to an astonishing degree. Furthermore, Japanese records are invariably at odds with the American version. Perhaps this is only to be expected. Confusion is a given in war. Even in normal circumstances it is rare for any two people to come away from any dramatic incident with the same story. And of course there is the fallibility of human memory. Few people are gifted with total recall, and events and conversations recorded after the fact, even only days after, can be expected to diverge from each other.

Every effort has been made to reconcile the various personal accounts. Every detail of the book is accurate in so far as it was in my power to make it so. The conversations are, of course, recreated but in roughly the words the participants remember using. By both necessity and inclination, this is a synthesis, an attempt to use the texture and devices of a novel to capture the true spirit and meaning of an actual adventure, and to honor the courage and devotion of the men who participated in it, so that, though only in a small way, perhaps, they are not forgotten.

CHAPTER I

The Darkest Hour

It is not much more than three miles long, with a round bulbous head and a spiny body and a narrow twisting tail, and from high above the little island looks like a tadpole swimming out of Manila Bay into the white-capped blue waters of the South China Sea. Before the war that began on December 7, 1941, it was a strikingly beautiful place, serene and peaceful. The huge guns of the coast artillery were not in plain view and what the casual visitor saw was this: gently wooded slopes containing trees of every shade, from dark glossy olive to the palest lettuce green; neat wooden bungalows with screened porches set amid a riot of red hibiscus, white frangipani, yellow oleander, purple bougainvillea; a dusty road which curved and twisted as it climbed from a sleepy barrio at sea level to a wide plateau six hundred feet above the cliffs, where the real purpose of the place finally met the eye in the form of a three-story concrete barracks that stretched, fantastically, for over a quarter of a mile and fronted a vast parade ground where sharply turned-out soldiers drilled. But as if to soften Topside's starkly military appearance there was also a minute but sporty golf course nearby, a library, a cinema, and a beautiful old lighthouse from Spanish days. All around the plateau, in the officers' houses that nestled among the trees and flowering shrubs, the raucous cries of banana birds would wake the inhabitants to a fresh, breezy morning, quite unlike the suffocating heat and humidity of Manila, thirty miles across the bay.

Now, in March 1942, the fortress island of Corregidor was a nightmare landscape of shattered buildings, smoking shell holes and charred, splintered trees from which tiny green shoots sprouted like false hope. The golf course was cratered beyond recognition. The huge barracks was gutted, rubble everywhere and its walls streaked with black scorch marks. Corrugated iron roofing rattled in the breeze that soughed through its ruins. Scraps of paper seemed to be everywhere, loose pages from a thousand books blown apart by a bomb that demolished the library. The big coastal guns were now nakedly exposed: each exploding bomb stripped the branches in a wide area around the crater it made, instantly erasing the protective camouflage afforded by the trees. It was the dry season and dust eddied and whirled about eternally, to mix with the smoke of smoldering fires. Together, it made a permanent haze that blotted out the stars and paled the sun. But with everything around it blasted and burned and smashed, with gaping craters encircling it, the hundred-foot wooden flagpole still stood in the middle of the parade ground—and the Stars and Stripes, a bit tattered, still flew.

On the evening of March 11, just after dark, a small boat approached the island at idling speed. She was a motor torpedo boat, designed to be the fastest warship afloat, the racehorse of the seas, but this one was falling apart. She badly needed hull repairs and replacement parts. Her three once-powerful engines could barely produce half the rpms they had when new. There were only seven men aboard, when there should have been twelve, because room had to be made for the passengers awaiting her. The men were not in much better shape than the boat. They were exhausted from constant night patrols and lack of sleep, and with the reduced ration they had not had much to eat. A few weeks before, one of them had shot a stray cat which was then boiled for several hours and devoured in minutes. There had been no meat for weeks before that, and none since. No vegetables. No fruit. They were all stick thin. Several owned wristwatches with expandable bands and the watches would slide up and down their now muscleless forearms.

The man standing at the wheel under a thin moon, with the stars doubling themselves in the shimmering water around him, had no idea he was already a national hero. His name was John Duncan Bulkeley and he had command of four PT boats. Six weeks before, on January 19, while leading a two-boat attack on what was thought to be a large Japanese warship anchored in a bay along the northern coast of Bataan, Bulkeley had lost sight of his wing boat in the darkness and had proceeded to ignore Japanese signal challenges and probing machine gun fire to creep in alone and fire two torpedoes, one of which made a hot run in its tube and failed to clear. But the other was seen to explode about a minute after being fired—proof enough for this aggressive young officer to claim a hit and a probable sinking. Observers high on a mountain claimed to have seen the ship sink, though it was not a big one, and perhaps not even a warship. In the communique released by the Navy Department in Washington it became a small armed merchantman. But these were grim times for America, after the stinging defeat and humiliation of Pearl Harbor, and the public was desperate for good news. And they got it.

The communique was like the primer that is used to set off a much larger explosion. The news of the attack made huge headlines across the nation: a little mosquito boat manned by bold American sailors had sunk a Japanese warship many times its size. Actually, no ship had been sunk, or even hit, but this was not discovered until Japanese records were examined after the war. As far as the American public was concerned, the country had a new hero—a dashing young PT boat captain who was tearing up the Japanese navy.

Bulkeley didn't know, couldn't know as he stood intently at the wheel of PT 41, easing her toward a bomb-shattered dock in the dark, that his picture had been in all the stateside papers. He was eight thousand miles from home and sealed up behind an enemy sea blockade—no newspapers could reach him now, no magazines, no mail, only the occasional shortwave radio broadcast, which very few were privy to because of the near absence of receiving sets. And in any case, though there was a sense throughout the besieged garrison of the growing fame of the PT boats, the fact that it was focused largely on one man was not apparent in the radio broadcasts. But there he was, John Duncan Bulkeley at thirty, his name and face now as instantly recognizable to the people at home as that of any movie star.

It was not Bulkeley's war face, though, that Americans were looking at over their breakfast or while sitting in an armchair in the parlor after supper. The round boyish-tough face was masked now by a long, unruly beard, the blue-gray eyes bloodshot and red-rimmed, the face as a whole gaunt and drawn. Bulkeley had not been eating or sleeping any better than anyone else. Like his men, he was not in much better shape physically than his clanky, worn-out boats. But that's where the similarities ended. John Bulkeley had always been a hyperactive, hyper-aggressive man. His nervous energy was tremendous and never seemed to give out, even in the face of near starvation and the bleak hopelessness of certain defeat. Bulkeley was still producing plenty of rpms.

Especially now. Easing the 41 in toward the dark, looming mass of Corregidor, he knew he was bound for either everlasting glory or oblivion, making just about everything else irrelevant.

***

Ten days before, on the morning of March 1, he had received a telephone message from General Headquarters on Corregidor. Bulkeley's telephone was in a nipa hut, one of about twenty that made up a tiny barrio in Sisiman Cove, on the tip of the Bataan Peninsula. Bulkeley had moved his boats to the secluded inlet after being bombed out of the Cavite navy base early in the war. The Filipino families living in the huts moved out and Bulkeley's men moved in, without much enthusiasm. A nipa hut is basically a single room with a thatched roof and sides, up off the ground four or five feet on bamboo stilts. Spiders, centipedes, and rats live in the thatch and often come out at night to visit the human occupants. Mosquitoes enter freely through the windows which are no more than open spaces in the walls.

No one seems to remember who had the phone watch that morning. Whoever it was, he took the message to Bulkeley, who was out on one of the boats that were tied up to a rickety coconut-log pier. It was an order to report to North Dock.

Bulkeley thought: *In daylight?* He was not questioning the order, he simply thought it a bit strange. Japanese planes dominated the skies and had taken to pouncing on everything that moved, even rowboats. This was well known at General Headquarters, and so was the fact that it was now PT doctrine to run the boats only at night. But Bulkeley only shrugged. He roused the crew of the 41 boat, minus several men, as instructed, and they set off.

It was clear and hot when they arrived at the dock that morning, all guns manned and ready, everyone tense. There was only three miles of water between Bataan and Corregidor but it was an especially dangerous trip in daylight, for this was a stretch of water that was kept under constant observation by the Japanese. Imagine everyone's surprise, then, when they saw General Douglas MacArthur and his wife waiting for them: the tall, imperious General in pressed suntans and Jean MacArthur, a small woman with a big smile, in a tan pantsuit and round sunglasses beneath a white turban.

"Buck, I'd like you to take us for a ride out on the bay," the General said.

Bulkeley did so. Manila Bay was placid, the ride pleasant with four P-40s now overhead—the entire American air force in the Islands—to quell the fear of being jumped by Japanese strafers. At one point a shark's fin cut close above the water. The bay was full of them. But they were of no concern to anyone aboard PT 41 that morning.

Morris Hancock was up in the port gun turret, thinking: *What the hell is this about?* There had to be a reason for it, you don't go joyriding like this in the middle of a war. But he couldn't figure it out. It was a mystery, to him and to everyone else aboard.

The mystery seemed to be solved after Bulkeley deposited the General and his wife back on the dock. There, MacArthur presented Bulkeley with the Distinguished Service Cross, second only to the Congressional Medal of Honor. The old General shook the young naval lieutenant's hand, praised his exploits, and returned with his wife to Malinta Tunnel.

"It pays to know the right people," Bulkeley quipped, getting a laugh from his crew, most of whom were frankly relieved it was over and that they could go back to the relative safety of Sisiman Cove. None of them, Bulkeley included, had any idea that this little excursion out on the bay was actually a prelude to the sacrificial destruction of their squadron and the imprisonment and death of many of the men in it.

***

That night Bulkeley was again summoned across the water. He was to have supper with the General. Perhaps it was here, as he hopped off the 41 at North Dock in the dark and climbed into the General's battered Chrysler, that he began to suspect something big was up.

Only a faint bluish-green light came from the painted headlamps, and the eerie glow did not extend more than three feet in front of the car. MacArthur had been living and working in the big tunnel under Malinta Hill, breathing the bad air like everyone else in that fetid, overcrowded concrete tube, dust sifting down onto his desk and onto him each time a bomb or a shell shook the ground above, the reverberating impacts a reminder of how trapped and helpless he was, his entire command locked now in a death struggle. But the commanding general had certain prerogatives, one of them being an evacuated officer's house a few minutes' walk from the tunnel entrance. There MacArthur could have some privacy, the one thing no one had inside the teeming tunnel. The house was completely defenseless from shelling, since there was no warning except the whistle of the shells themselves just before they hit. Yet, miraculously, after all the weeks of bombardment, it had not been touched.

The Chrysler stopped in front of the house. The dark form of a mango tree loomed on the small lawn, and Bulkeley walked past it, up to the porch where MacArthur and some of his staff were waiting. A flurry of saluting, a cordial welcome from the General, and Bulkeley was shown inside.

In one room a small lightbulb hung on a long cord. A black cloth funneled the light onto a small area in the center of a table set with china and silverware. The meal was rice with wheat germ in it, canned sauerkraut, and Vienna sausages. Nothing special for anyone on Corregidor but a feast for Bulkeley, the smell of the hot food instantly taking hold in his stomach like a pair of powerful hands. Shelling had been intermittent all day and occasionally a round would trundle in, shrieking over the roof to explode nearby as Bulkeley stuffed his shrunken stomach with sauerkraut and weiners while trying not to be too obvious about it.

When the meal was over, MacArthur asked Bulkeley to take a short stroll with him. Away from the others, he gave Bulkeley the momentous news.

"I'm leaving, Buck. I have been ordered to Australia by the president. Things have gotten to such a point that I must comply with those orders or get out of the army. My own preference is to go to Bataan and die there, fighting the Japanese, but that is being denied me."

MacArthur made no attempt to hide his dismay at being ordered to desert his men—and in their hour of need.

"There will be about twenty people in the evacuation party," he went on. "If we can get to Mindanao by boat, planes from Australia can pick us up there and fly us the rest of the way. Buck, do you think your boats can take us through the Japanese blockade to Mindanao?"

Bulkeley realized now the real reason for the morning's excursion out on the bay. Like any caring husband, MacArthur wanted to be sure his wife had no objection to riding the boats. The placid bay was a poor example of what they would face on the storm-tossed open sea, but Bulkeley carefully avoided mentioning this.

"Wouldn't it be safer if you went to Mindanao by submarine, or by air?" he asked.

"No, the Japanese will expect me to leave like that and will make every effort to intercept me. They won't be expecting me to make the breakout by PT boat. Besides, I have great faith in you and your boys."

We will never know if Bulkeley appreciated the essential absurdity of what MacArthur was telling him. The Japanese *were* expecting the General to make a run for it, and their surface and air patrols could detect the PT boats, with their thunderous engines and enormous wakes, much more easily than a submarine or an airplane. It was the absolute worst way to go.

As the two men walked a shell shrieked over. The explosion shook the ground beneath their feet.

"Well, Buck, do you think you can get us down to Mindanao?"

Unhesitatingly, Bulkeley answered, "General, it'll be a piece of cake."

Nothing could have been further from the truth. His four remaining boats were in no condition for a sea run of almost six hundred miles. They were so worn out that any Japanese destroyer could easily overtake them. The odds of one or more of the boats breaking down were high. Getting lost was a distinct possibility; none of the boats was equipped with a pelorus and so navigation would be by compass and dead reckoning. To make the run each boat would have to carry extra fuel, and the only place for it was in fifty-five-gallon drums strapped to the open deck. PT boats ran on the same super-flammable high-octane gasoline used in airplanes and one stray bullet or hot piece of shrapnel could turn a boat into an inferno, instantly incinerating everyone aboard.

But it was simply not in Bulkeley's nature to equivocate. Either he could do something or he couldn't. Add to that a very low threshold of fear and the kind of blind confidence that makes a man believe he can pull off just about anything and you have someone who can sincerely call a near-suicidal mission a piece of cake. Unfortunately, a man like that often takes others with him into the abyss, mere mortals who can see with terrifying clarity where they're going.

There were eighty-three officers and men in Bulkeley's squadron and unlike the rest of the trapped garrison they had a way out. In fact, the plan had already been submitted by Bulkeley and approved by the higher powers: when their gas was down to what they could carry on their decks they would make a run for the China coast, destroy the boats, and hike overland to Chungking. From there American planes could fly them back to the States. And getting these men home was far and away the best thing to do with them. They were the first crews to take PT boats into combat, in effect creating PT doctrine where none had existed, and they would be invaluable in any future training program. Home was where they could best be of use.

But getting home was now out of the question. The remaining gas needed for the squadron's own escape would now be used to serve the General. Once in Mindanao they would not have enough to go back. To the south the Japanese controlled everything as far as Australia, so they could not go forward either. With no hope of escaping, the men of Squadron 3—like the rest of the Americans on the besieged islands—faced death or capture at the hands of the enemy.

***

The four boat crews and the twenty or so evacuees accompanying the General are a grim bunch on this March evening. As the other three boats are picking up their passengers elsewhere Bulkeley steers the 41 carefully up to North Dock. Figures appear in the darkness. Sidney Huff, MacArthur's young aide, helps the General's wife aboard, stumbling a little on the charred timbers. Ah Cheu, the Chinese nanny, steps aboard. Arthur, the General's four-year-old son, hops on, clutching Old Friend, his stuffed panda. Bulkeley himself carries MacArthur's baggage onto the boat.

The General is the last to board. He stands on the deserted pier, his back to the boat, as he takes a long last look at the scene of his crushing defeat. Pause for a moment, as he is doing, and consider the humiliation he must be feeling.

Pride sits in this man like an anvil. He is America's most illustrious soldier, he had been brought down hard, and standing now amid the rubble in his worn khakis he looks like a grizzled old man, spindly and forlorn. His face is dead white, and there is a twitch, a kind of tic, at the corner of his mouth.

It is the darkest hour of his life. And the only hope that things will get any better lay squarely in the hands of a highly strung, wildly impulsive young man less than half his age, and about whom the General knew actually very little.

CHAPTER 2

Born for the Sea

There was never any question in John Bulkeley's mind that he would become a naval officer. He was aware from a very early age that one ancestor, Charles Bulkeley, had been second officer in the *Bonhomme Richard* under John Paul Jones and that another, Richard Bulkeley, had served as a seaman aboard HMS *Victory* under Horatio Nelson at the Battle of Trafalgar. His father had been an ordinary seaman in the U.S. Navy who had spent almost five months of his enlistment in a hospital bed recovering from typhoid fever contracted in Panama. Not much glamor there, but the father's stories of his life at sea must have been quite colorful, for the young boy never tired of listening to them. On many nights John would fall asleep clutching a book containing pictures of sailing schooners. From another book he taught himself how to navigate by the stars. At the age of twelve, to his sharp delight, his father managed to get him a berth as an ordinary seaman aboard a Columbia Steamship Lines freighter, and for three successive summers he traveled the high seas, mainly in the Caribbean, where he found out what ordinary seamen really do. He scraped rust, painted bulkheads, swabbed decks, cleaned the heads, scrubbed the chiefs' quarters, and at every port of call wrestled desperately with hawsers as thick as his leg. For all this he was paid a dollar a day. He would never admit it to his much older shipmates, who tended to grouse about the work, but he would have done it for free.

John Bulkeley grew up pugnacious and would box with anyone just for fun. In high school he played football and was elected captain of the wrestling team. One day, to win a five-dollar bet, he lay on his back on a trackbed and let a train run over him. A steam engine was pushing a string of boxcars ahead of it and he knew they would pass over him if he lay perfectly flat. He rolled out from under the boxcars just before the engine reached him. A week later he repeated the feat, simply on a dare. "He seemed almost immune to fear," a classmate remembered. It was not the last time someone was to make that observation.

At Hackettstown High School in New Jersey he earned satisfactory grades without being overly studious—satisfactory in the sense that he thought they were good enough to get him into the U.S. Naval Academy. For him, it was as though no other institution of higher learning existed. And in a sense, after his junior year, none did. On October 24, 1929, the stock market crashed. John's father was wiped out. He lost his business, then his house. Luckily, he also had a farm, bought during the fat years of the golden bubble and by now completely paid for. The family retreated there, father, mother, and son, where Fred Bulkeley grimly told them, "As long as we can raise our own food, we won't starve to death."

No one starved, but there was very little money, and certainly none for college. But the Naval Academy was free and that meant John's dream of going there was still intact. He was, however, faced with an enormous obstacle. Before sitting for the entrance examinations, candidates for the academy must be appointed by a United States senator or representative, and John's father knew no high-level politician he could buttonhole to get an appointment for his son. The father was in fact a broken man, unable to get his mind off his catastrophic losses, hating what had happened to him but seeing no possibility of doing anything about it. Resigned to disappointments, he flatly told the boy he had better forget about Annapolis.

But John was determined to get into the Naval Academy, and he decided to go to Washington and twist some arms among the members of Congress until someone gave him a recommendation.

His father thought this was hopelessly ridiculous and said so. "Besides," he added sourly, "you don't have the money to get there." John was prepared to beat his way there in a boxcar. Seeing him packing a bedroll, knowing she could not stop him, Elizabeth Bulkeley took her husband aside and persuaded him to sell off a few head of cattle to pay for the trip.

So here he is, arriving by train in Washington, the boy from a New Jersey farm, seventeen years old and with a fresh haircut that advertised the barber (his father) as an amateur, his round boyish-tough face set with untouristlike determination. He is here to get something done and so the grand monuments and museums and cherry trees of the capital go unvisited. From the day of his arrival, and all day every day for three weeks, he tramps the halls of Congress in his ill-fitting brown suit and worn black shoes, knocking on the office doors of one legislator after another and never getting beyond the secretaries and receptionists. The boy has only enough money for meals (Washington restaurants were then offering a meal of half a fried chicken, bread, butter, and coffee for twenty cents), and so he spends his nights sleeping on a courthouse lawn opposite police headquarters, with Washington's unemployed all around him, washing up at a public fountain as they do and paying fifteen cents every second day to shower at a YMCA (he only needs to shave once a week). Each night his brown suit lay neatly folded on the grass beside him. Miraculously, it does not rain.

Representative Morgan G. Sanders of the Third District of Texas was a big, bluff, hearty man fond of a joke or a good story. He was also a man in an awkward predicament: all of his district appointees had flunked the entrance examinations for both the Naval Academy and the Military Academy at West Point. When his secretary came in to tell him there was a persistent and rather scruffy-looking young man from New Jersey wanting to see him about a congressional appointment to Annapolis, Morgan Sanders decided it wouldn't hurt to talk to the boy, if only to set him straight.

The teenager sat in a chair on the other side of the big desk, looked the veteran politician in the eye and told him what he was doing in Washington, where he was staying, how he was living. As Sanders sat there listening, he had the impression there were not many people who could intimidate him. He was about to tell John that he wasn't going to find anyone in Congress not representing his state or home district who could do anything for him when the young man happened to mention that his father owned some land in Texas. The property turned out to be in Sanders's district. It was just a few acres of sagebrush Fred Bulkeley bought in the twenties, advertised in *Field and Stream* as investment property. With the Depression you could not get a nickel an acre for it, but it allowed Sanders to do a little finagling and make John an instant Texan, so to speak, after which Sanders appointed him to Annapolis from his district.

John breezed through the entrance exams. Back at the farm he received his notification of acceptance and in June, 1930, John Bulkeley entered the United States Naval Academy as a plebe.

***

It was the shock of his life. It was common among plebes even then to surreptitiously scratch the initials IHTP (I Hate This Place) or sometimes IHTFP on desktops and baseboards in a muted reaction to the sadistic hazing they were made to endure at the hands of upperclassmen. A plebe was a man in his first year at the Academy, and the hazing allegedly weeded out those who were physically or psychologically incapable of standing up to the pressures of military stress. But as Bulkeley saw it, the savagery had nothing to do with turning out first-rate naval leaders.

What happened to him on Hundredth Night was simply a more draconian version of the hazing he endured all through his plebe year. Hundredth Night marked one hundred days before graduation of first classmen. On this night it was traditional for small groups of firsties to form "tribunals of sea lords," the tribunals then competing with each other in inflicting pain and humiliation on plebes. Bulkeley was singled out by a particularly sadistic threesome of first classmen (all would eventually become admirals and well known in the navy but Bulkeley would always refer to them bitterly as "those three bastards"). They decreed that Bulkeley be "bound up"—bent over a desk with his wrists lashed down while he was beaten on the back with a broom handle. One hundred strokes. Near the end of it Bulkeley fainted. He passed blood for a week but refused medical attention and pushed himself through his daily routine. He believed the physical abuse was stupid and senseless but that had nothing to do with being able to take it.

***

John Bulkeley endured for the same reason they all did, those who made it to graduation and commissioning: they wanted it badly enough. Even the way he endured was not unique. Bulkeley retreated into a world of his own. It was not the world of books. He lost himself in boxing and in the Academy's machine shop.

Every midshipman mandatorily carried a sport during all three seasons of the academic year. Bulkeley's sport was boxing. He spent uncountable hours dancing around the heavy bag in MacDonough Hall's boxing area, perfecting his moves, throwing his greatest exertions at it, losing gallons of sweat to it. The bag helped Bulkeley work out his most unsolvable frustrations, taking on the faces of his tormentors, allowing him to pound on them and exhaust his anger before it made trouble for him back in Bancroft Hall. It made him strong, and gave him dignity. He won most of his bouts, simply by giving better than he got, by being more courageous and intense than most of his opponents. The only drawback to his flailing style was that it cost him dearly. In swarming over other fighters he would leave himself open to blows, and he was hit more often, and with better shots, than less aggressive men. Fortunately, he could take a punch.

The machine shop was his mental resting place, his purist respite. Bulkeley would disappear into it like a man stepping into a vault and closing the door on himself. He had great mechanical talents. He once made a poppet valve model engine that could turn 10,000 rpms. He also transformed the engine of an old Ford into a diesel.

Scholastically, however, he was at the bottom of his class. There is little doubt he could have done better but he preferred to do just enough. Where he excelled was in leadership. As an upperclassman he is remembered by those below him as a strict disciplinarian who at the same time took no part in the worst aspects of hazing. Nor could he bring himself to join in the small, spiteful acts that were so common: undoing ten hours of spitshining by stepping on a plebe's shoes, slowly grinding the polish off each mirrorlike toe as the helpless plebe stood at attention. Instead, after bracing a plebe, he would often ask questions about the younger man's classes, his girlfriend, his aspirations. He rarely cited a plebe for a conduct offense. It seemed more effective to counsel a wrongdoer, to attempt to affect his future conduct rather than merely mete out punishment. Not a few of Bulkeley's contemporaries at the Academy thought that the underclassmen responded to his offhand, nonregulation sort of leadership in the best way, by giving him genuine respect.

Bulkeley did not equate scholastic excellence with leadership, but he seriously underestimated the practical value of good grades. When President Franklin Roosevelt went to Annapolis in the spring of 1934 to personally hand a diploma to each member of that year's graduating class, perhaps it was his way of apologizing to those in the bottom half of the class standings. With the country gripped by the Great Depression the military budget had been cut yet again, and 215 out of 430 graduates were not given commissions. "It was like taking those four long, grinding years we went through," one of those graduates would later remark, "and flushing them down the toilet."

***

On the train back to the family farm Bulkeley tried to decide what he should do. He found himself in a twilight world, a civilian with a Naval Academy diploma. A *civilian*. It was hard to take in. There were millions of unemployed and he had no prospects. Anyway, he did not have the heart to look for work. It was painful even to think about a civilian job, when the only thing he wanted in this world was the ensign's rank he had dreamed of since early childhood.

His stay in purgatory lasted almost nine months, during which he did indeed do nothing more than think about getting a job. Fred Bulkeley seemed content not to push his son in that direction, as long as he continued to do most of the work on the farm.

Then, on a cold day in December, with snow sifting against the panes of the kitchen window, Bulkeley was sitting at the table with a newspaper when he read something that sent him bolting to his feet. President Roosevelt was going to recall to active duty the Naval Academy graduates of 1934 who had not been commissioned.

In due time his orders arrived and he reported to the cruiser *Indianapolis* at Provincetown, Massachusetts as the ship's fire control officer. He became such an accomplished "spotter" with the new optical range finders that the *Indy* brought home the coveted E (for battle efficiency) for her main gun batteries during the navy's annual battle practice.

His next assignment was something of a disappointment: second officer on a gunboat plying the Yangtze River in China. He would be doing all his sailing on a river, and for Bulkeley there was something unnavylike about it. But as the transport *Chaumont* made her slow way across the Pacific, he consoled himself with the thought that at least he was back in the navy. At the time, the gunboats on the China Station were the smallest boats in the navy, and if anyone had told him that he would go from serving on a gunboat to a boat that was even smaller he could have taken it only as a joke.

CHAPTER 3

Sons of the Country

They came from farms, small towns, the teeming cities. For most of them, growing up in the depths of the Great Depression, life had always been flint hard, not a nickel to spare. Enlisting in the navy was a release from the iron grip of poverty. If not quite heedless of peril and risk, inherent in them was a dash of recklessness. The oldest was in his late twenties, the youngest all of nineteen. As varied in age and temperament as they were, the one thing they all had in common was the pride they had in themselves and in the work they did. The navy sent some of them to technical schools, others learned on the job, and despite the fact that a number of them had not finished high school, all were a cut above average in their ability to learn and absorb new skills.

The blue-water navy ran on engines, and the men who maintained them, the motor machinists, the MMs, were its mainstay, and among them, with a destiny to fulfill, were Joseph Chalker, Ralph Brendlinger, Leroy Conn, William Cook, Rudolph Ballough, Howard Fisher, Paul Eichelberger, Herbert Grizzard, Velt Hunter, John Lawless, John Lewis, James McEvoy, Hayward Miller, Robert Monroe, Theodore Morgan, Elwood Offrett, Paul Owen, Carl Richardson, George Shepard, John Tuggle, Arthur Waters, George Winget, Dale Guyot, Morris Hancock, and Richard Regan.

Torpedoes had always been associated with submarines but the navy was about to put them in a different realm entirely, and among the first torpedomen, the TMs, to follow them there were John Houlihan, Robert Burnett, Marvin DeVries, Charles Dimaio, David Harris, James Light, and John Martino.

Quartermasters, the QMs, are trained in navigation and stand off-watches at the helm and are indispensable on small boats where there are only one or two officers. The QMs were Clayton Beliveau, William Dean, DeWitt Glover, Otis Noel, Albert Ross, and Doyle Smart.

Boatswain's mates, the BMs, train and supervise damage control parties and are responsible for maintenance and security, among other things. The BMs were Robert Caudell, Jesse Clark, Ernest Pierson, and John Shambora.

The radiomen, the RMs, were David Goodman, William Konko, Robert Langer, Harry Tripp, Stewart Willever, and Watson Sims.

Gunner's mates, the GMs, do the obvious, they man the guns. There was only one GM, James Culp, but that was because, in the intimate, unconventional niche in the naval service that was being created, every man, no matter what his rating, would learn how to fire the guns.

The pharmacist's mates, the PhMs, were John Balog and Charles Beckner. George Bartlett was a fireman, to be put to work anywhere. Joseph Boudolf was a carpenter's mate. John Clift, William Stambaugh, and Herbert Hough were yeomen, responsible for ship's logs and records. As coxswain, Clem Langston was usually at the wheel. Ned Cobb and William Johnson were signalmen. Floyd Giaccani was rated as baker, which made him especially valuable, and alongside him, more humble perhaps but absolutely essential, were the SKs, the ship's cooks: Harry Keith, Ben Licodo, Edward Morey, Francis Napolillo, William Posey, Willard Reynolds, Henry Rooke, and Densil Stroud.

Full of simple courage and youth, most of them, though just how much courage even they had yet to learn. They had been scattered throughout the navy, and with few exceptions had volunteered for what might well turn out to be hazardous duty, though for quite some time no one could see the true shape of things to come.

CHAPTER 4

Ron 3

Dead in the water, a PT is squat and beamy. It is designed for speed, and in speed lies its beauty. As a PT gains momentum, its bow lifts clear of the water and it planes gracefully over the surface, throwing out a great wave from the chine on either side and a rooster tail of white water astern. The men destined to ride PTs would curse them for their pounding and discomfort but love them for the beauty that is born of their speed.

Italy and Britain used motor torpedo boats to great effect in World War I. In Britain, during the twenties and thirties, experiments continued in their design and construction. The U.S. Navy showed little interest in the type until the day in June 1939 when boat designer and professional speedboat racer Hubert Scott-Payne unveiled a seventy-foot model that could carry four torpedoes and machine guns in power-driven turrets—the first modern PT boat—and crossed the English Channel with it in a Force 8 gale: winds at forty knots, seas running 12 to 18 feet, through which the boat was able to average an astonishing thirty-two knots. Orders immediately poured in to Scott-Payne's company, British Power Boat, from Britain and other European powers. Among them was an order for one boat from a private purchaser that would have a profound effect on the PT program in the United States.

Henry Sutphen, president of the Electric Boat Company, was fifty-six years old that year, a tall, handsome man with exquisite manners and a quiet intimacy about him that many people found quite seductive. He could also be as ruthless and manipulative as a robber baron.

The U.S. Navy's reaction to the new Scott-Payne design was to launch a development program of its own, starting with a design competition. Sutphen's company already held a number of navy contracts and so it was barred from submitting a design. This of course effectively blocked Elco from participating in the navy's PT program, but Sutphen was not about to sit still for that. The profit potential was huge, and he was resolved to circumvent the design competition and land the navy contract for PTs.

He went to England and bought a Scott-Payne boat at his own expense and had it shipped back to New York as deck cargo aboard the SS *President Roosevelt.* Then he paid Scott-Payne himself to come to America and put the boat through its paces for a navy trial board. The board was impressed. Sutphen took the results of the sea trials to Acting Secretary of the Navy Charles Edison, an old friend of his. He convinced Edison that an American design would never surpass the British model.

"My company can use the Scott-Payne boat as a working model," Sutphen told Edison. "We'll measure each part and make an entire set of blueprints from the measurements, with modifications if necessary. You know Elco's record. You know we can produce whatever you need, and fast."

Edison smiled at that. Sutphen was the Henry Ford of boatbuilding. During World War I his company turned out 550 eighty-foot motor launches for Britain's Royal Navy in 488 days. War had again broken out in Europe (as Sutphen thought it would) and Edison was not willing to wait the many months it would take to get an American prototype PT into the water. He went directly to *his* friend, Franklin Roosevelt (Sutphen had anticipated this too) and got the president to approve a contract for Elco to build thirty seventy-seven-foot boats of modified Scott-Payne design. The contract was worth twenty million dollars.

For the suave, smiling Henry Sutphen it was a spectacular business coup. For the navy, however, the new "wonder weapon" soon began to look like nothing so much as an unmitigated disaster.

***

The first six boats to come off the Elco assembly line were sent to the Brooklyn Navy Yard and specially equipped to detect and sink submarines. It was this semi-secret, highly experimental "subchaser squadron" that became John Bulkeley's first command. Bulkeley had no idea what he was doing. No one did. The PT service was new and PT doctrine did not exist. No one was sure exactly how the boats should be used. No one knew what would work and what wouldn't. But on a cold, windy day in February 1941, as he stood on the dock in Brooklyn looking at his first PT boat, Bulkeley felt something turn inside him. She was all menace and power. Slight wave action from the wakes of ships passing in the harbor made the boat pull against the mooring lines as if she were telling him she wanted to go out and do some damage. Bulkeley knew he was hooked.

***

The boat was seventy-seven feet long with a twenty-foot beam just forward of the cockpit that tapered down to fourteen feet at the stern. From a distance, she looked smaller than she was because her lines were those of a racing boat. She was as big as a luxury yacht but there the resemblance ended, because engines and gas tanks took up nearly half her belowdecks.

Those three 1,250 horsepower engines that were so critical to her existence were the product of two decades of development by the Packard Motor Car Company. This engine generated enough power to propel an eighty-foot, fifty-ton boat across the water at close to fifty knots. (There was to be the famous instance when one of Bulkeley's boats would cross the wake of a battleship and sail completely out of the water for almost fifty yards, becoming in effect an airplane, a sight hundreds of amazed sailors on the battleship would never forget.) PT boat engines had unforgettable voices, ranging from a low, bubbling rumble at idling speed to a pitch and volume at full throttle that sounded like giant, howling tomcats.

Forward of the engine room were three 1,000-gallon tanks holding 100-octane aviation gasoline. Directly above the tanks was a low cabin, the dayroom, and forward of the tanks was the captain's cabin, with a broad bunk, a small closet, bureau, and a desk with a chair fixed to the deck. Next to it was the radio room. Forward of that was the wardroom, with just enough space for a two-man table, then the exec's stateroom and the galley. The galley was equipped with an electric stove, oven, and an eight-cubic-foot refrigerator.

The crew's quarters were in the forepart of the boat. With its eight bunks and a table amidships, it reminded more than one sailor of the forecastle in *Treasure Island*. The bunks were stacked four high along each side of the curving hull. They looked like long wooden shelves and each had a mattress and pillow and plenty of headroom.

***

These were the boats Bulkeley took to Key West, Florida, to conduct anti-submarine trials. Through the spring of 1941 and into early summer they pounded through the Caribbean Sea in one exercise after another.

The results were disastrous.

Equipped with racks from which depth charges could be dropped astern, and two Y guns that could throw four depth charges at a time, two on either side, the boats were able to lay down a good pattern. It was the experimental sonar that failed. Though each boat was fitted with a different type of sound gear, none worked. If the boat was underway the noise of its engines drowned out the echoes of the sound equipment. If the boat shut off its engines and lay to, it developed such a short, sharp roll that it couldn't pick up the echoes. With the boats at speed the sonar heads often broke off and fell to the ocean floor. Not a single sonar head survived. Although admirably armed against submarines, the boats had no way of locating them.

The idea of PT as subchaser was scrapped, but Bulkeley's enthusiasm for the boats was higher than ever. Their speed and power had seduced him. All through the trials, the big Packard engines ran perfectly, ramming the boats through the water at speeds of over fifty knots, close to sixty land miles an hour.

He wasn't the only one to fall in love with the boats, if that is the proper word for it. Many of the men who manned them had volunteered for the PT service because of its informality. There was nothing hard and fast about crew rosters; men sometimes traded berths among the six boats, as long as it was all right with the officers, and it usually was. Dress codes and saluting were nonexistent. Young officers were captains of their own ships and enjoyed a reputation for being dashing and independent. The men were all skilled ratings and they were treated with respect. Many would find the informality to be a problem, in a way. It made it almost impossible to go back to the impersonal routine of a big ship, the rigid discipline, the endless inspections, the strict adherence to regulations.

In fact, everyone was a little worried. Bulkeley had reported the dismal results of the sea trials and had been told by the Navy Department that the "experiment" was over and to bring his boats back to New York. The little squadron buzzed with scuttlebutt. It was going to be disbanded. The boats were going to be sent to Britain as Lend-Lease. The men were going to be sent back to the fleet.

But not if Bulkeley could help it. By now he had developed an almost mystical belief in the boats as a new and potent weapon and he was determined to prove their worth. He had an idea, and he spent his last weeks in Florida preparing his pitch. He would be going before a Navy board in Washington—three senior admirals—to make a formal report on the subchaser experiment, and he intended to use the occasion to persuade them that PT boats would be highly effective against large surface ships, enemy destroyers, and cruisers, *in direct attacks*. Their speed and maneuverability, which had to be experienced to be believed, was the key. Never mind that a PT boat was one-fiftieth the size of a cruiser. In capable hands she could get in close, fire her torpedoes, and make a clean getaway. Later in the war, events would show this to be something close to a juvenile fantasy, but it was something Bulkeley had come to believe in with the fervor of a religious convert.

***

In July 1941, at the very moment Bulkeley was in Washington making his pitch, a decision was being made to reinforce the Philippines. A crisis with Japan was brewing in the Pacific and the small American garrison there, headed by General Douglas MacArthur, was directly in the path of Japanese aggression. But there was little to send. Months before, President Roosevelt had signed into law the Lend-Lease bill that he had ramrodded through Congress in record time. Most of what the country's still-dormant arms industry was producing was being sent to beleaguered England in return for nominal payments.

MacArthur knew about torpedo boats, in theory at least, from his extensive study of military history. He knew about their use in World War I by the European navies. The United States could not permanently station enough capital ships in the Philippines to defend against Japanese attack, and he believed that a large number of torpedo boats could deter the big Japanese warships long enough for our own big ships to arrive. By the summer of 1941 he was aware of the U.S. Navy's experiments with PT boats. He asked that as many as possible be sent to him. He was a persuasive man in a powerful position, and he was listened to.

As many as possible, however, was not very many.

There is no way of knowing how effective Bulkeley's presentation was on that hot July day in Washington when he addressed the Navy board. It's impossible to say whether he would have been able to keep the PT program going and turn it in the direction he envisioned for it. It would hardly seem to matter. A much more persuasive personality and the forces of history intervened.

Early in August the Chief of Naval Operations directed the formation of Motor Torpedo Boat Squadron 3, John Bulkeley's six boats, for immediate shipment to the Philippines. They would be PTs 31 to 35, and PT 41.

Ron 3. The Expendables, destined for incandescent fame and ultimate destruction, although mercifully there was no hint of the dreadful ordeal that lay ahead for all but a lucky few.

***

As the transport *Guadalupe* took them through the Panama Canal and on to Pearl Harbor and beyond, Bulkeley preached his new doctrine of direct attacks against large warships with more fervor than ever. Now that they were crossing the Pacific there could be no doubt who the enemy was going to be—the Imperial Japanese Navy—and he was absolutely determined that one of his boats be the first to sink a Japanese capital ship. There were sessions on strategy and tactics every day, at which his officers would hear the same refrain, over and over: "Get in. Hit 'em fast. Hit 'em hard. And get out." That basically was going to be the strategy. As for actually getting *in* there, close to a big warship, the tactics for that had to be improvised, as there was no established doctrine for the tactical deployment of PT boats in combat.

So much for Bulkeley and his officers. The men were left pretty much alone. Gunner's mates, radiomen, torpedomen, engineers, they all knew their jobs. On the long sea voyage they had little to do except amuse themselves. Ned Cobb, from Mathis, Texas, who had never done any fishing, caught two dolphins, a small marlin, and a 600-pound shark in an informal contest between himself and Floyd Giaccani, who came from San Francisco and liked to brag about catching stripers in the surf and steelhead in the rivers. Ned aced him; Floyd caught nothing. John Martino, George Winget, Charlie Beckner, and Bill Cook played a running game of poker that lasted for the entire voyage, with conflicting claims about who lost the most. Clem Langston brought a dozen Mickey Spillane paperbacks with him that were eventually passed around and read until the pages started falling out. Most wrote letters home, but ship movements were kept as secret as possible and they knew that much of what they wrote would be censored.

The little half-squadron arrived in Manila Bay on September 28, 1941. Twelve officers and sixty-nine enlisted men. They had exactly seventy days of peace before them.

CHAPTER 5

The General

In 1941 the most important and influential publisher of news and current affairs in the United States was undoubtedly Henry Luce, owner and founder of *Time*, *Life* and *Fortune*. Early that year *Time* produced an article on the Philippine Army and its prospects. It was not an optimistic report, which might be why it attracted Luce's attention, and with his wife, the writer Claire Booth Luce, he visited the Philippines in July—that busy month—to ascertain the facts for himself. The Luces were dinner guests of General Douglas MacArthur and his wife, Jean, in their penthouse in the Manila Hotel. Apparently, the General held forth for the duration of the entire meal, which annoyed Luce who himself, given half a chance, was inclined to dominate table talk. After bidding farewell, the Luces descended in the MacArthur private elevator when suddenly Luce pressed the stop button between floors.

He stood there, his brow furrowed in quiet meditation.

"What are you doing?" his wife wanted to know.

"I'm trying to decide whether MacArthur is a great fraud or a genius."

A good twenty seconds later Luce pushed the elevator's down button.

"Well?" his wife pressed.

"He's both," concluded Luce.

***

That's probably as close to the truth as anyone will come. Douglas MacArthur "was a great thundering paradox of a man, noble and ignoble, inspiring and outrageous, arrogant and shy, the best of men and the worst of men, the most protean, most ridiculous and most sublime," one of the General's biographers would write. He was, in fact, a deeply flawed personality whose behavior throughout his career, in whatever capacity he served, clearly reflected those flaws. That is not to say he was without complexity, without intellectual talent, without insight, without some of the qualities of greatness.

And MacArthur had a vision of himself that never changed from childhood to old age: He had a destiny to fulfill.

He was first in his class at West Point. Many consider him to be the greatest frontline general of World War I. He had walked around wearing a soft cap in place of a helmet—the Germans had not made and could not make the bullet that would hit him—and had gone over the top at the head of his troops with nothing but a riding crop as a weapon. In 1919 he became the youngest officer ever appointed as superintendent of West Point. In 1925 he became the youngest major general in the army. In 1930 he became the youngest Chief of Staff in American history. The newspapers had always paid attention to him—"America's greatest soldier" was the often repeated phrase—and he reveled in it. Indeed, he could never get enough of it.

But where was destiny taking him now that he had reached the summit, where the only place to go was down? By 1935 he would be on his way out, not only as Chief of Staff of the Army but also as a major player on history's stage. Surely it was the most dismal of futures imaginable to him. Where could he go now, other than into retirement? What could he do, this man with a congenital need to be at the center of things? No immediate limelight, comparative obscurity—what would become of him? What would save him from what, for Douglas MacArthur, was a fate worse than death: that of being forgotten, of simply fading away.

***

At first glance the Philippines would not seem to be a place where anyone, let alone America's greatest soldier, could find salvation. Here was a conglomeration of over 7,000 islands with close to sixteen million people speaking over a hundred dialects but no national language. It hardly qualified as a civilization, let alone a nation. Spain had occupied the Philippines for almost four hundred years, getting hardly anything out of the place except converts to Catholicism. The United States seized the Islands at the turn of the century from the collapsing Spanish empire, but almost immediately even table-thumping imperialists like Theodore Roosevelt were questioning the wisdom of this decision. The Islands were half a world away, produced nothing of consequence on any worthwhile scale, and yet would have to be defended. "As long as our flag remains in these waters," Roosevelt himself stated during a visit to Manila, "it goes without saying that it must not be hauled down at the will of any foreign power without a fight to the finish."

In 1935 a decade-long debate ended when the U.S. Congress passed a Philippine independence bill. The Islands were to be cut loose in ten years. In the meantime they would be a commonwealth of the United States, self-governing as it felt its way toward full independence but with America still responsible for its defense. The elected president of the new commonwealth was Manuel Quezon, brilliant, mercurial, tubercular, and a great friend of Douglas MacArthur, who had served two tours of duty in the Philippines.

Quezon was consumed by one major concern: defense of the archipelago. The United States maintained a token garrison of about 10,000 men—a weak force that for a variety of reasons was not to be increased. It wasn't nearly sufficient to defend the Islands and everyone knew it. And in any case, Quezon wanted the Filipinos to defend themselves. He went to see President Roosevelt in Washington just before the independence bill was passed. He asked Roosevelt to make Douglas MacArthur, whose term as Chief of Staff was ending, U.S. military advisor to the commonwealth government. MacArthur was to create a Philippine army capable of defending the Islands on its own. In addition to generous pay, MacArthur was to become "Field Marshal" in the Philippine Army.

This was MacArthur's idea and it was non-negotiable. Here was his salvation. As soon as he ceased to be Chief of Staff he would revert to his permanent rank, that is, he would lose two stars, falling in rank from four-star general to two-star major general. A meteor descending, burning out. However, now he would become a *five*-star general—a field marshal. Never previously had any American held five-star rank. The young major who was to serve as MacArthur's aide, Dwight Eisenhower, tried to talk his superior out of accepting the title. Eisenhower thought it was pompous and ridiculous to be field marshal of a nonexistent army, and he couldn't understand how an officer holding top rank in the U.S. Army could possibly desire such an honor.

He did not yet know MacArthur. No member of the American military was ever more self-centered or self-absorbed. Had MacArthur gone to Uruguay rather than the Philippines there is little doubt that South America would have become strategically the most important part of the world. As it was, he assigned that quality to East Asia, with the Philippines at the center, "the key that turns the lock that opens the door to the mastery of the Pacific." For everyone else, including official Washington, the Islands were still a tropical backwater, 8,000 miles from the U.S. West Coast and at the very periphery of

American interests, and the garrison there continued to be almost criminally neglected. It remained a dumping ground for obsolete airplanes, obsolete weapons, and aging army officers awaiting retirement.

***

When Henry Luce showed up in Manila in July 1941 to have a look at things, MacArthur had been there for six years. At an annual salary of $36,000 (equivalent to $600,000 in the year 2000), he was the most highly paid military officer in the world. He lived like a merchant prince, in a six-room air-conditioned penthouse on the top floor of the Manila Hotel, for which he paid no rent. He received visitors in a large formal dining room with red drapes and many French mirrors. Two balconies overlooked the city and the lovely curve of the bay. The General's favorite balcony opened off the dining room and afforded a spectacular view of Bataan and Corregidor. A wife shared his luxurious nest. He had married Jean Faircloth in 1937, his second marriage. A small wisp of a woman with a large flashing smile, she was a daughter of the South, as was MacArthur's mother. The marriage appeared to be happy but it would have been hard to determine, because Ms. Faircloth had been raised from girlhood to subordinate her own interests and desires to those of her husband. She never called him "Doug" or "Douglas" or "sweetie" or other terms of endearment, but rather "Sir Boss" or "ginral." She never criticized him, kept in the background, allowed him to dominate every situation, and indulged his ludicrous behavior. The couple, twenty-six years apart in age, produced a son, young Arthur MacArthur, now three years old and living with them in the penthouse.

The General's lunch with the Luces lasted five hours. MacArthur did all the talking, most of it on his feet. He was always a tremendous pacer. Luce was not the first to observe that the General "cannot talk sitting down." On this day he paced the floor of the dining room in his outlandish field marshal's uniform, white tunic festooned with medals, stars, and gold cord, as he held forth on the military situation in Asia. The confident, sonorous voice that many found almost hypnotic went on and on.

Luce couldn't get a word in. He didn't even try. But as he listened, unease seeped into his annoyance. The subject was Japan's aggressive intentions, and at one point MacArthur boasted that his Philippine Army of 100,000 men could defend the entire archipelago. He would "crush" the Japanese on the beaches.

This was completely at odds with the pessimistic report Luce had read in the March issue of *Time*. As MacArthur went on about the formidable force he had built—"It has changed the entire strategic plan in this part of the world"—Luce grew increasingly skeptical. His instincts told him that something was very wrong, and like any good journalist he decided to have a look for himself. He arranged an inspection tour, not through MacArthur's office but through the U.S. garrison commander, who was independent of MacArthur, the Philippine Army and the U.S. Army being two distinct entities.

What Luce saw profoundly shocked him. There was an army but it was an army with untrained personnel, inadequate equipment, inexperienced leadership, and antiquated weapons. It was an army on paper; actually, an organized mob. The attitude of the soldiers he talked to, conscripts from the rice paddies and sugar plantations, reflected the attitude of the Filipino civilians he met. He did not meet a Filipino who felt he should fight for his country. It was all up to the Americans. A Filipino would fight for his family, maybe for his barrio, but he had no larger loyalty. In all his travels in the Islands Luce did not hear any feeling of nationalism expressed. And the last thing any of the soldiers seemed willing to fight for was someone *else's* barrio.

Douglas MacArthur was living a fantasy. Who can truly explain what was going on in his mind? It should be noted, however, that no one had ever seen him make an inspection trip to any of the training camps. Not once did he go out to "the field" and see for himself what was transpiring. All his working hours were spent in his well-appointed office in Fort Santiago, surrounded by a fawning staff who prepared their reports according to what they knew the General wished to see. It's highly likely that the men grinding out the reports came to believe them. And with the eloquent MacArthur, public delusion and even self-delusion was always possible because he was himself the most persuasive of men.

Henry Luce was of a mind to correct the record but desisted. He had seen how, in the Far East, America's military prestige—what little there was of it—was linked inextricably with the personal prestige of the General. He needn't have been concerned; events were about to do the correcting.

***

On July 23 the pro-Nazi Vichy government allowed the Japanese to occupy French air and naval bases in Indochina. President Roosevelt responded with an oil embargo, cutting off at a stroke Japan's main source of petroleum. It was an act so provocative as to be practically a declaration of war. The Japanese would now be forced to seize the oil fields of the Dutch Indies or knuckle under to American demands and withdraw from Indochina. Under Hirohito's new minister of war, Hideki Tojo, the Japanese were not likely to knuckle under. And if they struck at the Dutch Indies they would also strike the Philippines, which quite literally blocked the way.

In Washington, Secretary of War Henry Stimson recognized the danger immediately. He urged Roosevelt to take immediate steps to strengthen the Philippine defenses. Two days after Stimson's meeting with the president, on July 25, MacArthur was having breakfast when his penthouse doorbell rang. A houseboy brought two War Department cables to the table, both marked "Urgent." One called him back to active duty and gave him command of all U.S. army forces in the Far East. The other federalized the Philippine Army—MacArthur's native troops were now part of the army of the United States.

He showed the cables to his wife. "I feel like an old dog in a new uniform," he told her exultantly. To a reporter the next day he exclaimed, "By God, it is destiny that brought me here."

***

Luce and his wife were on their way home when all this happened, with no plans for an article about the fast-fading General. But MacArthur's new command changed everything. No longer was it only in his own mind; suddenly he was at the very heart of America's Pacific defenses.

Late in September, Claire Booth Luce returned to Manila to write a profile of MacArthur for *Life*. She was a shrewd observer of the man whose "temperament was flawed by an egotism that demanded obedience not only to his orders, but to his ideas and his person as well." She noted the pallor of his skin, indicating how little time he spent outside, his trembling hands and the vanity which required him to comb his thinning black hair from left ear to right, thereby covering a large bald spot. She took some photographs of the man who said he never posed for photographs. Just for her, he stood on the walls of Intramuros, outside his office, his eyes fixed beyond the horizon as though challenging the Japanese to come and try him.

As promised, Mrs. Luce sent MacArthur the draft article. He was greatly upset by many of the personal comments, and after the deletions he demanded what was left was a fawning, reverential profile. The article appeared in the December 6 issue of the magazine with the General on the cover in a heroic pose above the legend "MacArthur of the Far East."

Suddenly he was famous again. In fact, more famous than ever. *Life* had a circulation of over five million and its influence on popular culture was immense. With the new crisis in the Pacific, radio commentators and newspaper columnists picked up on the theme. MacArthur was once again "America's greatest soldier." The effect was like being on prime-time television a generation later. His name was now as instantly recognizable to the American public as Roosevelt's or Churchill's. He was in the limelight again, center stage, this man with an addiction, really, to fame. He was not going to fade away and *be* history, he was going to *make* history.

***

The challenge was overwhelming. The Japanese had six million men under arms; their elite divisions were veterans of four years' fighting in China. MacArthur had 12,000 U.S. soldiers, mostly support troops with no combat training, and his commonwealth army of 80,000 Filipinos, many of whom had yet to even see a rifle and whose military knowledge was limited to saluting.

Help was on the way. In Washington, a last-minute decision had been made to reinforce the garrison. But America's prewar army was tiny and the country was only just beginning to mobilize, with Lend-Lease drawing off a lot of what was being produced, and what trickled across the Pacific between August and December was pitiful. A coast artillery unit with obsolescent cannons. Two battalions of light tanks with untrained crews. Thirty-five heavy bombers, whose effectiveness was vastly overrated. Fifty pursuit planes that could not compete in any way with the new Japanese "Zero" fighter.

And the six PT boats of Motor Torpedo Boat Squadron 3.

CHAPTER 6

Prelude to War

On the morning of Ron 3's arrival in the Islands, MacArthur was in his penthouse when he heard a sound that he mistook for low-flying aircraft. He stepped onto his favorite balcony, the one that overlooked Manila Bay, and saw it was the roar of torpedo boats. He sent word that he wanted to meet the squadron commander.

That same morning Douglas MacArthur and John Bulkeley came face to face. It was like voltage jumping a gap—each man took an immediate and strong liking to the other. The unusually close friendship that developed between the legendary sixty-two-year-old army general and the brash thirty-year-old navy lieutenant seems as improbable as something from a bad novel. One was a man of enormous stature, at one time or another the confidant of Presidents Coolidge and Hoover, the head of the American Olympic Committee, the superintendent of West Point, the Chief of Staff of the Army, and now, with war looming, the commander of all U.S. forces in the Far East. The other was a man thirty-two years younger who had bounced around at the bottom of his class at Annapolis, gotten into serious trouble for unauthorized spying, and been shanghaied into an assignment no one in the navy particularly wanted because no one saw any future in it—the PT boat.

Nor, would it seem, were they particularly compatible. The older man was infuriatingly vain, egotistical, flamboyant, brilliant, eloquent, arrogant, sensitive to criticism, and extremely well read. The younger man did not have a vain bone in his body, could take criticism from anyone without batting an eye, was blunt, eager, a bit crude, and favored mechanical devices of any sort over books. But the friendship was real enough and in the end it was the basis of this friendship—their mutual admiration and trust—that sealed Squadron 3's doom.

MacArthur talked for forty-five minutes. Bulkeley listened reverentially, not venturing to say anything. MacArthur explained that he intended to meet any Japanese invasion force at the beaches. He had a native army of 80,000 men to bolster his single division of regulars—two regiments of dependable Philippine Scouts and one American infantry regiment, poorly trained and badly understrength with less than 2,000 men. "When and if the Japanese attempt to land, I will advance to attack them," he told Bulkeley.

This flew in the face of the standard army war plan for the defense of the Islands. War Plan Orange called for an immediate withdrawal by the garrison into the Bataan Peninsula, where the defenders were expected to hold out until the navy could bring reinforcements from the States. But as soon as MacArthur saw War Plan Orange he mentally shelved it. It was defensive, and therefore defeatist. Only the offensive is decisive in war, he believed. And he abhorred the idea of the army hunkering down and waiting to be rescued by the navy. With his new Philippine Army, he was going to take the fight to the enemy.

Bulkeley sat listening in silent admiration. He had never heard of War Plan Orange and being an extremely aggressive officer himself, he heartily approved of taking the fight to the enemy. But he had no firsthand experience with the Philippine Army. The American officers assigned to train the Filipinos, had they been present, would have been astonished by the grandiose notion of their men meeting the Japanese on the beaches and slugging it out toe to toe. The 80,000 men upon whom MacArthur was depending had an average of one month's training. Most had never fired their old, decrepit Enfield rifles, the ones who had rifles. There were no entrenching tools, no gas masks, no steel helmets, no cartridge belts, no field packs, no mosquito nets, no radios. Most of the sergeants and company clerks, the mainstays of any functioning military unit, were illiterate. Officers and men could not talk to each other without interpreters to translate the various dialects.

The explanation most often given by historians for MacArthur's tragically unfounded optimism is that he was simply blind to the realities around him. But there exists in the archives a private letter to a friend in which MacArthur admitted that his program for training a native army had fallen short. There was some doubt in his mind as to the abilities of the untried and poorly trained Filipino soldiers—but clearly not enough to prevent him from sending them out to meet the Japanese head on. This suggests something additional was at work: a marked racial attitude common to people of that time. He was going up against what was thought of as a half-civilized coolie army, a horde of little yellow men who did not command his respect as, say, the German army might. MacArthur didn't have complete disdain for the Japanese, he was too good a soldier for that, but he clearly believed that as long as they were led by American officers his Filipinos would prevail. It would prove to be the most serious miscalculation of his career.

The meeting ended with MacArthur shaking Bulkeley's hand. "As long as our flag flies over these islands, America has a responsibility, a duty, to defend the Philippines," he told Bulkeley. "We have a moral obligation to protect the Filipino people."

***

For Americans who were in the Philippines in 1941 the scents, scenery, sounds, weather, people, customs, the vivid contrasts, the unadorned pleasures, were unlike anything at home. Their letters invariably mention the lovely strangeness of the place—the huge, extravagantly shaped, brilliantly colored butterflies that weaved among the hibiscus and bougainvillea, the jasmine and the wild orchids; the cone-shaped umbrella trees that cast perfect circles of shade fifty feet across; the small doll-like tarsiers people kept in their gardens sleeping through the day upside down with their arms folded and their tails curled around a tree branch; the robber crabs that climbed the coconut palms to clip off the nuts and husk them with a big, sharp claw. You could drift down a river at night and suddenly, as if by magic, a huge dark tree would blossom with tiny fires, with an immense mass of shimmering, dancing lights, to become a tree of golden flame in the night, the doing of a swarm of tropical fireflies. Less than a hundred miles from Manila lived Stone Age tribes who had never seen the outside world. Everything was cheap—housing, handcrafted furniture, fine china and linens, food, clothes, liquor, and the native help, the houseboys, cooks, maids, lavanderas, chauffeurs, and gardeners who could be found serving even the meanest of white households.

A lot to see, a lot to do. But Bulkeley was stingy with liberty. He wanted all the boats manned and ready at all times. They were based at the Cavite navy yard, ten miles south of Manila. The yard was on a spit of land that jutted out into the bay. Its newer buildings sprawled around an old Spanish fort with ancient lichened walls. Many of the original thick-walled Spanish buildings were still being used, including the barracks that housed Ron 3's crews, though with Bulkeley's obsession for readiness they were practically living on the boats. The men went to the barracks only to take showers.

Bulkeley felt certain an attack on the Philippines was imminent and that it would be a surprise attack. He didn't have access to top-secret intelligence reports, and he had no special insight with regard to Japanese intentions. His certainty about those intentions was based on his belief, as deeply held as religious faith, that the Japanese were a treacherous race, "the meanest, dirtiest, sneakiest sons of bitches alive," he would say later. "It was like walking around among crowds of people in the street and knowing you had an enemy there who would hit you from behind without warning."

He had them doing speed runs from the very first day. The six boats would roar up and down the bay, planing gracefully over the water, throwing out huge wakes, engines thundering. Manila residents came by the hundreds to watch. The new "wonder weapon," the city's newspapers took to calling them.

Far out in the bay, they would practice their gunnery. Bulkeley had acquired some large red balloons. These were launched from the bow of his boat, the 41, and when they had risen about two hundred feet each boat in turn would open fire. A single boat's firepower was prodigious: four .50 caliber machine guns, a linked pair in each of two gun turrets, the so-called "twin fifties." (A single .50 caliber bullet could cut down a sapling.) To this was added a .30 caliber Lewis gun in the bow. Even when fired in short bursts, all the guns together could pump out close to a thousand bullets in the space of a minute.

On the 32 boat the guns jammed after one short burst. Jim Culp came aboard from the 31 and cleared them in a few seconds, but that would be too long when a plane was coming in on them. Bulkeley happened to be aboard the 32 that day. As squadron commander he rode all the boats in turn. There was no doctrine that required him to do this, it was he who was creating PT doctrine every day, but he was quite adamant that the boats had distinct animal characteristics that set each apart from the others, and he wanted to be intimate with every boat, know it and how it performed, as well as the boat captain did. He took Culp aside and told him that the two of them were going to spend the rest of their days trying to figure out what had caused the guns to jam, and that was all they were going to do. For three days he watched Culp taking the guns apart and putting them back together. Right then, Culp hated him, this man who was hanging over him all day, breathing down his neck, as if he, James Culp, gunner's mate first class, didn't know his job.

Culp finally found the problem. The oil being used in the firing mechanism was too gummy and some of the tolerances were too tight. He added some thinner to the oil and loosened the sliding parts a bit. Then he fired the guns into the air in a continuous burst that ran through five hundred rounds. He looked at Bulkeley then, as if to say, "Satisfied?"

Bulkeley's doctrine was to get within four hundred yards of the enemy, which could be done only at night. In broad daylight, a destroyer or cruiser would blow them out of the water at 10,000 yards. For "practice," the boats would take turns sneaking up at night on merchant ships anchored off the breakwater, idling in on one engine to cut down on the noise, "firing" two torpedoes, and then racing away in a thunderous roar with all engines full ahead. It was unfortunate that they couldn't actually fire a few torpedoes, for they would have discovered, before it would cost some of them their lives, that many of the torpedoes were duds.

Bulkeley demanded precision and excellence in maneuvers and meticulous maintenance once they docked. He was a hard-driving commander and a perfectionist in all things concerning the boats. On the other hand, he dispensed with most of the military formalities, including saluting. Because of the tropical heat and humidity most of the men, Bulkeley included, went shirtless and often shoeless while conducting drills. Bulkeley grew a fierce black beard and took to wrapping a bandana around his head to soak up the sweat. Admiral Thomas Hart, commanding the Asiatic Fleet, of which the PT boats were a part, thought he had never seen a unit so unnavylike as Ron 3. "A bunch of pirates!" he complained in his diary. He felt certain the boats would prove worthless against large enemy surface vessels. He issued an order that the squadron conform to standard navy regulations. Bulkeley ignored it.

Hart resented the fact that the boats were to be used in close cooperation with the army—it was largely General MacArthur's urging that had brought them out to the Islands—and he knew about the new PT "doctrine" of attacking large surface vessels only because Bulkeley had told him. Never one to restrain himself, Bulkeley had reported to the stiff, dour little admiral on the day Squadron 3 arrived and had stated flatly that he was going to sink a Japanese battleship. Hart was a tart-tongued officer who never wasted a word and always said what was on his mind.

"Rank nonsense!" he assured Bulkeley.

***

Opposites in almost everything, Hart and Bulkeley shared the belief that a Japanese strike was imminent. Hart watched political developments closely, and the menace seemed to be growing all the time. He had sent most of his ships to the southern Philippines, away from the danger of air attack. It was not a fighting fleet in any case. The Asiatic Fleet was one aging cruiser, thirteen World War I-era destroyers, and a handful of ancient submarines. It was not a war fleet. It was strictly a fleet for showing the flag.

Incredibly, the army, with which the navy had almost no contact, remained "tropical." In all departments the workday ended at noon, and the general prewar torpor was still evident. Most of the resident American civilians—there were about five thousand in Manila—did not believe there would be a war. The Philippines, despite commonwealth status, was still United States territory, like Hawaii or Puerto Rico, and the Japanese would not dare attack the most powerful nation in the world and start a war they would be certain to lose in a few weeks. It was just saber rattling, they told each other. The Japanese would compromise in the end.

CHAPTER 7

"It's Here!"

Thanksgiving came and went, and November gave way to the last month of the year. The hourglass was down to its last grains of sand.

At three-thirty in the morning on Monday, December 8, a young sailor from the navy yard's communications center ran into the old Spanish barracks near the boat sheds and woke Bulkeley from a sound sleep. "It's here!" the sailor yelled excitedly. "It's war! The Japs bombed Hawaii!"

Bulkeley put on his uniform in record time and rushed over to the boat sheds to rouse the PT crews. Tony Akers was the captain of the 35 boat, a soft-spoken Texan and the tallest man in the squadron at 6 feet 4 inches. When Bulkeley shook Akers awake, he didn't believe it. Bulkeley was not known for practical jokes but that's what Akers thought it was. "It's a hell of time to declare war," he muttered peevishly, and rolled over, but he never did get back to sleep. Too many men were making too much noise, and it didn't take long for him to realize this was it.

Bob Kelly, the squadron's second in command, knew instantly that it was no joke. He was a thoughtful man who had been following events closely and he had been as certain as Bulkeley that a Japanese attack was imminent. Of course he didn't know exactly what day it would come, only that it would be very soon, and so it was sheer coincidence that took him to the Army and Navy Club and its very good restaurant the night before, where he ordered a charcoal-broiled steak, the club's proprietary french fries, golden brown and thick as your middle finger, and a big tomato with Roquefort dressing, finishing with brandy and a cigar. He was under no illusions about what war would bring, and at least he would have that meal to remember.

The young sailor from the communications center had brought a message for Bulkeley. He was to report immediately to the *comandancia*, the old thick-walled Spanish building where the commander of the navy yard, Admiral Francis Rockwell, had his headquarters. When Bulkeley got there Rockwell, tall, silver-haired, slender as bamboo, and his chief of staff, Captain Herbert Ray, were standing at the window of Rockwell's office, watching the sky as dawn, with its faint tint of pink, was just beginning to break over Manila Bay.

"Prepare your boats for war stations," Rockwell told Bulkeley, without taking his eyes off the sky. "They ought to be here any minute."

He was a little ahead of himself, but he wasn't wrong about them coming.

***

It was twenty minutes past noon at Clark Field. Sixty miles north of Manila, Clark was by far the biggest airbase in the Islands. The news about Pearl Harbor had come nine hours earlier, and it had been a strange, unsettling morning. At eight o'clock all the bombers, fifteen four-engine Flying Fortresses, had been ordered into the air. They flew in circles for two hours, with a squadron of P-40 fighters flying cover. Then all the planes landed, to be serviced and refueled. The fighters, eighteen of them, were sitting on the turf field, engines turning, ready to go up again. Just outside the hangars, the Fortresses were taking on their bomb loads. The order had finally been given: they were going to hit the Japanese airfields on Formosa.

A bomber pilot, George Strong, had just finished lunch and was walking to his quarters when he heard someone yell, "Hey, look at that!"

The man was pointing, and Strong shaded his eyes and found them. The planes were very high and looked like little silver toys against the deep blue of the sky as they came steadily on from the north in two big Vs. They were almost directly over the field.

Then something appeared beneath them. Tiny black specks, like pepper.

Strong ran for a nearby slit trench. As he jumped into it the bombs began to hit. About five hundred yards away columns of dirt began springing up, like a row of trees, only moving, coming straight at him from across the wide grass field, straight through the P-40s that were still waiting to take off. With each new dust tree the noise grew louder until it became a huge, all-engulfing roar. Strong lay at the bottom of the trench with his teeth gritted and his hands covering his head as the explosions thundered over him, tremendous ear-splitting blasts, the earth beneath him bucking and heaving. There was a shower of dirt and stones and clods of earth as the explosions moved on and then, quite suddenly, there was only silence.

It seemed to be over. Strong was about to climb out of the trench when he heard someone shout, "Jesus, here they come again!"

Black, oily smoke was rolling over the field, so thick it shut out the sun. Strong watched as a single-engine plane broke sharply out of the smoke and roared by almost directly overhead, wing guns rattling and nose cannon thumping. He heard the rising, hissing *pfffo-O-OFF* of exploding fuel—and suddenly it came to him what was happening. Strafers were going after the Fortresses that were parked on the field and that the bombs must have missed.

Most of the planes at Clark were destroyed on the ground. Late that afternoon Captain Bill Dyess, a P-40 pilot sent from Manila's Nichols Field, flew over Clark and reported that planes, oil dumps, and hangars were still burning fiercely. "It's a real mess down there," he radioed back.

***

At twelve-thirty that afternoon a formation of fifty-four Japanese bombers and fifty Zeros, the best fighter plane in the air at that time, caught the defenders similarly off guard at Iba Field, a small fighter strip on the coast forty miles west of Clark. The bombers were directly overhead before anyone saw them. Everything was flattened, even the palm trees that stood between the airstrip and the beach. The single P-40 squadron based there, eighteen fighters, were just returning from combat patrols. Not knowing that enemy bombers were at that moment high overhead, the pilots brought their planes in, touching down just as the bombs began to hit, and were blown to pieces.

By midafternoon on December 8 the Far East Air Force, which MacArthur had counted on heavily in his plans for the defense of the Philippines, had been eliminated as an effective combat force.

The war was not yet one day old.

***

The PT crews knew none of this, and would never know the details until after the war. News reports, such as they were, were heavily censored. All that day the men loaded the boats with food, mostly canned goods, along with coffee, sugar, tinned butter, whatever they could get their hands on. Five of the boats were dispersed along the shoreline at Cavite, about a hundred yards apart. The sixth was patrolling out in the bay.

At noon on the following day, for one heart-stopping moment, it appeared that the worst was upon them. A large formation of planes flew over Cavite, and then over the boats as all six raced out into the bay. But nothing dropped. The antiaircraft batteries at Cavite opened up but the brown puffballs of exploding shells did not reach even halfway to the planes, which were at 20,000 feet. It was just a reconnaissance raid—and the Japanese had learned what they needed to know. The antiaircraft defenses at Cavite were antiquated and posed no danger to their bombers.

Seeing that, Bulkeley immediately perceived the danger. Cavite was exposed, and if it was bombed he would need another base from which to operate.

"Take three boats over to Bataan and scout out a new location for us," he told Bob Kelly. "There's a submarine tender at Mariveles. Report there for food, water, and torpedoes, and stand by for orders. You're to attack anything I tell you to attack."

Kelly wasn't underway yet when word came that he was to take some passengers to Corregidor. Waiting for them delayed his departure. It was almost five o'clock when the three boats left Cavite, and pitch dark by the time they were outside the minefields, feeling their way into the little port of Mariveles, on the southern tip of the Bataan Peninsula.

Aboard the 34 boat, Ensign Illif Richardson was steering. They had a chart of the minefields but in the dark, with the minefield lights turned off and no lights on the boat, he was blind. As he gripped the little spoked wheel all he could think of was being responsible for the boat, and the lives of eleven other men.

But at that point the army took over. Shore batteries all around the harbor heard the roar of the PT engines, which echoed against the mountains and were mistaken for airplanes. Searchlights felt up into the night sky, bright wands of light, and there was some shooting by nervous gun crews, the red tracers arcing up toward the stars. The 34 boat had a searchlight, not a big one, and Richardson thought the odds were good that if he turned it on they wouldn't be shot at, not with everyone's attention focused on the sky.

No one shot at them, and the light made it much easier to negotiate the minefield. They snaked through finally and tied up alongside the sub tender.

On the following morning the three boats idled into Sisiman Cove, a short distance along the coast from Mariveles. The moment Kelly saw the little secluded inlet he knew he'd found what Bulkeley wanted. The inlet was home to a tiny barrio, about twenty nipa huts. Some were already abandoned. The remaining Filipino families, fearing that the boats would bring a shower of Japanese bombs down upon them, did not have to be persuaded to move out.

Later that same day all three boats were fueled from barges that originally had been waiting for them at the wharves in Mariveles but had been towed out into the bay as a precaution. The barges were loaded with drums of 100-octane gasoline—airplane grade and more volatile than dynamite. The tiniest bit of static could set off an explosion, and in the tradition of leading from the front, only the officers fueled the boats. It was no small job. Each boat held three thousand gallons, and the gas had to be poured from the fifty-five-gallon drums through a funnel, one drum at a time.

***

On the other side of the bay, the 31 boat was taking a bag of dispatches from Cavite to Manila. As they were coming in, the enormous bulk of Pier 7 was just off to port and all the Filipino dock workers there paused in their tasks to watch the boat go by. There were dozens of them and they all smiled and waved. Of all the men aboard only Rudy Ballough didn't wave back. He was down in the engine room and had no idea what was going on topside.

They idled in toward the fleet landing on one engine, the engine making a low throaty rumble above the burbling exhaust. As they approached the broad concrete pier Ed DeLong, the boat captain, put the center engine in neutral, the starboard engine ahead, and the port engine back, with the rudders hard over. Docking a PT boat was an acquired art, and DeLong had mastered it. In the open cockpit, standing before the control panel, one hand on the wheel as the other worked the throttles, he played the wing engines and rudders lightly and deftly and the boat swung about and nuzzled up broadside to the rubber fenders all in one easy motion.

They tied up with only one line. When it was secured Bill Dean, the quartermaster, went down the gangway with the canvas pouch. Behind him came Bill Plant, the boat's second officer. Dean was wearing brand-new dungarees and a newly bleached white hat. He was freshly shaved and his shoes were shined. He had a .45 pistol strapped to his hip. Plant, heading in the opposite direction, running, really, was dressed in immaculate khakis, complete with cap and a two-blocked tie.

Dean ambled as slowly as he could across the concrete pier, to give Plant more time. Then across the street to a five-story building of pink brick that had a black metal fire escape zigzagging up one side—Admiral Thomas Hart's headquarters.

Three hundred yards south of the Marsman Building was the white concrete, red-roofed Manila Hotel and its parquet-floored outdoor restaurant that looked out on the waterfront. That's where Plant was headed, to meet his girlfriend for lunch. She was the daughter of a prominent Spanish–Filipino family, the highest social class in the Islands. Nieva was in her last year at the University of the Philippines and was thinking about becoming a lawyer.

Bill Plant was in love with Nieva, with all that that implied. He could not take her to the Army and Navy Club. He couldn't take her into the Manila Hotel either, but its outdoor restaurant was tacitly exempt from racial restrictions, if you didn't mind being stared at by the overwhelmingly white clientele, the city's prominent businessmen and their wives, army and navy officers and *their* wives.

Dean had formed a friendship with Plant that would not have been possible outside the PT service. Officers and men lived together on the boats, and almost from necessity each boat became a family. The men did not call the officers by their first names, a small gap between them being essential to discipline, but it was an easy, relaxed relationship. Dean and Plant played dozens of chess games, which Plant, in the beginning, mostly won. Then Dean racked up a long winning streak, his skill on the chess board suddenly leaping well ahead of Plant's. Dean had acquired a book, which he tried to keep hidden, called *Twenty Great Chess Moves*. Plant was indignant when he discovered the book, feeling as though Dean had secretly hired a tutor just to be able to beat him. Dean explained that Plant, a college graduate, was so much smarter than him that he needed the book to make the games more interesting. Plant laughed at that, and the games went on, and they were more interesting.

Plant had not been granted liberty to see his girlfriend, he was using a courier run to do it, and so he faced a time constraint. He couldn't stay longer than it took Dean to deliver the pouch and get back to the boat. But Dean wanted to help Plant, and he'd had an idea. He could not play around with the pouch, he had to go straight to the Marsman Building with it. But before leaving Cavite he'd gone up to DeLong and asked if he could take a smoke break after delivering the dispatches.

"You don't smoke," said a puzzled DeLong.

"I do now," Dean told him.

DeLong was not an unperceptive man. He gave Dean a pack of cigarettes. "You have my permission to take a smoke break," he said. "In fact, smoke as many as you like. Just keep smoking until you see Bill heading back for the boat."

CHAPTER 8

Calamity

It came at noon on December 10, in the form of a 125-plane flotilla at 20,000 feet. Later in the war the formations of Allied aircraft bombing Germany and Japan would far exceed that, numbering up to a thousand planes, but early in 1942 the formation that bombed Cavite was the largest anyone had ever seen.

When the air raid sirens sounded at the navy yard three of the boats were at Mariveles. The three at Cavite immediately raced out into the bay, where they would have room to maneuver. At their battle stations, the boat crews watched as a shower of bombs fell. They could see the blasts shooting up like ugly black mushrooms. Above the black smoke small brown puffballs of antiaircraft fire blossomed in great numbers, but well under the enemy bombers.

The bombers circled over the bay and came in again for a second traverse, the big formation moving with the stately precision of an air show. Everything below them was blotted out by thick, billowing smoke. The entire yard seemed to be burning.

About a dozen P-40 interceptors were scrambled from Nichols Field, in the suburbs of Manila. Forty Zeros were waiting for them. In seconds there was a swirling dogfight that tumbled back and forth across the Manila sky at furious speed. Parachutes blossomed, far out over the bay and off toward the eastern hills, the few surviving American planes finally scattering in all directions. It was over in minutes, and it left everyone on the boats stunned. Many would remember it as their first big shock of the war. It was the opposite of what they'd been expecting—that if Japanese planes ever did show up over Manila they would be met by swarms of American fighters and shot out of the sky. With the strict censorship they couldn't know that over two-thirds of America's air strength in the Islands had been destroyed on the first day of the war.

The bombers droned away, untouched. But the yard was still blowing up. On the boats they could hear the deep booming explosions and see the fires, orange at the bottom of twisting pillars of smoke.

The men on the boats were helpless witnesses to this, and would remember it always, but they saw it at a distance. For a better appreciation of the destruction and loss of life that occurred that day there is this account, compiled from a number of sources, though the emotions and impressions are attributed to one individual, a young officer from the fleet radio station, who at noon on that day was on his way to the *comandancia* with a decoded top-secret message that he carried in a worn leather pouch.

As he approaches the *comandancia* the air raid sirens go off. On the graveled walkway ahead of him a sailor looks up, shading his eyes. "Well, what do you know … there they are!" the sailor exclaims. Since the start of the war there have been two days of false alarms, no one even sighting an enemy plane.

The young officer stops and looks up, searching. It takes a moment to find them. They look like V-shaped flocks of tiny silver birds high in a sky white with heat. He can hear them now, a faint, uneven droning, and feels a little flutter in his stomach. It is his first sight of the enemy.

Along with dozens of others, some standing in the middle of the street, he watches as the huge formation passes above Manila and wheels out over the bay toward Cavite.

They are almost overhead and yet all of them, dozens of sailors and yard workers, stand there watching as something appears beneath the planes. Tiny black specks …

"Christ in heaven!" someone cries, and the spell is broken, all of them scattering like a flock of sparrows. What follows for the young officer, huddled at the bottom of a slit trench that had been dug on the lawn fronting the *comandancia*, is a debilitating fear, deep and clutching, like a seizure. The explosions are tremendous, each one shaking the ground. He holds his hands over his ears and keeps his mouth open, to keep his eardrums from bursting from the concussion. He feels his insides loosen, and alarmed at the shame of it, he prays he won't soil himself. Something drops into the trench but he is immobilized, he can't move, can't even turn his head to see what it is. A good thing too, because at this moment it is the last thing he can afford to see. It is a mass of coiled intestines tenuously attached to a lower torso from which the legs had been sheared off just below the hips.

When finally the explosions stop and he climbs from the trench, still shaking, even worse sights await him. The base seems to be one sheet of flame. Everything is burning. The *comandancia* is throwing off so much heat that he has to move away from it, the flames curling out of windows and shooting up through what is left of the roof. There are three bodies on the lawn, burned black and still smoking, men who had run out of the building with their clothes on fire. They lay in grotesque positions, arms and legs at unnatural angles, their teeth showing whitely.

A man in officer khaki stumbles along the street toward him, stooped over, half his face burned away and what is left of his right arm, mostly just white bone, hanging like a stick. His face is so distorted that it takes the young officer a second or two to recognize this pitiful figure as a friend of his who works at Central Wharf. He starts toward his friend but hasn't taken more than a few steps when the man stops—and then pitches over, falling on his face in a way that can never be done by anyone who isn't dead. There is nothing for it but for the young officer to leave him there. He is suddenly aware of the top-secret message in the pouch on his hip. It doesn't seem to him that there is anyone left to deliver it to, and he takes it out of the pouch and conscientiously tears it into tiny pieces.

Along with dozens of others who worked there, Admiral Hart watched the destruction of Cavite from the roof of the Marsman Building. He watched for as long as he could bear it, which wasn't long. He left the roof before anyone else. General MacArthur had not bothered to inform him of the huge losses sustained on the opening day of the war, and he was stunned by the almost total absence of army fighter protection. But it was clear to him that the air war was being lost, "and we shall be blockaded here, for a long time," he confided to his diary.

From the roof Hart went straight to his office and gave the order that would send the Asiatic Fleet south to the relative safety of the Dutch Indies. Only the PT boats would remain behind, as the only ships deemed equal to the task or risk of combat under skies controlled by the Japanese.

***

After the bombing the three PT boats that had been out in the bay raced back into the yard to see how bad the damage was and to help with the wounded. Everything was on fire, and there were mangled and scorched bodies everywhere, and parts of bodies. As they fanned out from the wharf area, looking for wounded, they were nauseated by the horrible debris of severed limbs and heads.

The three boats took scores of wounded to the Canacao naval hospital. Back and forth they went, all afternoon. There was an inch of blood on the landing platform at Canacao, and the men could hardly stay on their feet, the blood being as slippery as crude oil. The white aprons of the hospital corpsmen who came out to load the wounded onto gurneys were so blood-spattered they looked like butchers. Tony Akers saw a young Filipino woman, every stitch of clothing blown off by a bomb, running in circles, screaming, the wild light of insanity in her eyes. He was too busy gathering up the wounded to try to catch her and get her out of there, but seeing that young woman unsettled him even more than the dead and injured.

Cavite burned for days in the windless weather, stinking smoke hanging over the bay, a dirty, thick rope winding up as far as you could see into the sky. Two days after the fires were out George Cox took the 41 boat in to see if anything useful could be salvaged from the boat sheds. One look at what little was left of them told him it was hopeless.

He was a young man with a strong stomach and he found himself both repelled and fascinated by what was going on. Filipino yard workers were burying the dead, which consisted of collecting heads and arms and legs and tossing them into the nearest bomb crater and shoveling debris over them. They were under the supervision of a few navy petty officers who, they claimed, had to ply the Filipinos with grain alcohol to make them work. A week before, Cox had purchased a bicycle, and the night before the raid he left it locked against a wall. The wall was now a jagged ruin but the bike was untouched, and he unlocked it and rode all over the yard, watching staggering Filipinos dragging a chunk of torso toward a crater, pulling it by its one remaining leg, or rolling a head along as if it were a soccer ball.

It was later estimated that almost a thousand people had been killed in the raid, most of them Filipino yard workers. The bombs had caught them at their dinner hour. The submarine *Sealion*, tied up for repairs, took a direct hit and sank at its moorings. All the tugs and barges along the waterfront were destroyed. And for the PT boats there was the crippling loss of over two hundred torpedoes, thousands of gallons of high-octane fuel, and all their spare parts. Not so much as a gasket was left to see them through the war.

***

The permanent home of all six boats was now Sisiman Cove, thirty miles across the bay from Manila. Bulkeley's orders were to report to Admiral Rockwell every morning. Rockwell was his immediate superior, and with no functioning navy yard to command he had moved his headquarters to the Marsman Building, on Manila's waterfront.

On his first morning there Rockwell informed him that his boats were to provide a messenger service to Bataan, Corregidor, and Manila to make up for the loss of the navy's prime radio station at Cavite. They were also to patrol the entrance to Manila Bay and along the west coast of Bataan, which faced the South China Sea. That request had come from General MacArthur, who thought the Japanese might attempt an end run behind his lines with an amphibious assault on Corregidor. If they did, he was counting on Bulkeley to intercept the landing barges, since he no longer had an air force to do it. MacArthur was right about Japanese intentions, but the assault would not come for some time, and it would not be against Corregidor.

CHAPTER 9

A Maritime Tragedy

During the first week of patrolling the nights were quiet. There were exceptions, but with the shortage of gasoline usually only two boats at a time went out. With no spares, the boats couldn't be kept at peak efficiency and the inevitable deterioration began. Bulkeley managed to bring the men some navy issue to replace what they had lost at their quarters in Cavite—a shirt each, underwear, a few tubes of toothpaste, and razors, two for each boat. But blades were in short supply and it was only a matter of time before beards would be making their appearance.

On December 17 came their first big test, though it had nothing to do with combat. The SS *Corregidor* was one of several interisland steamers operating in the Philippines. She was not quite decrepit, but certainly old, having started her life before World War I as a British seaplane tender. On the evening of December 16 she was at her berth on the Manila waterfront, her captain watching uneasily as passengers frantically piled aboard. The fighting in the north was getting closer to the city and there was panic in the air. In the Chinese cities that fell under their control the Japanese had not hesitated to rape and loot and kill. A lot of people in Manila wanted out, and an estimated 1,500 of them crowded onto a vessel whose capacity was about a third of that. Most were Filipino families. Seven Americans were thought to be aboard, heading for their homes in the southern islands.

At 8 p.m. *Corregidor* pulled away from the dock, sluggishly, her engines straining. It was a clear night with a half-moon. Under it, the waters of the bay were calm and glassy. It took her a bit over four hours to cross the bay. At a few minutes past midnight, with many of the passengers now asleep, she was passing tiny La Monja Island, just south of Sisiman Cove and west of Corregidor, heading for the entrance to Manila Bay and the open sea beyond. Here, near the entrance to the bay, minefields had been in place since the summer.

On Corregidor there was a control station that would temporarily deactivate the mines to allow for the passage of friendly ships. But something had gone terribly wrong in Manila. *Corregidor* had not been properly cleared for departure, and so the electronic mechanism that deactivated the mines wasn't working.

Elton and Dode Fee were among the Americans aboard. A married couple, they were going back to Mindanao, where Fee was a manager for the Standard Oil Company. The explosion sent them tumbling out of their beds and onto the floor of their cabin. They picked themselves up, put on life belts, and in the utter darkness hurried to the deck above. There was chaos—no chance of getting into a lifeboat.

The ship had struck a mine on the starboard side near her stern. Through the gaping hole the sea cascaded in, swirling about the pipes and valves of the boiler room, which filled with water so rapidly the three crewmen on duty there could not get out in time to save themselves. The ship immediately began to sink by the stern, the bow rising slowly until it was pointing toward the sky. The Fees somehow made it through a screaming, clawing, panic-stricken mob of passengers to the top deck. While struggling to get to the rail they became separated—and then they jumped into the darkness below, like hundreds of other passengers. *Corregidor* went down by the stern with people still aboard, the suction pulling many more already in the water down with her, the sea closing over all of them.

***

The explosion reached Sisiman Cove as a deep, muffled boom. A few men were in the nipa huts but most were sleeping on the boats, not below in their bunks but on the decks, where it was cooler. The sound was loud enough to bring most of them awake. Not a few thought it was a bomb going off and instinctively went to their battle stations.

Bulkeley was on the 41 boat, staring out at the darkness beyond the little inlet. George Cox, the boat captain, was standing next to him. They could see the faint outline of a ship and some flickering lights on the surface.

"That wasn't a bomb," Bulkeley decided. "Some ship out there hit a mine."

Cox agreed with him.

Bulkeley passed the word: "Boats 32, 34, and 35, make ready to get underway." He jumped aboard the 32 and nine 1,250-horsepower Packard engines started up with a whine, a cough, and a low rumble. In seconds a thunderous roar filled the air as the three boats headed out into the bay.

They were approaching the edge of the minefield when the smell of fuel oil came to them. The water was soon thick with it. Then came the bobbing heads of survivors, a sea of heads rising and falling in the gentle swell, so many that the boats had to lay to. Even the slimmest of canoes could not enter that dense mass of humanity without running into people. The sound of the PT engines triggered cries for help that seemed to come out of the night from all directions. No one on the boats heard any English, it was all in Tagalog, but no translation was needed. Help me. Oh God, please help me. Individual voices were lost in a steady, overwhelming clamor.

On the 34 boat George Shepard, John Martino, and Henry Rooke were already rigging ladders and tossing lines over the side. Men on the other boats were doing the same. Even Bill Konko, big and muscular, had trouble pulling his line in. Up to a dozen people fought for every line tossed over the side. "Christ," Konko heard someone yell, "it's like casting for trout!" What disturbed Konko the most was the way women were often pushed aside by men grabbing for the lines. Whenever he saw children in the water he would throw his line in their direction, but it wasn't always the children who ended up holding onto the rope.

An American man remembered by those present only as Ellis was pulled out. Immediately he asked for a rope. Covered with fuel oil and wearing only his undershorts, he joined the sailors in pulling out survivors, never mentioning that his wife was out there somewhere. As it happened, the 34 boat pulled her out. She too was covered with oil, and wearing only a bra and panties. Henry Rooke handed her his bandana so she could clean the oil from her face and then headed off to find a pair of dungarees and a shirt for her. "Come back here, young man," she called after him, "this is no time for modesty. Wipe off my back."

***

The boats quickly filled up with rescued passengers, lying, sitting, standing. They were taken to the hospital on Corregidor, the empty boats immediately returning for another load.

Bob Kelly happened to be in the hospital at the time. A week earlier he'd somehow sliced open the index finger on his right hand while conning the 34 boat during a patrol. Overnight the finger swelled to the size of a hot dog. Kelly ignored it, until that was no longer possible. Blood poisoning spread up his arm almost to the shoulder, and his entire hand swelled up until it was the size of a catcher's mitt. He couldn't lie down for any length of time and had to constantly hold his arm up to keep it from throbbing. He refused morphine, and he refused to go to a hospital. This was when there were still only three boats at Sisiman Cove. He was in charge, and they might be asked to go on a mission at any time. When Bulkeley brought the other three boats over after the destruction of Cavite and saw the condition Kelly was in, he immediately ordered his executive officer to the hospital on Corregidor.

It was in Malinta Tunnel, deep underground. Branching off from the tunnel were the laterals, lower-ceilinged and narrower and open only at one end. The main hospital lateral contained two parallel rows of white iron beds. Other laterals were marked Surgery, Pharmacy, Dental, Dispensary. There was a lateral where the doctors lived and another for the nurses. All of it was lit by garish blue lights that cast deep shadows on the faces of the occupants and hollowed out their eye sockets.

Kelly lay there and watched them being brought in, covered with oil, some with burns, most of them in shock. Some walked in unassisted, some had to be helped, and a good many were carried in on stretchers. Nurses and corpsmen began a frantic search for blankets to cover those who were almost naked.

The tragedy was brought home to Kelly with overwhelming force when a young woman and her two-year-old child were put in the bunk next to his. She had lost her husband and another child, a baby, who had slipped out of her arms in the water. She was inconsolable, and kept blaming herself because her arms had gotten so weak she couldn't keep the infant from sliding away from her. She was Filipino but she kept moaning in English, tears streaming down her face, "My little boy, oh, my little baby." Kelly was not a sentimental man, and he was being toughened even more by war, but listening to the pitiful lament of that young woman broke his heart.

***

Out in the minefield the rescue work continued. The boat crews were pulling survivors up the sea ladders at such a rate that their shoulders and arms were getting tired. A Filipino woman in need of clothes was pulled aboard one boat. Someone gave her a clean white navy uniform and she was sent below to rest. Later, Clem Langston caught sight of her and whacked her on the back, thinking she was a PT sailor taking a nap while everyone else was hard at work pulling survivors out of the water. The terrified woman bolted upright in the bunk, and when Langston saw his mistake he was so mortified words failed him, and he quickly left the dimly lit compartment.

All night they worked. There was a freighter and several smaller boats in Mariveles harbor but no one came to help. Perhaps it was the minefield, and the very real possibility of ending up like the *Corregidor*. When their lives are at risk one must be slow to judge the actions of others. At the same time it must be said that the officers and men of those three PT boats, which pulled aboard a total of 296 survivors, never hesitated for a moment to sail into a minefield in an effort to aid a ship in distress.

***

Progress was measured by the gradually lessening cries for help. It came down finally to lone voices here and there, off in the darkness. Even at idling speed the engines made a throaty rumble and they had to be shut down to allow the men to hear anything. As night gave way to the mauve and coral of a beautiful dawn it seemed to be over. No more cries for help, no drifting survivors to be seen. For another hour the boats plied back and forth, heedless of the mines, the crews wanting to be sure that no one was left behind in the water.

They were exhausted, and smeared all over with oil from the people they had saved. Bulkeley at last gave the order and the three boats returned to Sisiman Cove.

But there was no time to rest. Fuel oil from the rescued passengers had also smeared the boats, everywhere it seemed—decks, the charthouse, passageways, the below-deck compartments, even the engine room, so tightly had the survivors been jammed aboard. The clean-up lasted until noon, when the boat captains were at last satisfied. A quick meal, and the men and officers of the rescue force settled down to try and get some sleep, though as usual most found real sleep impossible in the stupefying heat of the tropical day.

***

The total number of those lost in the *Corregidor* disaster has never been accurately established, but by any measure it was a tragedy of immense proportions, rivaling the loss of life when the *Titanic* went down. But the *Corregidor* carried no internationally prominent personalities, and very few Americans, and it occurred in the midst of a world war, in a far-off corner of the world, and except for those who survived, and those who played a role in helping them survive, it was quickly forgotten.

CHAPTER 10

Retreat

For the boat crews the rescue effort had been charged with emotion. Even the men who had not taken part in it felt a curious kind of excitement. Awful as it was, at last *something* was happening. Feelings like that made not a few of them realize just how dull the routine at Sisiman Cove had become. The nightly patrols were uneventful. The daylight hours were spent in upkeep, overhauling carburetors, fuel pumps, gas strainers, and refueling from the gas drums, duties so repetitive they numbed the mind. The heat was oppressive, and there were no newspapers or radio broadcasts or movies to distract them. Nothing to read, nothing to listen to except each other. Twelve to fourteen men were living and working on each boat, and in such close quarters small irritations grew larger even between friends.

The lack of news may have been a blessing. From the first day of the war it had been uniformly bad.

The Japanese had made their first landing on December 10, far up on the northern tip of Luzon. A modest force of about 10,000 men, it was clearly not the main invasion. There was nothing up there to stop them from coming ashore. Only air power could do that, and there were hardly any planes left. But a blocking force, skillfully handled, might confine them to the northern mountains. And in any case, they were not the real threat.

General MacArthur felt certain the main invasion would come at Lingayen Gulf. Ninety miles north of Manila, this great indentation in the coast of Luzon was a natural harbor with broad, low beaches that opened directly onto the central plain. Flat, open country all the way to the capital city. Lingayen Gulf was where *he* would land an amphibious force.

As usual, he was not lacking in strategic insight.

On the morning of December 20 the submarine *Stingray* sighted a fleet of Japanese troopships, escorted by heavy cruisers, fifty miles off the coast of northern Luzon. The American response was, there is no other word for it, pathetic. Four Flying Fortresses dropped their bombs on the transports, scoring no hits, turned away, and flew off to Australia. Six submarines fired torpedoes but only one enemy ship, out of some twenty warships and eighty-five transports, was sunk.

At 2 a.m. on December 22 General Masaharu Homma's veterans of the China war started going over the side, and the gray light of dawn found them ashore at three points in the gulf. On only one beach were they resisted, and even that was short-lived and feeble. The untrained, undisciplined Filipinos dropped their rifles and literally ran for the hills. There was a hopeless holding action at Damortis, where the coast road turned inland, by a regiment of Scout cavalry. Filipinos but highly trained and motivated, the Scouts were exemplary soldiers, and they fought with great valor, but the Japanese had control of the air and the regiment was all but destroyed by dive bombers and strafers. By afternoon long columns of Japanese infantry and tanks were streaming down the central plain, the roads taking them past dry rice paddies and through fields of man-high cogon grass that ran off to the horizon.

Recall War Plan Orange, then. Should the Japanese invade, it called for a withdrawal into the Bataan Peninsula, where the garrison would fight it out until a relief force arrived from the States—a plan MacArthur so disdained that upon seeing it he immediately put it out of his mind. It was defensive, a concept he abhorred. He would meet the enemy head on at the beaches and crush them.

Only now, it was *his* army that was being crushed.

What to do?

MacArthur was, if nothing else, a decisive man. He didn't acquire his reputation as America's greatest soldier by vacillating. But for two crucial days that's what he did, so deeply repulsive was the idea of retreat, to be followed by defensive warfare—very likely a long, drawn-out siege—as he waited to be rescued by the navy. The humiliation of *that* would seem too great to be borne.

What forced him to a decision was another Japanese landing, at Lamon Bay, sixty miles south of Manila. There, resistance melted away, as it had in the north. The enemy was now advancing on Manila from the north *and* south. Once glance at the map showed him that unless he moved quickly he would be trapped by two gigantic pincers. And that would mean defeat, final and irredeemable.

At last he radioed all commanders: "WPO is in effect." The next day he declared Manila an open city.

Those two decisions would change the complexion of the entire war in the Philippines, but not for the better. It was too late, and too little had been done. The only effect would be to prolong the agony. But that of course is hindsight. Filipinos and Americans, soldiers and civilians, they were going to make a fight of it.

***

A retreat is the most difficult of military maneuvers, under any circumstances. In MacArthur's case the odds seemed insurmountable. The retreat into Bataan depended on precise timing between two large forces of demoralized soldiers approaching each other from opposite directions but not in contact with each other. A double withdrawal, really, and one slip in this complicated maneuver would leave the South Luzon Force cut off and cornered in Manila. The retreat went on for almost two weeks, and it was executed brilliantly. To MacArthur should go a fair share of the credit, to his field commanders a larger share. But something has been lost in the historical record—a thumping piece of good luck.

"We got there," Dave Alexander, an officer who was in the thick of the retreat, remembered, "only because the Japanese air force, with complete control of the skies, failed to bomb the highway bridge over the Pampanga River. Destruction of that *one* bridge would have stopped the retreat cold. Bombing the long columns of retreating troops would have been just as effective, and even that wasn't done. And it wouldn't have taken many bombs either, because the discipline of those Filipino troops was practically nonexistent. They would abandon their vehicles at the mere sound of an airplane engine, throw away their gear when they got tired, even their rifles. It was not a withdrawal, it was a rout." But MacArthur radioed the War Department—incredibly—that "I have effected a fighting retreat in the face of a determined enemy now estimated at 150,000 troops and without the loss of a man or an ounce of material." In fact, Japanese forces never added up to more than 38,000 men.

So the escape to Bataan succeeded. But the preparation of Bataan failed miserably. A retreat into Bataan was not all of War Plan Orange. The peninsula was to be stocked with ample supplies of food and medicines, field hospitals established, communications lines laid, defensive positions prepared, all the things required for a successful defense. When MacArthur abandoned the plan nothing of the sort was done, and in fact supplies were moved *out* of Bataan and scattered among the forward locations close to the beaches.

Much of it was lost. Filipino workers at these supply depots would flee at the mere rumor of approaching Japanese. Some truck drivers simply took off in the stampede to get to Bataan—with empty trucks. There was a mad rush to get supplies from Manila to Bataan that was only partially successful. When the dust settled one thing was clear: on Bataan there was plenty of ammunition but little in the way of medicines—and almost no food.

***

Meanwhile, Manila was abandoned by the armed forces. An open city means a demilitarized city, and a demilitarized city *might* not be bombed. MacArthur was determined to save the city he cherished not from the Japanese but from complete devastation. But his open city declaration put Manila's 750,000 Filipinos and 5,000 resident Americans at the mercy of an army that had never shown any mercy to either soldiers or civilians.

The news that the city would not be defended came on the day after Christmas. Most of the city's residents were terrified. On everyone's mind was the Rape of Nanking. It had made headlines around the world. After they captured the city the Japanese soldiers looted homes, burned churches and temples, and rounded up groups of men—a hundred, two hundred, five hundred at a time; old men, young men, boys, it didn't matter—and, point blank, executed them. Then the soldiers went house to house, neighborhood by neighborhood, seeking out women, and, in an almost methodical way, raping every one of them. Thousands of Chinese men, women, and children were shot, stabbed, raped, beheaded. Now it was about to happen in Manila.

Fear spread quickly. Most businesses immediately closed their doors, and thousands of people poured out of the city in all manner of conveyances—taxis, trucks, buses, horse-drawn carriages, limousines, oxcarts, anything, in fact, with wheels. The retreat to Bataan had only just begun and this mass exodus from the city created a ten-mile-long traffic jam at the Calumpit Bridge, another headache for MacArthur's field commanders, who needed the bridge to get their troops to Bataan.

From the moment he made his decision to give Manila to the Japanese, in his headquarters at Fort Santiago, MacArthur worked furiously on orders directing the razing of all supply depots and storage tanks. Not far from the small tin-roofed building where he worked, in their penthouse in the Manila Hotel, Jean MacArthur was decorating a Christmas tree for Arthur, who was as excited as any three-year-old would be by the knowledge that a closet was filled with presents for him. Jean had a pretty good idea of what was coming, but for Arthur's sake she pretended they would all be celebrating Christmas at home. Which in fact they did do, a day early. Little Arthur, elated, pedaled through the rooms of the penthouse on his new tricycle. Colonel Sidney Huff, MacArthur's longtime aide, had been sent to Heacock's Department Store to buy presents for Jean. She opened her beribboned packages and cried out in delight as she held up each article of lingerie and each of the four dresses Huff had bought. To her husband she said, "Sir Boss, they're beautiful. Thank you so much." Then she carefully rewrapped them and put them away, as if she would wear them sometime.

The blow fell on Christmas Eve. At five that afternoon MacArthur called his wife. "Jean," he told her, "we're going to Corregidor."

It was time to pack. One suitcase only. Jean took almost nothing of her own. Most of the space was taken by food and clothes for Arthur. Huff carried Arthur's tricycle. Ah Cheu, the amah, was holding Old Friend, the child's stuffed rabbit. "Ready to go to Corregidor?" Jean said. The boy nodded. Ah Cheu opened the door. As they entered the elevator the air raid sirens began wailing.

At Fort Santiago the General cleared his desk, as though he expected to return in the morning. Then he picked up his family and Huff in his battered Packard. At Manila's Pier 7 the MacArthurs, Philippine President Manuel Quezon and his family, and a hundred others awaited the arrival of the interisland steamer *Don Esteban.* The sun was down, the light was failing fast. Out of the gloom a naval officer approached them. It was Admiral Hart, there to say goodbye. He was going south, to the Dutch Indies, taking with him every U.S. naval vessel except some submarines—and the six PT boats. Admiral Rockwell, already on Corregidor, would be staying behind to command these.

***

At last they cast off. It was a balmy, moonlit tropical evening. Behind them Manila lay dark and quiet under a dense pall of smoke drifting over the city from the burning Pandacan oil tanks. Thirty miles ahead, blacked-out Corregidor was invisible. Off the port bow they could see Cavite burning brightly. American demolition squads had blown up what remained of the navy yard. It was hard to believe it was Christmas Eve. Someone started to sing "Silent Night." Nobody joined in, and after a few bars the voice died away. There was no conversation, no sound at all except the chugging of the *Don Esteban*'s engines and the soft plash of water at the bow. Almost everyone stayed on deck. MacArthur felt the urge to pace but they were all standing so close to each other there was no room for him to walk.

The escape party settled into Corregidor's maze of tunnels. From there the General directed the retreat to Bataan—two weeks of intense anxiety, victory or defeat hanging in the balance. He pours over every message from the field, pacing like a caged lion, almost never sitting. Having developed the plan of withdrawal in detail and studied it again and again, having carefully selected the commanders, the participating units, and those to be held in reserve, he can do nothing now except send messages to his field commanders, prodding them to move faster, urging them to hold a little longer here, warning them of a threat to their flank there. Now the outcome depended on other men far removed from Corregidor.

They did it. On January 6, when the last bridge was blown, sealing off the peninsula, he had 80,000 fighting men on Bataan—65,000 Filipinos and 15,000 Americans. There were also 20,000 refugees to feed.

Even more than the enemy, the problem now was food.

CHAPTER 11

A Boat is Lost

It was a routine mission to a place they had been before. The Verde Island Passage, fifty miles south of the entrance to Manila Bay, was a narrow channel that separated Luzon from the island of Mindoro, and if the Japanese decided to mount a seaborne attack on the bay their ships would have to pass through it. It had to be watched, and night patrols to the passage had become commonplace.

On Christmas Eve Henry Brantingham got his orders. He was boat captain of PT 33 and he was to patrol the passage and attack any vessel encountered. "It will be Japanese," Bulkeley assured him, "because no friendly ships are operating in the area." Ed DeLong with the 31 boat would be going with him.

Off they went, with 33 in the lead. They idled out of Sisiman Cove and through the minefields and then laid on speed. Iliff Richardson was on the 33 as executive officer and he kept a nervous eye on their luminous wake. In tropical seas millions of tiny phosphorescent organisms, like tiny glowing fish, swim near the surface and at high speed the propellers seem to excite them so that they glow even brighter. At speed the wake is very broad and several feet high and the illuminated spray goes much higher. It is a gigantic glowing arrow pointing directly at the boat, something no Japanese pilot or ship's lookout could fail to see. It is among nature's most lovely displays, but Richardson felt they could do without it.

The two boats planed over the night sea at close to forty knots, the usual bouncing, jarring ride, everyone holding on to something to keep from being flung overboard. Then it happened. At exactly eight-thirty all three engines of PT 33 suddenly stopped.

Below, in the engine room, Howard Fisher muttered a profanity. He had detected sputterings and hesitations in the engines before this. They were like tiny skips of the heart, barely noticeable and seemingly harmless, but when they persisted he was pretty sure he knew what it was: dirty gasoline. He'd been hoping they could run through it before anything serious happened.

After about five minutes of fooling with them he got the engines started again. But they were not yet at the designated patrol area and the 31 boat had kept going. In the cockpit, in an effort to catch up, Brantingham rammed his throttles all the way forward. The stern went down, the bow rose, and the boat took off. Staying on his previous course, Brantingham ran at maximum speed for several minutes, looking for any sign of the 31.

Then, up in the port gun turret, John Tuggle cupped his hands and yelled over the thunder of the engines, "Lights on the port bow!"

Richardson was in the cockpit with Brantingham. He saw a flashing light and pointed, and Brantingham swung the wheel and headed that way.

A few moments later they both saw something phosphorescent.

"Could be the 31's wake," Richardson speculated.

Brantingham thought it was. He was heading directly for it when a tremendous jolt knocked him loose from the wheel. Richardson was almost flung from the cockpit. Herb Hough, standing near the aft torpedo tube, was sent flying half the length of the boat. In that moment everyone aboard became a human projectile. Accompanying this was a long, deep, metallic howl, as if the boat were in pain.

The phosphorescence was surf breaking over a shallow coral reef. Brantingham had struck it at maximum speed and the momentum carried the boat almost sixty feet onto the reef.

Except for bruises, none of the crew was injured. Richardson grabbed a flashlight to check for damage. He found the hull intact but screws, shafts, and rudders were badly bent. He went into the charthouse to consult the tide tables.

"High tide," he informed the skipper.

Brantingham frowned at that. A PT boat has a relatively shallow draft and a rising tide would be enough to lift them off the reef. Already at high tide, the water under them was now going out, lodging the boat even more solidly. They were in hostile waters and about as vulnerable to attack as they could be, and they couldn't sit there and wait hours for the tide to reverse itself.

"All hands in the water," Brantingham ordered.

Over the side they went, two officers and ten men. The coral beneath their feet was knife sharp and it cut into their shoes as they rocked the boat and tried to push her off the reef. After about ten minutes they gave up. She was stuck fast.

What now? Brantingham thought. He was in command, but he was out of ideas.

Just then the sound of engines broke the silence. A moment later the 31 boat came into view. It was going by them astern. Everyone crowded into the stern of the 33 and started yelling as loud as they could as Richardson frantically waved his flashlight. The 31 swung about and began to approach. She was heading for the reef. More screaming and yelling from the 33, with Richardson blinking the flashlight, sending DANGER in Morse. The 31 finally stopped twenty yards from the coral shelf.

DeLong jumped over the side and waded over to the 33, two men pulling him aboard.

"We thought you were Japs," he said to Brantingham. "My guys in the gun turrets were this close to opening up on you." He held his thumb and forefinger an inch apart.

The two young boat captains conferred. At high tide 31 might be able to pull her sister boat free. DeLong returned to his boat and sent over towing cables. Hooked up, he slowly revved his engines. But it was not to be—there was a sound like the crack of a rifle as the tow lines parted.

DeLong went over to the 33. "I'd better go back and report the situation," he said to Hank Brantingham. "You'll have to hang in here for a while."

Brantingham didn't like it, he was desperate to get his boat free before the enemy found him. But he had no choice.

Gloomily, all hands watched the 31 disappear into the night.

***

For the men on the 33 boat, alone and helpless in enemy territory, it was the longest night of their lives, and few of them got any sleep. At daylight the next morning—Christmas Day—Richardson went over the side for another inspection. The entire boat rested on only one spot on her hull forward and on the propellers aft. There seemed to be opportunity there. The coral formations were like soft limestone and could be cut and cleared. Brantingham gave the order and all hands went to work trying to cut a channel to deep water.

They were just off the coast of Luzon, a white sand beach a quarter mile away, palm trees leaning over it, scrub jungle farther in. No one noticed the soldiers in blue denim uniforms, all of them barefoot, as they quickly formed a firing line on the beach. The men in the water heard a shout, and a moment later there was the smack of bullets striking the 33's hull and the hollow droning of bullets tumbling and keyholing through the air as they glanced up from the sea.

The soldiers were Filipinos. Richardson scrambled aboard and fired off a Very pistol, as a signal that they were shooting at a friendly boat, but the orange flare arcing above the beach had the opposite effect. The soldiers started firing faster.

Everyone scrambled aboard the boat, where they were less exposed. Crouching behind a torpedo tube, Tuggle had an idea. He and Ed Morey tied the American flag to the boat's antenna, the highest point possible—but the flag was riddled.

The two officers were hunkered down in the cockpit, bullets zinging by just overhead. Art Waters had found shelter in the crew's head. A bullet hit the mirror inches above him. Torpedo warheads, fuel tanks, that's what everyone was thinking about. One hit in the wrong place and it was very likely all of them would die. Something had to be done to stop the firing.

An unlikely hero emerged. On the day Cavite was bombed the 33 boat had run out into Manila Bay where it could maneuver. During the raid some planes passed directly over the boat. A single bomb fell. It landed almost three hundred yards behind the speeding boat, but as it was coming down Ernest Pierson lost his head and dove overboard. He became the object of mirth for everyone aboard, but it was deeply humiliating. Pierson felt he had demeaned himself. And it wasn't enough for it never to happen again. Somehow he would have to make up for it.

Now was the time. He ran below and pulled the bedsheet from his bunk, tore off a strip, and tied it to the end of a long-handled ladle snatched from the galley. With the white flag he slid over the side and began wading slowly toward the beach, stumbling at times on the sharp coral. Bullets were flying all around him, and every time he stumbled the men on the boat thought he'd been hit. But each time he regained his balance and kept going, into rifle fire dense as bees. Incredibly, he wasn't hit.

When he was about halfway to the beach the firing stopped and a dugout canoe put out from shore. Two soldiers were paddling it. They came to Pierson but didn't get out of the boat, holding it in place with their paddles. They spoke almost no English, and Pierson didn't know a word of Tagalog. He was obviously not Japanese but despite his repeated attempts to explain the situation the soldiers remained wary. Perhaps they didn't understand, or didn't believe him.

The three of them were getting nowhere when a Filipino officer showed up and waded out to join them. He looked younger than Pierson, who was twenty-one. He had a bright smile. Imagine Pierson's relief when he said, "Good morning. Are you in trouble?" He went on to explain in his perfect English that the local mayor, seeing lights and hearing engine noises during the night, had called an army post to report a Japanese invasion. The troops had arrived that morning and it was the mayor who had ordered them to open fire. He was obviously in a panic, as he had also ordered local residents to evacuate, disrupting their Christmas holiday.

***

Around noon, PT 31 returned with the 41 boat, an impatient Bulkeley aboard. They had been delayed by a crisis of their own: a loose barge loaded with mines drifting in Mariveles harbor. After a long struggle against an incoming tide the barge had finally been secured.

Bulkeley took one look at the stranded boat and ordered the four torpedoes and all ammunition unloaded. That was a lot of weight, but it wasn't enough. When the 31 and 41 together tried to pull the 33 free the tow ropes broke.

Bulkeley made his decision. "Scuttle her," he told Brantingham.

In shallow water there was only one way to do that. As he supervised the unloading of all that was removable Brantingham was in genuine despair. He was about to destroy the only boat he had ever commanded in his navy career, and, after this, the only one he was likely to command. The navy was unforgiving when it came to ship command. All it took was one false move, one piece of bad luck, to forever blight an officer's career.

With everything unloaded the crew of the 33 was transferred to the 41 boat, leaving only the boat captain and Richardson aboard. The 41 and the 31 stood back at a safe distance. In the forward crew compartment the two officers piled wood, cloth, anything flammable they could find, and doused it with high-octane gasoline. "It's your boat, Hank," Richardson said, and he retreated to a small boat just off the stern. Standing in the punt, he held on to a deck cleat and kept his head just above the level of the deck, to watch what was going on.

Brantingham decided it was best to set off the blaze with the help of a broom. He set it on fire up in the cockpit, went down below deck, and gingerly tossed the flaming stick onto the pile—and was instantly blinded by a great flash as a tremendous explosion blew him through the deck over the forward compartment. At the stern, Richardson saw the deck section rise some seventy feet in the air. He watched it with almost hypnotic fascination, until he realized it was going to fall on him and dove into the water. The decking came down on the punt in such a way as to almost cover it.

Richardson pushed the decking out of the way and climbed back into the punt. He couldn't see Brantingham anywhere, but what he did see seized his eyes like a fishhook. Small fires radiating out from the burning inferno forward were heading for the stern—and the gas tanks. He had to get as far away as possible before they blew, but couldn't bring himself to leave before making certain Brantingham was dead. He was about to climb aboard to look for him when he saw the object of his concern stumbling through the flames toward the stern.

Brantingham had been temporarily knocked out, but by some miracle he wasn't seriously hurt. Richardson helped him into the punt and they paddled like mad. If one gallon of high-octane fumes could make that explosion, imagine what would happen when the fire reached the main gas tanks.

They reached the 41 boat and were hoisted aboard. A grinning Bulkeley clapped Brantingham on the back. "I didn't think you were going to make it, Hank," he said jovially.

The 41 and the 31 backed off even farther from the burning 33, and everyone waited for the big explosion. It never came. When the flames reached the gas tanks they simply rose higher, their tops barely visible in the bright sunlight, and black smoke boiled up into the still, hot air, looking like a gnarled, twisted tree trunk. In the cockpit of the 41 Bulkeley rotated a hand above his head, engines were engaged, and the two boats turned about and left the burning hulk behind.

CHAPTER 12

Into the Abyss

The last days of Manila before the Japanese occupation were eerily quiet. Church bells, the cry of vendors in the early morning, the roar of traffic on the boulevards, the incessant *clop clop* of the calesa ponies were not to be heard. The streets were deserted, the shops boarded up. A thick, oily haze hung over the city, blotting out the sun. Garbage began to pile up in the streets. Swarms of flies settled on the rotting refuse, and when dogs came to root in it the flies would rise and quickly settle again. Weeds began to sprout in the gutters. The city's resident Japanese were released from internment and Quiapo, the district where most of them lived, blossomed with Rising Sun flags.

This was the city George Cox entered on the morning of December 27, the day after the open city declaration went into effect. As if to announce his intent, the guns on his boat had their canvas covers on. The Japanese had just bombed the harbor, provoked no doubt by the presence of several small freighters. Abandoned by their crews, all were on fire and sinking as Cox's boat glided by.

He tied up at the landing near the Marsman Building.

"If the sirens go off again, you know what to do," he said to Bond Murray, who in his absence would be in command. Murray understood completely. He was to run out into the bay and not wait for Cox to come back.

Cox was on a rescue mission of sorts. He walked into the city and tried every store and shop he came to. Practically all of them were shuttered but even with the streets deserted many were still open, though he often had to knock loudly to bring someone down from the upstairs living quarters. He was hunting for those small necessaries that would ease their situation at Sisiman Cove—soap, toilet paper, needles, thread, scissors, shaving cream, razors, nail clippers, combs. Common items that had become uncommonly hard to procure. Bulkeley saw a long siege ahead and whatever Cox could find would have to be nursed along indefinitely, because there would soon be no more trips to Manila.

He didn't find much. There had been a run on the stores. But what he did find he didn't have to pay for. Without exception the Filipino storekeepers asked only for his signature on a piece of paper. They trusted him. Or more precisely, they had a blind faith that the country whose uniform he wore would soon liberate the city.

***

For Tony Akers, leaving Manila was particularly painful. He had gotten involved with a girl he liked very much. She had been elected Miss Philippines a year or so before. There was that, and there was her wealth and her intelligence to make her even more interesting. Her family had a big house in the suburbs and whenever Akers was invited to visit, which was often, she would send a car for him. The one time he ventured there by himself he couldn't remember all the streets but the family name was so well known that every traffic cop he met knew where the house was and had no trouble directing him. He had been stationed at the waterfront since December 12, on courier duty, but with the departure of Admiral Hart and Admiral Rockwell's move to Corregidor a courier boat was no longer needed.

Cox had reported seeing piles of supplies and equipment, unguarded, on one of the docks. It belonged to the army, but that didn't stop Bulkeley from sending Akers to see what he could pilfer. Working fast, the crew loaded the boat, mostly with crates of canned goods, but no one came by to stop them. There was another reason to hurry, though. The Japanese columns were now ten miles north and less than eight miles south of Manila.

But for some reason they paused there. It was New Year's morning and perhaps General Homma, known for his humanity, was being considerate of any possible late-night revelers who had hangovers to deal with. All that morning black rain fell on the city. The next day, at six o'clock in the evening, just as the sun was setting, from both the north and the south, marching down the long broad boulevards with the swagger of veteran infantry, the Japanese entered the capital.

***

In darkness the water sped past. Behind were the white swirls of foam and the great glowing wake. Directly ahead was the distant glow of fires. There was no moon. Down in the engine room, a separate world of heat and noise, there was the *ping* of a bell as the signal panel shifted from "Full Ahead" to "Stop." Carl Richardson, clad only in a pair of khaki shorts, quickly pulled the three throttles all the way back. He could feel the speed drop dramatically. Another *ping*, and the panel read "Idle Speed." Ross engaged only the center engine and nudged the throttle forward until the red needle on the tachometer met with his approval.

On deck they could smell oil on the water. The sky, lowered by a thick haze of smoke, glowed faintly. The blackened piers, the charred walls where buildings once stood, these were invisible as the boat glided into the harbor, hardly seeming to part the water. All was quiet, foreboding, like the eerie silence that precedes a coming storm. The smell of scorched debris, acrid and death-filled, hung in the air.

"Off to port," someone called quietly. A half turn of the wheel and John Shambora, an axe in his hand, jumped onto a small two-masted schooner as the 41 boat slid by. He hacked a hole in her bottom, Bulkeley swinging the 41 about and coming back to pick him up as water gushed in around his ankles. This was repeated several times, all small wooden boats, until finally they came upon something larger, a 6,000-ton freighter, abandoned by her captain and crew and somehow still afloat. This one required a demolition charge, and that was for officers only, not because the men couldn't be trusted to do a good job but because the dynamite they were using, long in storage, was unstable and dangerous.

Standing in the bow, Shambora tossed a grappling hook up to the freighter's rail. He brought in the slack and when the rope stiffened he handed it to George Cox, who had dynamite, caps, and fuses in a satchel hung over his shoulder. Everyone watched as Cox went up the rope and onto the deck of the freighter. He went below and set a charge in the engine room, and another, for good measure, in a belowdecks compartment that was near the waterline. He lit the fuse on the charge in the engine room, ran to the compartment and lit that fuse, and then, moving about as fast he would ever move, he ran back on deck and lowered himself onto the 41. One foot of fuse burned for one minute, and he had given himself only five feet of time. And even that might be too much fuse. The engineers who had provided the fuses and the charges had told him that if the fuse was too long it sometimes sputtered out before it got to the blasting cap. But sometimes it would restart on its own, and there you were, going back to make sure it *was* out.

Cox was lucky. The 41 was already moving away from the freighter when there were two huge explosions, one right after the other. Twin pillars of flame a hundred feet high rose, and the sky was filled with red-hot pieces of steel coming down like rain. The freighter promptly sank to the bottom of the harbor, with only her funnel showing.

The work continued, from nine o'clock that night until three the next morning. They were there to destroy harbor shipping, what was left of it, before it could fall into Japanese hands. It was nervy work. In the glow of fires the men could see columns of Japanese infantry moving along the streets near the waterfront. Sometimes they were on bicycles. Sporadic gunfire could be heard. Luckily, most of the boats they found were small and wooden and could be sunk with an axe, which did not advertise their presence anywhere near as much as thunderous explosions and pillars of flame.

As the work neared its end the Army and Navy Club, directly facing the waterfront and dark until now, suddenly blazed with light. It had been a favorite haunt of all the officers, a source of fond memories, listening to a shortwave broadcast of the Army–Navy game, the Olympic-size swimming pool, dancing in the open-air ballroom, the fantastic meals, the Filipino bartenders who knew how to make any drink you could name, and some you'd never heard of. The handsomely appointed Reading Room with its huge library. All of it now coming under alien hands. It's going to be their headquarters, some of the men speculated. No, said others, a whorehouse for officers. Seeing those lights come on saddened everyone, and angered not a few.

Mission accomplished, the 41 started for home. Even before they were out of the harbor Paul Owen got the message: "Full Ahead." He pushed the three throttles all the way forward and felt the boat jump with the surge of power, the engines thundering through his earplugs as they raced to get back to Sisiman Cove before dawn, leaving behind a ruined city and a terrified citizenry.

***

On New Year's Day it started. In the American community, in its enclaves scattered throughout the city, there was a frantic exchange of rumors, each taken for the truth until a new one displaced the one previously passed on. Japanese troops were landing in the port area. Japanese parachutists were dropping on Corregidor. The Japanese had taken over the Manila Hotel. There were Japanese tanks on Taft Boulevard. All this before there was a single Japanese soldier in the city.

When they did come in, in long columns that headed directly for the government buildings and radio stations, the rumors turned into everyone's worst imaginings. All the white women were being put in brothels. The men were being put to work as slave labor on the docks. Hundreds of men, women, and children had been taken to North Cemetery and executed. During the first week of January there *was* a roundup of enemy aliens—Americans, British, Dutch—but no one was harmed. The Japanese were acting with restraint. Names were recorded and then everyone was dumped into the walled campus of Santo Tomas University. Close to five thousand people were interned there, imprisoned really, for no one could leave the grounds.

The Japanese were not harming them but they weren't helping either. There was no food, no medicines, nothing except what the internees brought in with them, and most had been restricted to one suitcase each. Starvation and sickness lay ahead, but with heartbreaking loyalty the Filipino people rallied to them. They came by the hundreds every day, lining up at the gates in what came to be called the package line, where they deposited their parcels of food and clothing and bedding and so much more for inspection by the Japanese before it was distributed to the internees behind the wall. Most were never paid, and never asked to be paid. It was a clear demonstration that their minds and hearts were not with the conquerors but with the conquered. In this, through an often brutal three-and-a-half-year occupation, they never wavered. Thousands of Americans would owe their lives to the generosity and devotion of ordinary Filipinos.

But Santo Tomas *was* a prison, and no one in it ever imagined it would be three and a half years before they were liberated. For a week they were trucked in, until five thousand people were crammed into three buildings. Women with children under twelve were put into the Annex, a one-story structure behind the huge, towering Main Building. There were only fifteen rooms in it, and almost four hundred women and children. Each mother had a space three feet by eight feet to live in, along with her children. Baggage and a cot or mattress took up most of the space, with about a square foot left. The days were long and hot and crowded with a horde of small children constantly underfoot, and by the seven o'clock curfew all the mothers were exhausted. At seven-thirty the lights went out, but it always took another hour or so for the children to settle down and the rooms to get quiet.

That's when they would hear it, like the far-off rumble of thunder, and be reminded that heavy fighting was going on just across the bay on Bataan. Every night the sound came to them, and it made everything bearable: as soon as help came from the States the army would be fighting its way back to Manila. One woman had three young sons and when she heard the oldest tell the other two that they were still going to be here next Christmas she sat the boy down roughly, even though she knew he was only teasing, and said, "You know who General MacArthur is, don't you? Well, just you wait. He'll be flying the good old Stars and Stripes over this joint in two weeks!"

CHAPTER 13

A Matter of Time

All through the opening weeks of January the fighting raged. Perhaps because they knew there was nowhere to go now, the young, untrained, poorly equipped Filipino soldiers who had been so undependable up on the Luzon plain were holding on behind makeshift defenses. Lack of food was the main problem. On Bataan, a little thumb of a peninsula thirty miles long and twenty miles wide, MacArthur had a hundred thousand mouths to feed—his army of 80,000 men and 20,000 refugees. That there wasn't enough to feed them was his fault. His decision to meet the Japanese at the beaches meant stockpiling food and supplies far from Bataan instead of on the peninsula itself. It was a major blunder. Having saved his army by ordering a last-minute retreat, he had to put them on half rations—about thirty ounces of food a day. Later, this would be reduced to three-eighths of a ration—about what a man could hold in the palm of his hand.

Most of those palms were brown. A false impression persists to this day about who did the fighting on Bataan. Except for one understrength infantry regiment, the Americans in MacArthur's ragtag army consisted of about 12,000 air corps technicians, beached sailors, civilian engineers, and the flotsam and jetsam of rear-echelon supply and support units, none of whom had ever fired a rifle before being turned into makeshift infantry. The bulk of the Bataan army was made up of Filipinos. But practically all the voices that come to us from that time and place, the monographs and memoirs and the numerous "I was there" stories, as well as the formal histories—are American, and they leave the distinct impression (and some actually make the claim outright) that Americans did most of the fighting on Bataan, when it was the Filipinos who did practically all of it.

On Corregidor their commander worked in one of the laterals that angled back from Malinta Tunnel. The tunnel was thirty feet high and wide enough for three trucks abreast without crowding. As soon as you stepped into it you were hit by the stench: unwashed bodies, dirty clothes, overused and undercleaned latrines, creosote, diesel fumes, and the rotten-egg dead-animal stink of gas gangrene that seeped from the underground hospital. Giant fans were supposed to move the bad air out, but they weren't doing the job. Soldiers slept along each side of the tunnel, on ammunition crates or cots or on the damp cement floor, shoes in each other's faces. Many men were in there who were not supposed to be, trying to escape the daily air raids.

From this main shaft, with its railroad track running through it, extended twenty-five laterals, narrower 400-foot-long branches that held the various offices: Quartermaster, Paymaster, Records Office, Ordinance, Transport, Operations, Intelligence, and on and on through a sprawling military bureaucracy that even here, in the midst of a shortage of almost everything, was awash in paper.

MacArthur worked in lateral No. 3, not far from the tunnel's east entrance. The lateral was only ten feet high and six feet across, with rough concrete walls and a curved ceiling, painted white with a bucket of paint scrounged from the hospital. At the end of a long row of wooden desks was MacArthur's. Behind it, he spent much of his time pacing, looking at the floor, thinking, thinking, occasionally brooding. When not pacing, he sat at his desk reading reports, writing messages, or poring over a map of Bataan.

And he composed communiques—every day, and more often than not, several in a single day. Nearly all of them mentioned only one soldier, Douglas MacArthur. Most found their way directly into the nation's newspapers, and with no other reporting coming out of the Philippines, it was MacArthur stopping a Japanese drive, MacArthur counterattacking, MacArthur holding firm against an estimated 200,000 Japanese troops (on Bataan there were never more than 25,000). MacArthur. MacArthur. MacArthur. A steady, persistent drumbeat. And it had its effect. In America streets, buildings, schools, even babies were named after him as he was quickly and enthusiastically enshrined as a national hero.

In fact, the communiques were usually inaccurate, and some nothing but blatant falsehoods disguising tragic errors of judgment. But at the time who could know? The impression at home was of a commander struggling valiantly against overwhelming odds, and who had already won a victory of sorts by being the only Allied military leader to face down the Japanese when all around him others had surrendered—Singapore, Hong Kong, the Dutch Indies. Here was an American holding a beacon of hope to the free world, and making his fellow Americans proud, and in the emotional context of the times that was what the country needed most.

Besides, Douglas MacArthur had plenty of military talent to go with his gift for self-promotion. But to be able to put it to use he would have to survive the Philippine campaign—and as the siege went on and the days turned into weeks with no sign of reinforcements, his survival was beginning to look less and less likely.

***

The same might be said of MTB Squadron 3. Slowly, the boats fell apart. There were no spare parts, not so much as a gasket. Meanwhile, both men and boats were being used hard. There were the nightly patrols, daily courier runs between Bataan and Corregidor, special rescue missions, and picket duty outside the minefields. All the boats had chronic engine problems. The effort to keep them in operating condition became a tedious around-the-clock chore.

Most of the work was done at Sisiman Cove. The little nipa huts were crowded and hot and there was only rice and salmon to eat, one cupful twice a day, and not much sleep for anyone, and as time went on nerves wore thin. Fights broke out. Beards sprouted. Skin rashes plagued everyone. Socks rotted off, underwear too. There was no clothing issue. No toothpaste. No soap. The standard uniform was a pair of khaki cutoffs. Not only spares had been lost at Cavite, but the men's personal gear as well.

But looming over everything, a threat to their very lives, was the fuel problem. The supply of the high-octane gasoline the boats ran on was dwindling, and what was available was stored in cans that had been brought over on a barge from Manila. Most of the cans had a waxy deposit in them, from whatever had been in them before they were used for storing the gas, and the wax would clog the gas strainers and carburetor jets. Someone discovered that they could get rid of a good bit of it by straining the gas through an old felt hat before fueling the boats, but never all of it, and so they could never be sure when the engines might clog up and stop. And if they stopped in a heavy sea, or, God help them, during a fight … it was nerve-racking, and only added to the tension felt by those aboard every time a boat went out.

***

Accidents, too, plagued them. On the morning of January 13, the 35 boat limped into Sisiman Cove on two engines after hitting something in the water, no one knew what, during a night patrol along the west coast of Bataan. Two of the boat's propellers were bent, damage that couldn't be repaired without spares and docking, though the boat could still do thirty knots if asked.

A few days later there was a gas explosion aboard the 32 boat, sudden and inexplicable—the 32 was not being refueled at the time. Gas fumes, perhaps a tiny leak in the seam of one of the tanks, though what set it off was a mystery, as no one had a cigarette going. Leroy Conn happened to be standing on a part of the deck that had been reinforced for a gun mount, and that bit of luck saved his life. The explosion ripped open the entire rear third of the boat and Conn was thrown thirty feet into the air to land stunned but unharmed in the water astern. But three of the crew were injured by flying debris. Henry Brantingham, formerly of the scuttled 33 boat, was now exec of the 32, and seeing this human cannonball brought back the memory of his own airborne experience, though he hadn't gone as high or as far as Conn. Over this accident Brantingham could only shake his head. Like Jonah, he thought. Every boat he was on seemed to attract bad luck.

The damaged 32 required extensive repairs. The stern was put back together, with glue and chicken wire mostly, but the after torpedo tubes had to be removed to lighten it and give it a chance of survival.

***

And then there were the air raids. With Bataan and Corregidor the only points of resistance, the entire Japanese air fleet could concentrate on this relatively small area. Bombers visited every day, Zeros too, strafing anything that looked remotely like a target, though Sisiman Cove itself, perhaps because it was so secluded, suffered no direct attacks. But no one knew how long that was going to last, and every time aircraft engines and machine gun fire was heard coming from the direction of Mariveles harbor, which took a pasting almost daily and was right next door, on the other side of a small hill, everyone on the boats ran to their battle stations. Sometimes Japanese planes would fly low along the eastern shore of the cove as they left Mariveles, providing the gun crews with some real-life target practice.

One morning, a single plane flew directly over the cove, so low it seemed possible to count the rivets in its fuselage. It flashed by so fast that the men who had scrambled into the gun turrets could get off only a few shorts bursts.

Everyone watched as it turned on a wing and headed back.

"Here she comes!" someone yelled happily. It didn't frighten anyone. They were eager to shoot one down, and actually it raised their spirits.

It came directly at the boats, with the bright morning sun at its back—a well-known trick used by enemy pilots to blind the gunners on ships. Six twin fifties—twelve .50 caliber machine guns—opened up at almost the same instant, a truly deafening noise that devoured the sound of the plane's engine. From the gun barrels smoke and flame stabbed out and such a blaze of tracers converged on the plane that it immediately altered course and was over the hill without any sign it had been hit.

The action was over almost as soon as it started. But only the action. There was a bit more to come. The next day Bulkeley received a formal complaint from the army, forwarded by Admiral Rockwell. The plane had been an American P-40. Miraculously, neither the engine nor the cockpit had been hit, but the fuselage had been riddled with bullets, stitched from cowling to tail fin, an uncountable number of holes. The pilot was understandably indignant but he should have realized that by coming at them out of the sun, no one on the boats could see the plane's markings. Not surprisingly, Admiral Rockwell, a great fan of the boats, did nothing about the complaint, and as is the nature of things in wartime, the boat crews found the entire incident hilarious.

***

Two of the boats experienced firsthand what Corregidor was enduring almost daily. The 32 and 34 were tied up at North Dock, waiting to be sent on a mission, when Japanese bombers arrived overhead. The two boat captains were in their respective cockpits, staring up.

"What do you say?" Barron Chandler called.

"They're too high for us to shoot any of them down," Vincent Schumacher called back. "I say we hit the air raid shelter pronto."

Even as they were saying this the bombs were coming down. No true sailor likes to abandon his ship, but it was the prudent thing to do.

The air raid shelter was a cavity dug into the side of a hill and shored up by timbers, like a mine tunnel. It didn't go very far back, and a bomb bursting at the entrance would likely kill everybody in it. Other than that, it afforded good protection. The boats were about 300 yards away. They couldn't be seen from the shelter, which made for an agonizing wait to find out if they had been hit. Everyone crowded as far back in as they could, and waited, and listened. There was the drone of the bomber engines, the *thump thump thump* of antiaircraft guns, the whistle of the bombs as they fell, and that eerie and in a way most frightening fraction of a second when a bomb fell silent before it exploded. Some exploded close enough to the entrance to send in a shock wave, the concussion whipping their pants and shirts.

Cone Johnson, ensign on the 32, had forgotten his helmet in the rush to get to the shelter, and during a brief lull he decided he would go back and get it. Bob Burnett, a young torpedoman on the 32, asked Johnson to bring back a pack of cigarettes. Most of the men smoked, and even those who didn't felt they could use one, hunkered in that shelter the way they were, dirt sifting down on them and the earth shaking with every explosion.

Johnson listened to the request but didn't say anything. He took off running for the boats and got there just as another formation of bombers arrived. To his immense relief he saw that neither boat had been hit. For a long, agonizing moment he debated with himself: Should I go aboard and get the helmet, or get out of here before it's too late? He could see the dense cluster of small black dots beneath the lead planes as they released their bomb loads. The helmet was forgotten and he sprinted back to the shelter, heavyset, short legged, feeling like he weighed a thousand pounds, the three hundred yards seeming like three miles. The first bombs began to hit and he ran through the smoke and dust and into the shelter, breathing hard, but alive and unhurt.

"Did you get the cigarettes?" Burnett asked him.

Johnson flopped down on the dirt floor. It was the way Burnett said it, as if all he'd done was take a stroll down the block to the corner store.

"Yeah, I did," Johnson said, "but I smoked them all on the way back."

The raid went on for a while longer. When at last they ventured out the air stank of cordite and the smoke and dust was so thick it paled the sun. There were bomb craters all the way back to the boats, but they hadn't been damaged, and the dock itself was still intact though hundreds of dead fish floated around it, where bombs had exploded in the water close by. It was clear that a number of bombs had straddled the boats without scoring a single hit.

Iliff Richardson, now serving aboard the 34 boat, thought he knew what was at work. "They'll never get the 34," he assured the others. "Three and four always make the lucky seven."

CHAPTER 14

The Action at Subic Bay

On the morning of January 18, Admiral Rockwell looked up from his desk in the navy tunnel on Corregidor and saw standing before him a man with a long, unruly beard and a red bandana around his head and wearing two pistols strapped to his hips and a big sheath knife like Jim Bowie's. His eyes were bloodshot and red-rimmed from lack of sleep and he was thinned down like everybody else, but nervous energy radiated from him like something incandescent.

"Good morning, John," Rockwell smiled.

"Good morning, Admiral," Bulkeley replied.

The same cordial exchange took place every morning, after which Rockwell, in an exchange just as brief, would give Bulkeley his orders for the day. Bulkeley had no reason to suspect that on this morning they would be any different: another monotonous patrol along the Bataan coast.

But on this morning Rockwell handed him a sheet of paper.

Looking at it, Bulkeley felt his heart skip. The first thing his eyes settled on was the word *Secret* stamped in block letters at the top. Below it was one concise paragraph: "Army reports four enemy ships in or lying off Binanga Bay. Force may include one destroyer, one large transport. Send two boats to attack between dusk and dawn."

Bulkeley felt an electric happiness. *An attack mission.* From the first day of the war, this was what he'd been waiting for.

Binanga Bay was little more than an inlet, hardly a mile across at its widest point and but an arm of Subic Bay, a large natural anchorage that was all the way up the west coast of Bataan, at the top of the peninsula, and once the home of a small American naval base, now abandoned.

Fashioning a plan of attack didn't take long. Among all the boats, the 31 and 34 were in the best shape, so that decision was easy. That meant he had

Barron Chandler and Ed DeLong as boat captains. Aboard Chandler's 34, Bulkeley unrolled the chart. His finger found the entrance to Subic Bay.

"We split up here. Ed, you go in on the eastern side, Barron, the western side. We'll meet half an hour later at the entrance to Binanga Bay for the attack. If one of us fails to make the meeting, the other will continue with the operation. We'll rendezvous at dawn off Corregidor, just outside the minefields."

All day, as the boat crews tuned the motors, re-strained the gasoline, cleaned the guns, greased torpedoes, there was the underlying, gnawing tension of waiting to go into action. Not a few of the men experienced a heightened sensitivity to everything around them: the sun playing on the water, the breeze stirring the palm trees along the cove's little white-sand beach, the cloud shadows racing each other across the grassy hillside above the cove. These things had always been there but never consciously absorbed or appreciated. Small things, but precious when there's a possibility you might not be seeing them ever again.

***

The two boats left the cove at 9 p.m. Just after midnight, at the mouth of Subic Bay, they separated in dead blackness. The weather was good and the seas were calm.

The 34 was just entering the bay when she was challenged by a signal light. Paul Owen, the 34's chief machinist mate, was watching tensely from the stern. "It won't be long now," he said to himself. He was expecting the enemy to open fire at any moment.

In the cockpit, Bulkeley took the helm from Chandler. It was not a lack of confidence in the younger man. This was by far the most important mission Bulkeley had ever had, and holding the little spoked wheel, he felt he was holding his fate in his hands, a thing he could not possibly share.

He throttled back from eighteen knots to ten. When he veered away from the light the blinking stopped. In the port and starboard gun turrets Jesse Clark and Willard Reynolds slipped their thumbs from the trigger bars.

A moment later a single cannon began firing. The sound carried across the water, but no shells came their way—for good reason. It wasn't the 34 that was being shot at, but the 31, on the other side of the bay.

***

Aboard the 31 all was frantic. They were stuck on a reef, the shell splashes edging closer. Bad luck had put them there. They were entering the bay when the two wing engines stopped running at precisely the same moment.

Wax was clogging the strainers. The two engineers, Ted Morgan and Rudy Ballough, worked desperately to clean them. While they were doing this the cooling system shut down, air bubbles had replaced the water, and now the center engine had to be turned off. The 31 drifted powerless in the night as men worked with buckets and hoses to refill the system from the galley tank. They were almost finished when there came what might be the most feared sound for a PT sailor—the obscene scraping of the wooden hull on coral.

Hardly a minute later the work was done. All three engines fired up, loud in the night. That's when the gun started shooting at them. White trees of water rose all around the boat. It took nerve to stay aboard, and DeLong had it. He did not panic. One shell landed so close that much of the water tree fell onto the boat—but only that one. It looked to DeLong like a random near-miss, and he waited it out. No shell hit that close again, and finally the gun stopped firing.

Now they had to get off the reef, fast—and as quietly as possible.

Walk the anchor out and try to pull her off, DeLong decided. He was about to give the order when they heard the distant rumble of engines.

"Sounds like the 34," Bill Plant, DeLong's exec, speculated.

"Might be," DeLong said, "but she's no help to us."

***

The 34 was heading east, away from the light that had challenged them and toward Binanga Bay. The cannon had stopped firing, and Bulkeley was keeping his speed low to cut down on the engine noise. Suddenly, out of the blackness, another challenge: an orange signal gun blinking out what was obviously a recognition code—dash-dash-dash-dot. Not knowing the answering signal, all Bulkeley could do was ignore it.

Hardly a minute later came yet another challenge, this one from what appeared to be a small vessel. Bulkeley swung the wheel and headed directly for it. Chandler had it in his binoculars.

"I can't make it out," he said to Bulkeley. "It's too dark. But whatever it is, it looks pretty small." The blinking stopped then.

"She's not worth a torpedo," Bulkeley decided, and he swung the boat 110 degrees, southeast toward Binanga Bay.

***

In the punt three men took the anchor out, the thick hawser trailing behind. The rest of the crew waited anxiously. Up in the cockpit, DeLong and Plant couldn't see a thing, the night was so black, though they were grateful there was no moon. They could hear the splash the anchor made, the softer splashing of paddles in the water, and then, at last, Jim Culp's voice from the forward deck: "We're ready, skipper."

"Everybody bear a hand," DeLong called out, and he and Plant stepped down from the cockpit.

Along the starboard side from bow to stern the hawser ran. Everyone aboard took hold of it, including the two officers, all in their bare feet, for better purchase on the metal deck.

"Heeeeve!" DeLong called, and again, and still again. The anchor did its job, it held fast as they pulled mightily on the hawser in rhythm with DeLong's commands.

Five times, six ...

They stopped at eight. The boat hadn't moved an inch. Plant offered to go over the side with a flashlight and take a look, but DeLong didn't want to show a light, and anyway, he knew what they would find down there, from the sound the boat had made when it went aground. The sharp coral had cut into the wooden hull and was holding them fast.

The tide was going out, leaving them with the terrifying prospect of having no water under the keel, and with daylight arriving before the tide reversed itself.

There was only one thing to do now, noise or no noise.

***

Two bright wands of light flailed the darkness, searching for the 34 as it crawled at ten knots toward Binanga Bay. One came from the north, from tiny Grande Island, in the middle of Subic Bay. The other came from the south, near Binanga Bay itself. In the blackness they lashed about, scissoring, separating, crossing each other, reaching out for that electrifying moment when they would have the boat illuminated, like a deer caught in the headlights of a car.

The searchlights didn't find them. But as they got close to Binanga Bay a machine gun began firing. Another joined in, then a third. The night sky quickly filled with a vast spray of flying red embers, the tracers arcing up and crisscrossing like wicker basketry—all of it far above the boat.

Barron Chandler gazed up at it. "They must think we're an airplane," he commented.

It had happened before. Whenever there were mountains in the near distance the echo of the boat engines seemed to confuse enemy gunners.

Chandler's reverie didn't last long. There was the deep boom of cannons, the shells whizzing overhead. But no shells landed near the 34. And the cannon flashes were like markers defining the shoreline in the dark, making navigation easier.

The 34 arrived at the mouth of Binanga Bay at one in the morning, right on time. Bulkeley ran the boat in slow circles, waiting for the 31 to arrive.

Ten minutes passed. Twenty. Yet DeLong's boat did not appear.

***

DeLong was racing his engines, trying to back off the reef. The noise was terrific, but no one shot at them. Desperate, DeLong persisted—until with a horrible grinding noise and a screeching whine, like a yowl of pain, the reverse gears burned out.

Nothing had worked. They were stuck for good. DeLong made the momentous decision. He turned to his exec, Bill Plant, and said, "It's time to abandon ship."

It was clear from the gunfire that Japanese were all around them, and two thoughts formed in DeLong's mind almost simultaneously—he had to destroy the boat, and he had to find a way to lead his men safely out of enemy territory.

And the best chance for that, he decided, was to get to land before daylight.

***

It was now one-thirty. Half an hour had passed and still no 31 boat. Bulkeley couldn't wait any longer. He went into Binanga Bay alone.

He went in at a slow eight knots. With him in the cockpit was Chandler, the boat captain, and Iliff Richardson, the exec. Bulkeley stood over the torpedo director, a crude device (from a 21st-century perspective) that was used to help aim the torpedoes. Chandler stood ready at the torpedo firing keys. Richardson was at the wheel.

They weren't the only ones feeling the tension. Everyone topside was silent, peering into the night from their battle stations, Clark and Reynolds with their thumbs on the trigger bars. Below, seated over the starboard engine with the three long levers of the gear shifts and buttons to start and stop each engine right at hand, enclosed in a cocoon of heat and sound, sweating in the stink of oil and grease, clad only in cutoffs, army shoes, and no socks, was Velt Hunter, who was feeling no tension at all. He never knew what was going on topside, and didn't care. All he had eyes for was the instrument panel and the signal panel.

Up in the cockpit, Bulkeley was peering through binoculars. They were 500 yards into the bay when he saw it: the faint outline of a ship. He quickly convinced himself it was a cruiser. Neither Chandler nor Richardson thought it was a big enough shape to be a cruiser, but without binoculars they could barely make it out, and so maybe it was a cruiser and they just couldn't see all of it.

Bulkeley alternated between looking through his binoculars and the torpedo director.

"Right a touch," he said.

"Right a touch," Richardson repeated, and nudged the wheel right.

"Steady."

"Steady."

Bulkeley was staring through the glasses when the night exploded into brilliant white day—a searchlight was full on them.

"Fire one!" he shouted.

Chandler hit the firing key for the port torpedo, and a heartbeat later, on Bulkeley's command, he sent off the starboard torpedo, which was heard to hit the water. Then all sounds disappeared inside the thunder of the engines as Bulkeley yelled for a hard right and full ahead. There was no time to linger. As they raced off several men, looking back, saw an explosion that was followed by an orange fireball mushrooming into the night sky.

Elation, quickly followed by alarm as someone yelled: "Port torpedo didn't fire! She's making a hot run!"

A high shrill screaming whine, now that they were listening for it, could be heard above the roar of the boat's engines. Richardson looked over the left side of the cockpit and saw the torpedo sticking out the end of the tube, stuck there with its motor running at maximum velocity. The small blast of the impulse charge had failed to eject it. It stayed in the tube, its motor running, the casings around the motor already becoming white hot. Full disintegration would follow, sending pieces of white-hot steel flying in all directions, like deadly bullets. Then the warhead would explode.

Every man aboard knew that the only way to avoid being blown out of the water was to stop the torpedo's propeller.

All engines were cut, and the 34 slowly drifted to a stop. Now there was only that unnerving, shrill, screaming whine. Many of the men found themselves moving to the starboard side of the boat, as if that might save them.

John Martino moved in a different direction, down to the crew's head for a roll of toilet paper. He possessed, among other attributes, assurance. Running back on deck, he straddled the roaring, hissing torpedo which might fly to pieces at any moment and stuffed wads of toilet paper into the vanes of the propeller. It only shredded at first, but he calmly kept at it, his fingers at risk of being cut off by the spinning blades, everyone else aboard hardly breathing with the suspense, until at last the blades, all wadded up, stopped. He deserved a medal, but he was quite satisfied with the cheers of his shipmates.

The 34 could not linger any longer. Gunfire was coming from the direction of Binanga Bay and searchlights were stabbing at the water and no one was being fooled by echoes. It was clear to the enemy that a boat of some sort had crawled into the bay and made an attack.

In the engine room, Velt Hunter saw the signal panel go to "Full Ahead." He engaged all three engines and gave each one everything it had. The stern settled in the water and then kicked up like a drag racer as the 34 went from a dead drift to forty knots in something like thirty seconds. Up in the cockpit, Richardson set a course for the rendezvous point off Corregidor, where they still hoped to meet up with the 31 boat.

CHAPTER 15

"We Can Do This"

They were in serious trouble.

Twelve men, two of whom couldn't swim, were crowded onto a makeshift raft that was drifting away, moving into ever-deeper water, as DeLong desperately tried to destroy the boat. He couldn't get it to burn. Using mattresses and clothing he had started a fire in the crew compartment, but it failed to spread to the rest of the boat.

As he was rummaging around for more flammable material he saw the short-handled axe, and it came to him. He grabbed the axe, chopped holes in the gas tanks, moved as far away from them as he could, and lobbed two grenades in their direction. As he lowered himself over the side there was the sudden *PFFFO-O-OFF* of exploding fuel and a great blast of heat that seemed to go by just above his head.

All around the boat firelight danced on the water. But a hundred yards away, at the edge of the reef, where the raft was supposed to be waiting for him, DeLong couldn't see three feet in front of his nose.

He shouted into the blackness but there was no reply. He stepped off into deep water and swam around for a while, using the breaststroke to keep his head out of the water and yelling for his men, but only silence answered him. He swam back to the reef and yelled some more. By now the heat from the fire was cooking the ammunition, sending .50 caliber bullets in all directions, and DeLong was in real danger of being shot. Still, it was some time before he could bring himself to abandon the search and leave the reef. As he waded over the coral shelf to the beach the warheads on the two remaining torpedoes exploded almost simultaneously, sending out a shock wave that DeLong felt like the shove of a giant's hand on his back.

***

Far out in deep water, beyond the range of DeLong's voice, the men on the raft saw the boat explode. It was in all their minds: *DeLong is gone*. They couldn't know he had been held up trying to get the boat to burn and thought he hadn't shown up at the raft because he'd been trapped by the fire.

But their own concerns overshadowed even that. They were far out in deep water because the raft was so unwieldy—the engine room canopy with mattresses lashed to it—and they hadn't been able to hold at the reef's edge. Now it was drifting out of control.

"We can't stay out here in daylight," Jim Culp said finally. He was a gunner's mate first class, his authority second only to that of Ensign Bill Plant. To him, Plant seemed unable to make a decision about what to do.

Plant said nothing. Culp was suggesting they abandon the raft and swim to shore, but on Plant's mind were his two non-swimmers, Rudy Ballough and Bill Dean. The decision he faced was perfectly clear to him. When nine out of the twelve men voted to swim to shore, Bill Plant, who was an excellent swimmer, said, "Fine. I'll stay on the raft with Rudy and Bill."

Off they went, led by Gunner Culp, as the raft drifted off into the darkness.

Plant would pay for his devotion. All three were captured and tied to trees for several days and interrogated. Perhaps because he was an officer, only Plant was kept as a prisoner. Rudy Ballough and Bill Dean were executed. All this, though, would become known only after the war. For Culp and the others, there was a raft out there with three men on it who might yet make it back.

***

Dawn came. From the clump of bushes where he had been hiding, sharing it with numerous biting insects, DeLong set off along the beach, looking for his men.

It wasn't long before he heard fighting off to the south, the direction he was heading. Machine gun and rifle fire was making a solid crackling sound, like burning timber. He was behind enemy lines, and the temptation was to hide until it got dark, but he was looking for tracks in the wet sand, and if he waited too long the tracks would be washed away by the incoming tide.

Tight with tension, expecting to see Japanese at any moment, he pushed on.

The gamble paid off. Not half a mile from where he started, he found the tracks of nine men. Heartened, DeLong began walking faster.

It was close to eight o'clock when Bob Caudell glanced up from the glittering arc coming out of him and saw a distant figure making its way along the beach.

"Hey, somebody's coming!" he called out.

The others were nearby, in a clump of trees and undergrowth. Caudell finished his business and rejoined them, and they all watched as the lone figure got closer.

Culp lowered his rifle. "It's him."

They stood there looking at DeLong as if he were Lazarus impossibly returned from the dead. When he got to them he received an especially warm welcome. He was both liked and respected by his men. Culp told him what had happened, and that Plant had stayed with the two men on the raft.

"Well, we can't worry about them," DeLong said. "We have to figure out what *we're* going to do." He estimated they were about three miles south of Binanga Bay, which would put them some four miles behind Japanese lines. Four miles, with the enemy between them and friendly forces, and with fighting going on that was getting louder by the minute.

"We can do this," DeLong said to them, and they believed him.

He laid out his plan. It wasn't complicated: they would stay where they were until dark and then make a run along the beach for their own lines. They couldn't afford to get into a fight with a sizeable force of Japanese. They had only one rifle and six pistols, all of which had gotten a good dose of saltwater during their swim, but the men had broken them down and cleaned them before too much corrosion could set in.

DeLong put a lookout up in a tree. Occasionally, planes flew low overhead. All morning they could hear the sound of fighting. When it seemed to be receding, DeLong decided to have a look around. He thought he might be able to find some food. He took Culp with him. Farther down the beach they came upon a nipa hut. No one was there, and there wasn't any food, but they found a pile of used coffee grounds and lit a small fire and they each had a cup of coffee, such as it was. It was disappointing, not finding anything to eat, but they discovered something better: two dugout canoes hidden in the scrub jungle nearby. And canvas for a sail. And two paddles, one board, and two shovels for paddling. And gear for rigging a sail. And just in time.

The Japanese were coming.

Soldiers appeared on the beach north of where DeLong and his men were hiding. They came down along the beach a short way, everyone in the clump of bushes waiting for the moment when they would see the tracks in the sand. But the surf must have washed them away; all the soldiers did was mill around for a few minutes before going back the way they had come. From up in the tree, though, Charles Dimaio could see more Japanese moving about to the east and south. So escaping south along the beach was now out of the question.

The two bancas gave them another way out. If they could sail or paddle five miles or so south along the coast they could put in behind friendly lines. It appeared now that they were surrounded by Japanese and some of the men wanted to leave right away, before they were discovered, but DeLong thought they would never make it in daylight.

"We'll wait for dark," he ordered.

As the sun was going down the lookout in the tree saw two small tanks heading down a trail to the north, coming toward them. It rattled them, and DeLong compromised. Rather than wait until full dark, he decided to leave with the setting sun.

This would prove to be a mistake.

***

One banca was larger than the other. DeLong divided the group. He and five others would go in the large one, Culp and three men in the small one. They had some line that DeLong intended to use as a tow rope. They rigged a sail on the larger boat and the small one was to be pulled along behind.

Dragging them down to the beach was the hard part. They were both equipped with outriggers, which snagged on every bush and clump of grass. Culp brought up the rear with the rifle. They got the large boat into the water but as the small one was being dragged over some sand dunes the men were silhouetted against the setting sun. For long moments they were moving figures etched blackly on the horizon, easily seen.

From behind them came a shout. It sounded like a command—and it wasn't in English.

"Go!" Culp told them. "Get that thing in the water, fast!" He flopped down behind the last dune and flipped up the leaf sight on the Springfield and put the rifle to his shoulder. He could hear scrabbling and excited chattering but couldn't see anyone. If he shot one of them, he was hoping it would hold them up long enough for the boats, and himself, to get away. If they kept coming he would keep shooting, and at least the boats might get away.

The men got the small boat in the water and DeLong hurriedly rigged the tow line. The voices were coming from more than one direction now, but no one appeared. The sun had gone down.

"Let's go, Gunner!" DeLong yelled, and Culp got up and ran for the boats.

They were barely wide enough to sit in and getting into them was a delicate matter, and if not a bit panicky, with the enemy so close, the men were rushed. Before they could get underway both boats capsized. Everyone ended up in the water, some of the equipment was lost, and the rudder on the large boat was damaged. DeLong quickly sorted it out, but now the small boat would have to tow the large one.

As they paddle frantically in the failing light the voices on the shore are quite distinct, and there is the rattle of equipment, canteens and bayonet scabbards bouncing and clacking—the enemy running toward them. But by the time the Japanese reach the beach the light has gotten so poor and the boats are so far away that neither side can see the other, and no shots are fired.

Two paddles are all they have. Both go to the small boat. The four men in it take turns with the crude paddles. They paddle until midnight, propelling their own boat and pulling the large one. Exhausted, their hands blistered and bleeding, they are replaced by four men from the large boat. The boats round a finger of land called Napo Point and are hit by a fierce headwind. For two more hours the men paddle until, exhausted, they are barely able to hold their own against the wind and tide. The decision is made to chance a landing in the dark. They manage to reach shore, a narrow, rocky beach. They leave the boats there. Moving inland, they find themselves entangled in barbed wire, through which they painfully pick their way, only to find themselves at the base of a cliff. Too tired to do anything else, there they huddle, to await daylight.

The gray light of dawn reveals a discouraging sight: the tide has come in. Deep water and swirling currents now trap them against the base of the cliff and make it impossible to move along the beach.

Then, seemingly out of nowhere, soldiers appear—but they are not Japanese. The Filipinos take them to their command post, where they are greeted by Captain George Cockburn of the United States Army, who tells them just how lucky they are. They had come ashore just inside the front lines, and also at the base of the only trail leading over the cliff.

And the final bit of luck: he has some vehicles that could take them back to their base at Sisiman Cove.

CHAPTER 16

An Appetite for Heroes

As Captain Cockburn was arranging breakfast for the ten exhausted and bedraggled American sailors, the 34 boat lay off the Corregidor minefields, waiting for them. The time for the rendezvous was set for 7 a.m., but the 31 did not appear. Bulkeley waited for an hour, until he finally decided the boat was lost, though with as capable an officer as Ed DeLong he and everyone else aboard the 34 still had hope the men would somehow make it back. He included that sentiment in his report of the action, along with John Martino's heroic conduct—though the torpedo with its still dangerous warhead had resisted all efforts at being dislodged and had hung halfway out of the tube all night, until, at six-thirty in the morning, it broke free and dropped into the sea, hitting the deck on its way overboard with a loud thump that for an instant stopped their hearts.

At ten-thirty that morning Bulkeley was in the navy tunnel on Corregidor, handing his report to Admiral Rockwell. Rockwell's experienced eye quickly isolated its essence: a ship that Bulkeley claimed was a cruiser had been hit and possibly sunk, and the 31 boat was missing.

"Buck, it wasn't a cruiser," Rockwell said, knowing he had to stop it there.

There is no record of Bulkeley's reaction to that, but he couldn't argue. Rockwell had already been informed that army observers high on Mariveles Mountain saw a ship sink, though the soldiers reported her to be a small armed merchantman. Frank Rockwell was as hungry for good news as anyone, but he was a man of integrity, and these were army people readily identifying a ship seen through binoculars from many, many miles away in total darkness, and he felt he had to weigh that against what Bulkeley, and they, claimed they saw.

Two days later, in another world, the *New York Times* ran a front-page story under a banner headline: NAVAL HERO SINKS JAP DESTROYER IN PHILIPPINE ACTION. The *New York Daily News* had this: U.S. HAMMERS JAP VESSELS. The *San Antonio Light*: NAVY HERO IN DARING BLOW AT JAPS. And so on, in newspapers all across the country.

The sensational press coverage was based on a brief Navy Department communique released in Washington, which was in turn based on Rockwell's official report, in which the admiral wrote "a probable hit on what appeared to be an enemy ship of undetermined size." Less cautious, and more PR-savvy, the admirals in Washington turned *that* into this: "A motor torpedo boat entered Binanga Bay, Philippine Islands, and torpedoed an unidentified enemy vessel of 5,000 tons in a night attack. Lt. John D. Bulkeley has been commended for executing his mission successfully."

It wasn't much, but starting with Pearl Harbor there had been an endless stream of bad news, the nation was weary of hearing about setbacks and defeats, and the nation's press ran with it, and somewhere along the way a shadowy, indeterminate form that might have been anything was turned into a destroyer, and in some accounts, more than one destroyer. Bulkeley and his men obviously saw *something* that night as their boat raced out of Subic Bay, but it was not the flash of a torpedo hit, nor was it a fire. Japanese records examined after the war clearly indicate that no ship was sunk in Subic Bay on the night in question. In fact, no ship was even hit.

No matter. Photographs of Bulkeley were in all the newspapers, and an entire country found its heroism in his face. The instant adulation was almost to be expected from a nation desperate for good news and wondering by this time if indeed it really possessed the kind of men who could stand up to the Jap—who had gone, in but a few weeks of war, from being subhuman to being superhuman.

***

The Jap (it was MacArthur's favorite word for his opponent, that or the singular "He") was by this time pressing him hard.

Stretching across the widest part of the peninsula, the main battle line was twenty miles long. The Japanese had sealed off the peninsula early in January and had been hammering at the line ever since. Everything would be over already if they had not paused for two days before launching the attack on Bataan. General Homma was forced to wait until his veteran 48th Division, the men who had landed at Lingayen Gulf, was put back aboard transports for the invasion of the Dutch Indies and the untried 65th Brigade put in position to replace them. The pause had given the Bataan army just enough time to dig in, but it was desperately short of food and medical supplies.

For two weeks now the Japanese had been systematically testing the line east to west, from the bay shore inward, and they had finally found the weakest part, where it dribbled off in a series of isolated foxholes to end completely in dense rainforest at the base of mile-high Mount Natib. From there the trenches and foxholes did not pick up again for another six miles, on the other side of Natib's steep, tangled slopes, which were thought, by the Americans at least, to be impassable.

This forbidding terrain didn't faze the commander of the 65th Brigade. General Nara sent a full regiment into it, with the mission of getting in behind the defenders. The regiment had marched off into the jungle on January 11 and then disappeared. The soldiers were young, many still in their teens, but they were imbued with military ardor. They had to have been, for they managed to cross a huge volcano, climbing over sheer cliffs, sliding into and pulling themselves out of deep, rocky gorges, hacking their way over nonexistent trails while dragging with them artillery pieces that weighed half a ton, along with all their other equipment, all on a few rice balls a day. They were not "creatures of the jungle," as the Americans liked to think of their adversary, but young men from farms and small towns and cities, many of them drafted into the army and given only rudimentary training but who possessed the kind of bone-deep spirit that would have been admired and praised by their enemy had they been white. For what they did was nothing less than a military masterpiece. Because the American commanders felt that no military force could possibly make its way over Mount Natib, it was undefended, and now, emerging out of nowhere, this regiment fell upon the exposed flank of the defenders, who retreated in panic, leaving a two-mile hole in the defense line.

The last available reinforcements were sent to plug the hole, and the line held. Meanwhile, on the other side of Natib, the west side of Bataan, fresh Japanese forces were attacking. (This was the fighting heard by DeLong and his men.) The line there began to crack. If it did, and the Japanese came through, the entire battle line would collapse. In his tunnel headquarters, receiving reports of renewed fighting on both sides of Natib, and the precarious state of the defenders, with no reserves left, MacArthur decided that the time had come for a general withdrawal to the reserve battle line.

He came within a hair's breadth of disaster. The retreat caused an eight-mile-long traffic jam along the main road that led south to the new defense line. The intermingled mass of men on foot and in trucks and buses had so slowed that those walking were moving faster than those riding. Had the Japanese chosen to interdict with artillery fire, they would have ignited the already shaky troops into a cattle-like stampede to the rear, causing hundreds of casualties and such confusion as to be fatal to any successful defense. Here darkness played a role, and luck. There was no stampede, but dawn on

January 25 found thousands of mostly Filipino soldiers still on the open roads and trails leading south. What the enemy artillery had failed to capitalize on during the night, the air force attempted to make up for throughout that long, hot, terrible day. Unopposed as usual, for twelve hours Japanese planes mercilessly bombed and strafed the slow-moving, dust-covered columns as they staggered down the roads of east and central Bataan. Hundreds were killed, hundreds more wounded before the men reached the new defense line that had been set up behind a cobblestone road that ran for fifteen miles across the peninsula. It was a strong position, being shorter than the previous line and therefore more easily defended. But it was also the last possible line. There could be no further retreat.

The withdrawal now complete, MacArthur sent this fairy-tale radiogram to Washington: "Under cover of darkness I broke contact with the enemy and without the loss of a single man or an ounce of material. Am now firmly established on my main battle position."

Though it had been a retreat, his army was still intact, still fighting, still a beacon of hope for the free world, a dimming beacon, perhaps, yet nevertheless keeping the dark from becoming absolute, and MacArthur's reputation spiked yet again, more MacArthur Buildings, more babies named Douglas, more accolades from an adoring press at home. More than ever, he was the nation's hero, side by side now, though, with John Bulkeley.

For a more realistic portrayal of the withdrawal we can turn to a poem, one of dozens written during the campaign by a young, sensitive lieutenant, Henry G. Lee of the U.S. 31st Infantry. The poems were found buried under a nipa hut in a prisoner of war camp on Luzon in February 1945 by American Rangers who liberated the prisoners. Lieutenant Lee, however, was not there. Just twenty days before he would have been rescued along with his poems he perished aboard a Japanese prison ship en route to Japan. Unlike MacArthur in his tunnel, Henry Lee had been in the thick of the withdrawal, and this is what *he* said about it:

> … saved for another day
> Saved for hunger and wounds and heat
> For slow exhaustion and grim retreat
> For a wasted hope and sure defeat …

***

Throughout all of this, the PT actions, the desperate fighting on land, the withdrawal to a new line, Bob Kelly remained in the hospital on

Corregidor. He couldn't get the doctors to release him and he was getting pretty mad about it, and Kelly had a temper. At times his voice could be heard throughout the hospital lateral and beyond as he told the doctors what he thought of them.

He was being unfair, his swollen arm and finger were resisting the various treatments, but he was being just as hard on himself for not healing fast enough to rejoin the squadron. There was a lot going on and time seemed to be slipping through his fingers like water.

Still, he managed to carry on a romance of sorts with one of the nurses, Beulah Greenwalt, "Peggy" everyone called her. Kelly had a lean, high-cheekboned, brooding face, almost like a male fashion model, and women found themselves pulled to him, though he had never paid all that much attention to them, somehow they seemed too distracting and perhaps even a bit silly, at least the ones he'd had casual dates with. But there was nothing silly about Peggy Greenwalt, an army nurse on the front lines, and pretty enough, and in his present situation what Kelly needed most was some distraction. The two hit it off and saw each other frequently. Peggy was dating an army officer at the time, one of the doctors, in fact, though nothing happened that might have alarmed him, unless he objected to long quiet talks between friends, and the party the two friends went to in the nurses' quarters, after which Peggy made certain her special patient was back in the ward and in bed by nine.

On the same morning that he delivered his Binanga Bay report to Admiral Rockwell, Bulkeley went to see Kelly in the hospital. Kelly, pale and clean-shaven, at first didn't recognize the wild-looking, bearded, bleary-eyed man with the red bandana around his head and the big Bowie knife tucked in his belt (Bulkeley had been reporting to Rockwell that way, causing consternation among the perfectly tailored staff officers in the navy tunnel, but Rockwell loved his PT boats and the men who rode them and he never said a word about it).

"John," Kelly said, "you've got to get me out of here."

"That's why I came." Bulkeley gave Kelly an account of the action in Binanga Bay. "We're down to four boats, and we're missing two officers. I need you back with us. How do you feel?"

Kelly had lost over thirty pounds, the long bed rest had taken away his strength and stamina, and there was still some swelling in his arm and a hole three inches long and an inch wide in his infected finger.

"I feel great," he said to Bulkeley. "I'm ready to go. But they won't let me out of here."

"Who's your doctor?"

Kelly gave the name.

"I'll be right back," Bulkeley promised.

Whatever was said between the pirate and the medical man lasted some fifteen minutes, but when Bulkeley left the hospital lateral it was with Kelly.

CHAPTER 17

The Twenty-Yard Shootout

It was January 22 and the 34 boat was scheduled for the evening patrol off the west coast of Bataan. The 34 was Kelly's boat, he was her captain, but he had been out of action for a month and that meant all the other boat captains had more combat experience than he did, and they knew what was working and what wasn't with boats that by now seemed to have personalities of their own, each a little different from the others in how the engines performed, how the wheel responded, how many repairs had been made and what effect the repairs had on the boat, and Bulkeley decided that Barron Chandler, who had been filling in for Kelly, should take the 34 out for one more mission as its captain, though both Kelly and Bulkeley would be coming along. It pleased Chandler to be going out, the nightly patrols, or more precisely the potential they had for action, were the only antidote to the crushing boredom of the daylight hours in Sisiman Cove, but this was a decision that would cost the young officer dearly.

It was a calm night, and chilly. Sweaters were comfortable over khaki shirts, though the men still had on only cutoffs or swimming trunks—the *only* thing they wore during the blistering heat of the day. Seeing how deeply tanned all the others were, in his own words "burned black as natives," Kelly was acutely conscious of his pale, almost prisonlike pallor.

There were four of them crowded into the cockpit: Bulkeley, Kelly, Chandler at the wheel, and Iliff Richardson, the boat's executive officer. At 2 a.m. Kelly took the wheel, to start the hands-on business of getting back in form, and also to relieve Chandler. Bulkeley stayed in the cockpit with Kelly, and Chandler and Richardson went below to get some sleep.

They were still asleep when Paul Owen, peering into the dark from up in the starboard gun turret, saw a dim light low on the water. "Skipper, there's something out there," he called to Kelly. "Off the starboard bow at ten o'clock. Looks like it might be a boat."

Bulkeley found it in his binoculars but could make out only a dark shape that seemed to be slowly drifting.

"Maybe it's Plant and the two guys who were with him," Kelly guessed. "Their raft might have drifted out to sea." DeLong and the other nine men had since returned to Sisiman Cove, to the relief of all, and everyone now knew what had happened to the 31 boat.

"Could be," Bulkeley said, "but why would he be showing a light? He wouldn't have any idea it was us."

Just then the light began to blink—dots and dashes, but no message they could read.

"General quarters," Bulkeley ordered, and Al Ross, who as quartermaster was standing by just outside the cockpit, worked his way to the stern and back, repeating the order. There was sudden movement all over the boat as men went to their battle stations, but it was all done so quietly that Richardson and Chandler were not awakened.

"Let's have a look," Bulkeley said, and Kelly cranked the wheel hard over and headed straight for the light. In the starboard turret Owen pulled back on the loading levers of the twin fifties and they slid forward with their distinctive clack. Jesse Clark in the port turret echoed the clack. Al Ross was now manning the Lewis gun in the bow. Kelly glanced about and saw what he wanted to see: all guns trained on whatever was out there.

As they closed, the light went out. Bulkeley stepped down from the cockpit and moved up to the bow, and when they got to within fifty yards of what was now clearly not a raft but a long low shape in the darkness he yelled out, "Boat ahoy!"

Silence followed.

Kelly put the engines in neutral and drifted closer.

At twenty yards Bulkeley called out again, "Boat ahoy!" An instant later there was an eruption of yellow-purple flashes along the entire length of the dark shape. The bullets passed so close to Bulkeley's head he could feel the suction. In almost the same instant every gun on the 34 opened fire. The noise was deafening, and it brought Chandler and Richardson bolting topside and into the cockpit.

What they saw made them blink: a long low boat lit by muzzle flashes that at times was almost hidden from view by the orange streams of tracers pouring from the 34. Hundreds of bullets were crossing each other's paths in the night. The firing was so intense that the barrels of the twin fifties glowed red. Bullets whined all around the cockpit and thudded into the 34's hull and spanged off the torpedo tubes. Showers of orange sparks flew off the boat they were firing at.

Then it began to move faster.

The enormous volume of gun flashes were lighting up the night enough for the men on the 34 to make out what they were shooting at. It was a landing craft, a long, low, barge-like boat, and it was full of helmeted men. And it had armor plating at the bow and stern. The orange sparks of ricocheting bullets told them that, and the way the boat was maneuvering, the man driving it trying to keep the armor facing the fire-breathing scourge that had descended on him out of the night. He was good at it, but Kelly countered by circling, coming in from one side and then the other and letting them have it where they couldn't take it.

Up in the cockpit they were all crouching a bit, almost involuntarily, against the storm of lead. Chandler was standing just behind Bulkeley when a round singed his cheek.

"Boy, that was close!" he said to no one in particular.

The words were hardly out of his mouth when something knocked his feet out from under him and he fell to the deck. He felt nothing at first, but as he lay there a blinding wave of pain suddenly surged through him. He looked down at his feet and all he saw was blood. A bullet had pierced the plywood and aluminum cockpit and both of his ankles.

Kelly took one look at all the blood and shouted, his voice almost drowned by the racket of gunfire, "Take the conn!" and Richardson stepped to the wheel. Kelly and Bulkeley not too gently picked Chandler up and carried him out of the cockpit and laid him on the engine room canopy, all under intense fire. On the way back Kelly stuck his head in the charthouse. "Reynolds, get out here with some morphine. Mr. Chandler's been hit."

Willard Reynolds was the boat's cook. He was also the medic, and he had been holding himself ready for just this kind of thing. He already had a morphine syrette in his hand and he stepped out of the charthouse, the air around him alive with the whine of bullets, and gave Chandler the shot. Then he picked Chandler up and awkwardly carried him below to the captain's cabin, leaving a trail of blood as he went, and laid him on the broad bunk. He put a tourniquet on each leg and proceeded to pour an entire bottle of iodine on Chandler's shattered ankles. The morphine hadn't yet taken effect and as the burning liquid entered his wounds Chandler's eyes widened and his mouth opened in a silent scream.

The noise above decks was tremendous. The air stank of sulfur. The two boats were twenty yards apart and blasting away at each other with all they had. The 34 was circling, its guns raking one side of the barge and then the other, the gun barrels glowing red and threatening to turn white with the heat.

Tracer ends streaked off the barge in all directions. The gunners on the 34 could see from their tracers that some of their rounds were hitting inside the barge, which was filled with men. A single .50 caliber bullet could blow a hole in a man the side of a pie plate, and as he was firing Jesse Clark thought about the human wreckage he was helping to create and was thankful it was dark and he wouldn't have to look at it. After exposing himself once to get Chandler below, young Reynolds did it again, scuttling up to Clark with a canister of .50 caliber ammo.

The brutal impact of those .50 caliber bullets sent debris flying from the barge, helmets too, from the heads of the men in it. The muzzle flashes coming from it gradually decreased until at last it fell completely silent. It had already started to sink, and now it went down fast.

Owen, Clark, and Al Ross in the bow stopped firing.

"Sweep the water!" Bulkeley ordered.

This wasn't something any of the three really cared to do, shooting at men helpless in the water, but they obeyed the order. "As I understand war," Bulkeley would say later, "you've got to kill the enemy, a lot of him." In his report of the action he would write: "Due to darkness it was impossible to rescue survivors."

***

Chandler was in danger of bleeding to death, and he was in great pain, but his agony was going to be prolonged. The fight was over but the 34 couldn't go back to Corregidor and its hospital until full daylight. Traversing the minefields at night was simply too dangerous. They would have to stay at sea for several more hours. Chandler might be forgiven for cursing his luck. Bulkeley had wanted him for one more mission as boat captain, instead of Kelly. But if it had been Kelly, Chandler would have had no place on the 34 boat and he would not have gone out that night.

"That boat was a landing craft," Kelly pointed out, as he and Bulkeley were talking it over. "It would be pretty odd if it was out here alone." Bulkeley agreed, and for the next two hours the 34 patrolled in the immediate area of the gunfight, looking for another target. They didn't see anything, and when their own shore guns began shooting at them, swarms of tracers arcing out into the night, Kelly set a course for home.

Paul Owen had the best night vision of anyone on the boat, and he proved it again. He was the first to see, just before it began to get light, a dark shape low in the water. Even with his binoculars Bulkeley couldn't make out more than that, but the silhouette was too familiar for him not to know what it was.

"Another one," he said to Kelly.

It was some distance away. As the 34 closed at idling speed the night gave way to gray dawn, and now they could see it clearly. It was another launch, though smaller than the first one, and it was moving away from the shore.

But they had a seriously wounded man aboard, and a horrendous fight already behind them in which they were fortunate not to have had anyone killed or anyone else wounded.

"I think we should put this to Barron, and the crew," Kelly suggested.

"I was thinking the same thing," Bulkeley agreed.

Before sending them to their battle stations, Bulkeley went to each man on the boat and asked if he wanted to go after the new target. It was as if he were taking a vote. This is a bit puzzling. He got a unanimous yes, but, really, what else could a man say, the fear being that you might be the only man to say no, and be branded a coward. Then he went below and asked Barron Chandler the same question. Chandler's answer would clinch it. If he said he didn't think he'd make it if they delayed any longer, they would immediately make a speed run for Corregidor. Throughout the fighting Bulkeley had dashed below to ask, "How are you doing, Barron?" Chandler wasn't doing well at all, and he knew it, but he would lie and say "I'm fine." And this time he lied again and said, "I'm feeling better. Go get them."

***

Just ahead of them now, the launch started to turn back toward shore. Bristling with guns, the PT boat bearing down on them must have been a frightening sight to the men in the launch and they were no doubt hoping to avoid getting shot up on the open sea.

Kelly changed course slightly to cut it off. At four hundred yards Bulkeley gave the order to commence firing and his gunners opened up. The guns were like fire hoses spraying molten ore, but the tracers seemed to be bouncing off iron plating, ricocheting a hundred feet in the air. The launch showed no signs of slowing. The return fire, though, was curiously light and sporadic.

The 34 closed to within ten yards of the launch, pounding it with gunfire, firing now almost diagonally down through her sides and bottom, the heavy bullets punching through steel, debris flying in all directions. It was a graphic demonstration of the awesome close-in firepower of a PT boat, and what both sides were witnessing, though neither side knew it, was the future. Later in the war it would not be torpedoes that did the most damage to the enemy—and in fact they rarely hit anything—but the PT boat's armament. The Japanese would use landing barges to shuttle men and supplies between the various islands they occupied, and with even more guns installed the PT boats would go out and routinely blow landing barges apart with a firestorm of gunfire.

Finally, with the 34 practically on top of the launch, a tracer hit the fuel tanks. They exploded in a ball of flame, the motor stopped, and now the launch was only drifting.

By now Bulkeley had two grenades in his hands. "Put us alongside," he said, and Kelly did so. When they were ten feet away Bulkeley tossed both grenades into the launch, which had started to sink, then jumped aboard with his pearl-handled .45 pistol, landing in a deep slop of water, blood, and oil.

At once he saw why resistance had been so light. There were only three men aboard: one dead and two badly wounded. The launch had delivered the soldiers it had been carrying to the beach and had been trying to make it home.

Al Ross tossed Bulkeley a line. Bulkeley tied a bowline and slipped the noose under the arms of one of the wounded men. Ross and another man pulled him aboard, and then, in the same way, the other prisoner. Bulkeley started tossing anything that might have intelligence value up onto the deck of the 34—briefcases, papers, knapsacks. He had to work fast, the launch was sinking under him. At last, with the water up to his chest, he waded to the launch's side, grasped Kelly's hand, and was hoisted out as the launch gurgled under.

Willard Reynolds, cook, medic, and now armed guard, stood over the two seriously wounded men with his .45 in his hand. One was an officer, who despite his wounds was holding himself up, kneeling with his eyes closed. Reynolds guessed he was expecting to be shot at any moment. The other was hardly more than a boy, a teenager in a uniform, so gravely wounded he couldn't sit up. Reynolds felt nothing but pity for them. He had never seen a Japanese before, let alone this close, and in their suffering they seemed to him all too human.

The younger one stirred and feebly asked for a cigarette. Reynolds didn't have one on him. He called out "Who's got a smoke?" and John Martino dug one out and came to the bow with it.

He offered it to Reynolds.

"It's for him," Reynolds said, pointing.

Martino looked at the young soldier lying there bleeding from his wounds. He lit the cigarette and knelt over him and put it in his mouth. But when he offered one to the officer, it was refused, the officer turning his head away.

Kelly was watching from the cockpit. "Surly bastard," he muttered, completely misreading the officer's reaction. Only later, after the war in the Pacific was over and was being written about with some insight, did Americans fully understand their adversary, the mortal shame a Japanese soldier felt if he was captured, the ultimate disgrace, death being preferable, indeed, mandatory. If a soldier *was* captured, usually due to incapacitating wounds, as with these two men, he considered himself already dead. And so how could a dead man smoke a cigarette? That the young soldier asked for one was almost certainly an indication that he knew life was ebbing, he was not to be among the living dead, but among the truly dead, and quite soon. In this, he was correct. When the 34 put in at Corregidor's North Dock both prisoners were given first-aid treatment by a doctor, but while on the way to the field hospital on Bataan the young soldier died.

Barron Chandler was carried into the hospital in Malinta Tunnel, dreadfully weak from loss of blood but still conscious. The decks of the 34, oily and bloody, were scrubbed down. The many bullet holes were counted. As a sign of victory, a Japanese bayonet and a helmet were wired to the top of the mainmast.

And so the war went on.

CHAPTER 18

Stalemate

It went on, but not well, not for the defenders, and not for the Japanese. Both sides were in a precarious position. By now malaria was rampant among the Japanese as well as the Americans and Filipinos, though the Japanese at least were not on a starvation diet and not running out of medicine.

In the last week of January, all along the cobblestone road that ran across the peninsula and that was now the main defense line, the Japanese had attacked and been thrown back with heavy losses. The young Filipino conscripts who only a month before had been not much more than an untrained mob were now battle hardened and combat wise, and though they still needed the steadying influence of experienced American officers and probably were still incapable of mounting a counterattack, next to a retreat the most challenging of military movements, they fought well on the defense, when they were behind adequate fortifications and supported by artillery.

General Homma was an experienced and competent commander but he had been betrayed by almost cruelly faulty intelligence estimates. They told him that after the precipitous retreat of the enemy forces down the Luzon plain he faced only a defeated remnant of those forces on Bataan. Homma had relayed that information to the high command in Tokyo, who promptly took away his crack 48th Division, the veterans who had landed on the beaches and who had proceeded to drive the defenders all the way back to Manila and into the Bataan Peninsula. The 48th was sent to Java and replaced by a brigade of troops intended only for occupation duties. A division was 20,000 men, a brigade 7,500. Homma now had fewer men with less experience to fight what had become a brutal contest of attrition in which the fighting spirit of these new men, every bit the equal of the departed veterans, would not be enough to overcome vastly superior numbers.

With the fighting along the front in deadlock, Homma decided on a tactic that had proved to be immensely successful against the British in Malaya.

On the first day of February he sent almost a thousand men to land behind the front lines on the west coast of Bataan.

This wasn't his first attempt. Two weeks before, he had sent small parties of troops, groups of 300 to 500, to land behind the lines, hoping to terrorize and confuse the defenders. This had always been a favorite Japanese tactic, it required men who were absolutely prepared to die, which almost by definition was every man in the Imperial Army. It was one of these landing parties that Bulkeley and Kelly in the 34 boat had stumbled upon on the night of January 22. There were three altogether and though they caught the defenders by surprise they confused no one, the American commanders sensing immediately what Homma was up to, and knowing what was going on, neither they nor the men under them felt any terror, a good deal of which is a fear of the unknown. Two of the landing parties were wiped out, but the landing at Quinauan Point (promptly dubbed "Quinine Point" by the Americans) had succeeded, and the Japanese were still there.

The mission of the latest landing party was to link up with the men at Quinauan and then drive south to seize the small port of Mariveles. All supplies and communications between Bataan and Corregidor ran through Mariveles. The defenders would be compelled to try to retake it, and to do that they would have to pull men off the main battle line, and when they did, Homma would smash through the weakened defenses and rout them. He would have the entire peninsula as his own, and with Bataan as a staging base, Corregidor was doomed.

***

A sound plan, unquestionably, but nothing went right. A squad of Filipino infantry patrolling along the main battle line found a copy of Homma's orders on a dead Japanese officer, a gift of incredible good fortune for the defenders, and General Jonathan Wainwright, tall, leathery, hard-drinking, the field commander who was running the show directly under MacArthur, wasted no time in getting what little reserves he had to the west coast of Bataan.

It was forbidding terrain, starkly different from the peninsula's relatively settled east coast that faced Manila Bay. Here, the coast faced the South China Sea and jungle-covered mountains sloped steeply down to end abruptly in high matted cliffs overlooking small beaches and coves. There were no settlements at all. It was dense jungle all the way to the cliff line. Into this semi-wilderness we see them move in and take up their positions, sealing off Quinauan Point, columns of infantry and tanks, the infantry the best the defenders had, Philippine Scouts, highly trained long-service soldiers with the best equipment available and a fierce pride in their fighting ability, which was prodigious. Every man was a marksman, and for each of them the army was his home. They were the last thing the Japanese in the landing party needed to have facing them. The tanks were manned by Americans and were probably the smallest tanks ever made, but they were tanks, armored vehicles that could not be hurt by small arms fire or grenades, which was all the Japanese had.

Once they got ashore, Homma's men were going to be in dire trouble.

But that's not where their travail started.

Forewarned, the lookouts on Mariveles Mountain spotted the landing barges while they were still out at sea. The alert was sounded and four P-40 fighters (all that was left of the American air force in the Philippines) rose from a small airstrip on Bataan, 100-pound bombs under their wings.

The little air armada had no trouble finding the barges in the night. Bombs fell, barges were sunk, the rest scattered, to remain scattered on a rough, heaving sea which even before the bombing had been giving them trouble. The planes circled and strafed until their ammunition ran out. Then the American artillery opened fire, the big shells landing among the scattered barges and the soldiers floundering in the water, the sea erupting all around them with hundreds of tall white waterspouts.

On the dark sea, under the thin moon and the stars, Homma's last great hope for a quick victory had already begun to unravel.

***

As this was going on, and oblivious to it, Bulkeley was gorging on homemade ice cream. He was aboard the USS *Canopus*, a submarine tender, a mother ship to a fleet of smaller vessels that depended on her for all sorts of supplies and services. The submarines were gone, having fled to the Dutch Indies early in the war, but the *Canopus* was still dispensing her favors. She had splendid machine shops and all over the peninsula anyone who needed something made or repaired tried to get to her. She had refrigeration and excellent cooking facilities, hot showers, and cold drinking water. Meals were served on white linen with fine china and silverware. She was moored along the eastern shoreline of Mariveles harbor, just over a big forest-covered hill from Sisiman Cove, and she looked like an abandoned hulk—listed over on her side, cargo booms hanging lifeless and black smoke wafting from charred bomb holes, as though fires were still smoldering inside her hull. The smoke was from oil-soaked rags placed in small cans, and the cargo booms had been intentionally cut loose.

The Japanese had bombed the ship twice with only superficial damage, and her captain had used the damage to create a ruse.

The disguise was working. There had been no more air attacks against the ship, and Bulkeley ate his ice cream with a splendid sense of security, a commodity not to be found anywhere else on the peninsula. He hadn't come to the *Canopus* just to eat ice cream. The generator on the 41 boat needed new bushings, and when the repair job was done he hopped aboard the 41 and went back to Sisiman Cove, where the 32 boat was just leaving for the nightly patrol along Bataan's west coast.

In the cockpit of the 32 Vincent Schumacher watched the 41 slide by off his port beam. He knew where Bulkeley had been and it made him think of his own visit to the *Canopus*, where he'd had a hot shower and a meal that was like something in a dream: Virginia ham, peas, glazed sweet potatoes, ice cream, coffee. When he got back to Sisiman Cove his twenty-year-old coxswain, Clem Langston, asked him what it was like, and Schumacher told him he felt like he'd gone to heaven and was sent back.

Langston was with him in the cockpit, along with Ed Delong. There were hints that DeLong was to get a medal for leading his men to safety after the loss of the 31 in Binanga Bay, which in a way troubled him. He had been in command, and the function of command was to make decisions and accept responsibility, and so why should he get a medal for simply doing his job?

Perhaps DeLong was pondering this, or maybe he wasn't thinking about anything at all, when Schumacher, binoculars to his eyes, saw a ship dead ahead at an estimated 5,000 yards. He handed the glasses to DeLong, and to Langston he said, "Battle stations." Langston surrendered the wheel and made his way to the stern, passing the order to all hands as he went.

In the binoculars DeLong found the dark shape.

"It looks pretty big," he commented.

"I'll bet you a cookie it's a cruiser," Schumacher said.

It was 9:15 p.m. and they were about five miles off the coast of Bataan and there was moonlight on the water. Schumacher began to stalk his prey, but he had a crippled boat. After the explosion that had sent Leroy Conn soaring high into the air, the 32's hull was being held together by a jury rig of wires and braces, and she was running on only two engines. When Schumacher pushed his throttles all the way forward, all he got was 22 knots, less than half the speed he would have with the boat in prime condition. Not surprisingly, the target gradually drew away from him. After half an hour it was hardly visible.

"Shit," or something close to that, Schumacher was heard to mutter.

Just then DeLong, straining to keep the dark shape in his glasses, saw it slow and then turn eastward, toward the Bataan coast—no longer heading away but now broadside to the 32.

Schumacher went straight at it, closing rapidly at full speed, the engines making their howling tomcat roar, phosphorescent bow wave up front, glowing wake behind, easily seen, easily heard. He was not stalking the target but was charging in, afraid that if he was too cautious it might turn again and he would lose it before getting within acceptable range for a torpedo attack, and only with hindsight can that be called bad judgment.

At 5,000 yards—still almost three miles from the target—the 32 was suddenly engulfed in brilliant white light, and a tremor of fear traveled the length of the boat. For the PT sailors there was nothing more terrifying than being caught in a Japanese searchlight.

Schumacher cranked the wheel hard over to bring the starboard gun turret to bear.

"Commence firing!" Jim McEvoy heard, and he squeezed the trigger bar and felt the heavy jolts as orange tracers poured out in a twin stream. There was a loud swoosh as a shell went by just above his head to explode in the water astern. McEvoy could see his tracers plunging dotted lines into the darkness and hitting the water and flying high into the air, and he cursed himself. He was firing too low, but the searchlight was full on them and his eyes felt blistered. It was like staring into the sun.

In the brilliantly illuminated cockpit Schumacher and DeLong could not see the target, it was lost in the glare. Using an estimate of the ship's last known angle and speed, Schumacher fired his starboard torpedo as two shells hit the water 200 yards ahead and the sea shot up in twin white pillars. Schumacher turned directly into the glare and fired his port torpedo as two shells hit the water 200 yards astern.

It was time to go. Schumacher cranked the wheel hard over with throttles to the wall, a hard ninety-degree turn, his gunners pounding away, trying to hit the light, which unnervingly stayed on them as Schumacher turned sharply again.

Suddenly there was an explosion below the searchlight and debris rose up into the searchlight beam. Schumacher would report this, and presumably others aboard also saw it. But whatever was out there kept firing at them, two-gun salvos as before, the searchlight staying on them, nothing had changed. It went on for ten more minutes, until another hard right turn lost the light. It passed over the 32 several times, playing back and forth, searching, and at last it went out, on its own. When Schumacher returned to Sisiman Cove at dawn, he reported a hit on a cruiser. As was only to be expected, his report generated yet another communique from Washington to the nation's press.

***

There would be one more night action before the four remaining PT boats would be called upon to perform their ultimate, sacrificial mission. Another hit would be claimed, on a destroyer. As these reports of successful PT actions came out of the Philippines the impression was that of a handful of mosquito boats holding half the Japanese navy at bay. It was the beginning of the PT legend, and no one questioned it. There were too many people eager to believe it for anyone to express publicly any doubt about the results of these actions. We were in a war, and losing, and to doubt was to be unpatriotic, patriotism having become a very real emotion, every bit as vivid and visible as hate or love or sorrow or joy. Questions would arise, and much doubt expressed, before the war was over, but not before it was absolutely clear we were winning. In the meantime, what passed for great victories was this:

January 24: Bulkeley in PT 41 again creeps into Subic Bay. Gunning the engines, he races at high speed and fires two torpedoes at what appears to be a large warship anchored six hundred yards away. Several crewmen observe one hit and see debris falling around the 41. Bulkeley is credited with another sinking, "probably a destroyer." Japanese records later show that a transport had been in the area but had not been hit.

February 1: the Schumacher mission. PT 32 fires two torpedoes at a ship believed to be a cruiser. Several men observe what they believe to be a hit, and Bulkeley's little squadron is credited with sinking a cruiser. Japanese records show conclusively that it was the minelayer *Yaeyama*, and that she was not hit.

February 17: PT 35 and PT 41 enter Subic Bay again and fire a torpedo at a large vessel near a pier. Bulkeley notices a fire near the pier. The next morning army observers high on Mariveles Mountain report what appears to be a large warship burning at the pier. Bulkeley is credited with sinking yet another destroyer. Japanese records show that a tanker had run aground and caught fire near the pier and had tied up there as her crew continued to fight the blaze. She had not been hit by a torpedo. (Bulkeley and the men of Ron 3 still didn't realize that their torpedoes were faulty; the ones that were not outright duds were passing underneath the hulls of enemy ships without detonating and then blowing up when they hit an object beyond, usually the shoreline. Not until well into the war would navy ordnance experts finally correct problems with the depth mechanisms and exploders.)

Nothing can diminish the courage of these men, who fully believed they were attacking big enemy warships. But it was all done in the black of night, with nothing seen clearly and with more hope than doubt riding invisible on every torpedo.

***

At Quinauan Point on that first day of February the Japanese who had survived the bombing and shelling of their landing craft, some 400 of them, were climbing the cliffs. In the dense jungle that covered the point, they found the 200 men who were already there from a previous landing.

The link-up had been accomplished, but moving south to seize the little port of Mariveles was not possible now. All 600 of them were trapped, hemmed in on three sides by tanks, Philippine Scouts, Constabulary troops, planeless American air corps men, beached sailors, anyone the hard-pressed Wainwright could find to throw into the fight.

What followed was a scene that would become familiar later in the war but that no one among the defenders had ever seen before, or could even imagine. Vastly outnumbered and outgunned, the Japanese fought savagely. Their grip on the little promontory had to be pried from them finger by iron finger, until every one of them was dead. Not one Japanese soldier surrendered. On the last day of the fighting a few dozen survivors were bottled up in an area the size of a football field, with the cliffs just behind them. Tanks, infantry, everything was blasting away at them, literally blowing the jungle apart, when suddenly there was shrieking and yelling that could be heard even above the din of battle. The surviving Japanese, having reached the threshold of human endurance, began jumping up and tearing off their uniforms and leaping off the cliffs. Incredibly, after their plunge some were still alive, though with broken bodies, and they crawled into small caves at the base of the cliffs, still refusing to surrender or be captured. American engineers were called in to seal them forever in the caves with charges of dynamite.

Among the defenders even MacArthur, pacing in his tunnel on Corregidor, was slow to realize what had happened. But General Homma knew. With the loss of the entire landing party his only hope of breaking the deadlock along the main battle line had vanished. He was in stalemate, and he would now have to suffer the humiliation of pleading for heavy reinforcements if he were to bring the Bataan campaign to a conclusion. With other Japanese armies advancing throughout the Far East, only actual defeat could have brought more shame upon him. It was not quite the time for ritual disembowelment, but at a staff conference on February 8 he burst into tears, and then fainted.

CHAPTER 19

Last Stand

Almost everyone in the besieged garrison called it The Aid, capitalized as if it were a name, the human entity who would be their savior. At a party in one of the field hospitals, doctors and nurses sipping from metal canteen cups the last of the hoarded whiskey brought over during the retreat from Manila, no one thought to raise a toast to the nurse whose birthday it was. Instead, it was "To The Aid." To which one of them responded with the standard reply: "And God help the Jap when it gets here."

The Aid was an armada of warships, divisions of trained soldiers, uncountable numbers of tanks and warplanes. It was the armed might of the United States descending on the invader. And no one was more anxious for it to arrive than Douglas MacArthur, for at stake was not only his life. For him, that was secondary to his reputation, which he had been striving mightily to protect, a sustained effort that revealed one of his least admirable traits, his mendacity.

His dispatches from Corregidor told the story of Bataan as he wanted it to be rather than how it was. The Japanese had used the jungle to outmaneuver him and he had been forced to withdraw to a reserve battle line lower on the peninsula. But even as the withdrawal was taking place, he was radioing the War Department that "our counterattack on the right was a smashing success." Another stated: "Our powerful artillery concentrations of one five fives was deadly," when in reality the American artillery was completely silenced by relentless Japanese dive bombing. Yet another said: "My infantry left the enemy completely disorganized; he left hundreds of dead on the field," when that would more accurately describe his own losses.

He had good reason to worry what others would think of him. He had blundered militarily, and lied repeatedly in an attempt to conceal it. And while victory can cover a multitude of sins, defeat exposes them all.

Malcolm Champlin was the naval liaison officer with the army on Bataan. He knew what was really happening and he was both shocked and offended as he glanced through the dispatches that arrived from the General's headquarters on Corregidor. To Champlin it was an unforgivable breach of an officer's code and honor to lie in such a manner. It was true that the Bataan army had stopped the Japanese on the reserve line, but Champlin knew from intelligence reports that the Japanese were suffering terribly from malaria and dysentery and were down to less than 9,000 men who could fight. In reality, they simply had run out of steam. MacArthur's claim, bannered in headlines all across America: "I have stopped them."

Even Champlin admitted that none of this was likely to be challenged, *if* MacArthur won the battle. And given adequate reinforcements, and the inability of the Japanese to immediately send more men to Bataan, there is little doubt he would have.

He had every reason to believe that immediate relief was on the way. There is Henry Stimson's cable to President Quezon, telling him "As soon as our power is organized we shall come in force and drive the invader from your soil." And what better encouragement than this: "We are doing our utmost to rush support to you. The President has seen all your messages and directs the navy to give you every possible support." George Marshall, that one came from, the Army Chief of Staff, a military man with a horror, a true abhorrence, of defeat, and therefore a man with deep empathy for MacArthur and the position he was in. And he was the one man above all others who could deliver the goods.

As if this wasn't enough, we have President Roosevelt himself, on December 28, hardly three weeks after the war began, electrifying the garrison and every loyal Filipino (and perhaps even the Japanese) with this announcement: "I give to the people of the Philippines my solemn pledge that their freedom will be retained and their independence established. The entire resources in men and materials of the United States stand behind that pledge."

Many people were to learn the old lesson, as old as time, that a solemn pledge coming from a master politician more often than not is an act of deceit. In the meantime, Roosevelt was taken at his word, and his words were interpreted by MacArthur as a promise that the siege of Luzon would be swiftly lifted. On January 15, brimming with optimism, his army still clinging tenaciously to the main battle line, he issued a proclamation and ordered that it be read by every commander to every unit on Bataan: "Help is on the way from the United States. Thousands of troops and hundreds of planes are being dispatched ..." It went on about honor and valor and sacrifice and the need to hold on until the reinforcements arrived, but it was that second sentence that everyone fastened on: *Thousands of troops and hundreds of planes.* Someone started calling it "the mile-long convoy," and those four words, so redolent with hope, quickly became embedded in the minds of practically everyone in the garrison.

The question now was, could the garrison hold out until The Aid arrived?

***

Carl Richardson bent over the paper and wrote, "Dearest—"

He looked at it. It was Valentine's Day and he was writing to his wife, but the letter was not going to be mailed. There was no mail, neither incoming nor outgoing. It was simply an attempt, however tenuous, to reconnect with a world once fully and happily inhabited but that was becoming increasingly more distant and unreal. That meant pretending the letter *was* going to be mailed. What would he write?

Richardson tried to think of something he could say about his life here that would not worry or alarm his wife. Absolutely nothing came to mind. Everything seemed worrisome or alarming. He had lost a good twenty-five pounds. Fresh food—meat, fruit, vegetables—were long gone. The PT men were eating better than the soldiers on the front line, but not by much: occasionally there were pancakes for breakfast (made without eggs or butter) to go with the cup of canned salmon and rice for supper. Everybody was trading for, stealing, or shooting anything edible. Richardson had eaten part of a monkey, part of an old tomcat, snails, iguana, and boiled roots to supplement the skimpy ration. And it was not only the food. Gasoline and ammunition was running low. A couple of the men had gotten sick, malaria, with its alternating, convulsive sweats and chills. One man's testicles had swollen to the size of a grapefruit, and no one knew what *that* was.

The squadron's troubles were simply a reflection of the condition of the Bataan army, which had been fighting on the peninsula steadily and desperately since early January. It had stopped the Japanese, but was in no condition to fight another battle. Along with everyone else, Richardson had gotten the grim report this very night from the woman whose laughter was even now coming to him from a nearby hut. Her name was Juanita Redmond and she was a nurse at Little Baguio. The field hospital was only a mile up the mountain from Sisiman Cove, along a trail through high grass and scrub jungle, and she had hiked down to see one of the officers she had befriended a few weeks before, during his brief visit to the hospital. Privacy was desirable, but in a place like this you could not possibly keep a young white woman to yourself, and so there was a party, with "pink lady" (raw alcohol flavored with the grapefruit juice brought by Miss Redmond) and everyone invited. They might be laughing over there now, but there was nothing jolly about what she had told them. In the hospital they had an incredible four thousand patients. Less than a thousand were battle casualties. The rest were down with malaria and dysentery, the twin scourges of the campaign. Field Hospital No. 2, at the base of the mountain near the bay shore, now had five thousand patients. Some nine thousand men were in the hospitals, and all of them ragged, starving shadows of the men they once were. It was absolutely astonishing to Richardson that these men had fought the Japanese army to a standstill.

***

With astonishing prescience, John Bulkeley seemed to have sensed, well before anyone else, that a destructive fate was hanging over the garrison. What else can explain the encounter he had with young Barron Chandler in early January, a week or so after President Roosevelt's promise of aid? Chandler was on patrol one night off Bataan when a ship was sighted. There had been no reports of enemy warships in the vicinity and Chandler sent out a signal challenge. There was a prompt reply: "American ship *Ranger*." Chandler yelled it out to everyone on the boat, and wild cheering followed. They knew the *Ranger* was an aircraft carrier and that it had not been in the Philippines at the start of the war.

Back at Sisiman Cove, Chandler rushed to the operations shack to tell Bulkeley that The Aid had arrived. Bulkeley looked at him for a long moment, as if in pity. "I don't know what you saw or thought you saw, but I want you to understand this," he said calmly. "Our entire air force has been wiped out, our ships and submarines have left, and no help is coming. Do you get the picture, Barron?"

A month after Chandler got this chilling intimation of the future, and after all the encouraging promises of immediate aid, came the first ominous signs that Bulkeley's instincts were correct. There was no more talk from Washington about convoys headed toward Manila. The opposite, in fact. Arthur Krock of the *New York Times* wrote after a visit to the White House that the siege of Luzon could not be raised unless the Japanese sea blockade was broken and American ships could enter Manila Bay, which simply could not be done. The chairman of the Senate Foreign Relations Committee, almost certainly with encouragement from the White House, stated publicly that "from a military point of view, the Philippines have long been regarded as a liability rather than an asset." For anyone paying attention, and MacArthur certainly was, it was clear that the American public was being prepared for yet another defeat.

At last, composed by George Marshall and signed by FDR, came the coup de grace—a cable ordering MacArthur to continue the struggle "so long as there remains any possibility of resistance. After that, capitulation is permissible."

One can imagine the blood coming to MacArthur's face as he read those lines. He was being abandoned after all. But though Roosevelt had approved of capitulation, there was never any possibility MacArthur would surrender to General Homma. He had long since cultivated an image of himself as a warrior knight, an image that by this time in his life he fully inhabited, and in the Middle Ages knights fought to the death. It was only as pride and honor demanded.

He needed a weapon, somehow his .45 Colt automatic had been misplaced or lost. He called for his aide, Sidney Huff, and pulled from his pocket a small ancient derringer, an antique with a polished wooden butt, two barrels, and two triggers. "This belonged to my father," he told Huff. "I want you to get a couple of bullets for it." Incredibly, Huff was able to find two cartridges that would work. MacArthur loaded the pistol and slipped it into his pocket, and said in a quiet voice, "They will never take me alive, Sid."

***

John Bulkeley was not made that way. Live to fight another day was more to his liking. No one knows except Bulkeley himself precisely when the idea came to him, but by February he had the plan in detail in his mind. He shared it only with Bob Kelly, his second officer, and the reporter Clark Lee, who had become friendly with Bulkeley and who had gone out on several patrols with him.

"We've got only enough gasoline for one good operation and we have only a few torpedoes left," he told Lee. "Then we'll be tied up here."

Implicit in that statement, as Lee was quick to discern, was Bulkeley's determination not to be taken prisoner should the garrison fall.

"What have you got in mind?" Lee asked.

"This doesn't go beyond the two of us."

"Understood," Lee said, and Bulkeley proceeded to lay out the plan. When their gas was down to just what they could carry on their decks, he would take the boats to China. The Japanese held most of the Chinese coast but Bulkeley knew China from the time he had spent there on a gunboat, and especially the region around Swatow. A cable from Chungking (brokered by Colonel Chi-Wang, the Chinese military observer with the Bataan army) reported that the region around Swatow was only thinly held by the Japanese. "So there it is. We make a run for the China coast with the last of our gas, burn the boats, then head overland to Chungking," the provisional capital of China, "and from there the American Ferry Command can fly us back to the States."

Lee asked if he could come along, and Bulkeley agreed to take him.

Reporting to the navy tunnel every morning for his orders, Bulkeley would occasionally drop in on his hero, who was always happy to see him. With his fierce pirate beard, double holsters, Bowie knife, a red bandana around his head instead of a helmet, he appealed to the unconventional streak that lay not so deeply buried within MacArthur—the grommetless hat, the corncob pipe, the plain, unadorned uniforms that made him look more like a private soldier than a general. Perhaps there might even have been a bit of envy.

It was only natural that a much younger man should want to take this hugely admired figure into his confidence, and during a brief visit shortly after his conversation with Clark Lee, Bulkeley said, "General, what if I could get the squadron out?"

"How in God's name would you do it?"

Bulkeley revealed his plan.

"Well, Buck, you will have to take that up with the navy," MacArthur said. Something in his voice told Bulkeley that if it were up to the General, and as close as the two of them had become, he would not let the squadron go. MacArthur would never forgive or forget his abandonment by the Asiatic Fleet early in the war, and the vindictiveness that was as much a part of him as his physical courage would manifest itself in strange and often spiteful ways.

But it was not his decision to make, it was Admiral Rockwell's.

And Rockwell said yes.

And so, in all the garrison, there was hope at least for the men of Motor Torpedo Boat Squadron 3.

CHAPTER 20

The Imperatives of War

Anyone's life can take the most astounding turns, but should you happen to be a major figure on history's stage such abrupt turnabouts can change the course of history itself. So with Douglas MacArthur. Unknown to him, George Marshall was having second thoughts about the prospect of losing his Far East commander. Marshall was a thoughtful man with a rare gift when it came to global military strategy, especially as it related to domestic politics, and it is no small wonder that he didn't see it before he wrote the cable that in effect was MacArthur's death warrant. Here was the only Allied general who had proved that he knew how to fight the Japanese, and in whom the public therefore had confidence. He was America's hero, whose dramatic communiques (though mostly inaccurate and self-serving) had captured the imagination of the country. And should he be captured or killed it would give the Japanese a tremendous psychological victory at a time when America could least afford it. And so Marshall reversed himself, believing now that the General's loss would be catastrophic.

Roosevelt agreed, though he was thinking more along the lines of a political catastrophe. The demands that MacArthur be brought out had grown to a great wave that was washing noisily over the White House, with its consequent effects on presidential politics. He already knew he wanted another term as president and the responsibility for the loss of Douglas MacArthur was certain to haunt him, not just into the next presidential campaign but for the rest of his days. It would never be forgotten, and he would never be forgiven.

But getting MacArthur out would be a very delicate business. All those who knew him well agreed that he would never obey an order to leave his men. He would ignore any such instruction unless it came directly from the president. It is not clear why, but this Roosevelt seemed reluctant to do. Perhaps it was a fear that MacArthur, headstrong, imperious, his pride sitting in him like an anvil, would do the unthinkable and disobey a direct order from the commander in chief. That kind of confrontation would do no one any good, with its spectacle of a court martial for America's first soldier, a far more dreadful prospect, politically, than leaving MacArthur to his fate. But a decision had to be made, and Roosevelt was struggling with it.

We see him in the Oval Study, at his desk in his wheelchair, a striking, blue-eyed man with a huge chest and shoulders and thinning gray hair atop a large head which at the moment does not contain his famous incandescent smile. It is February 22, Washington's birthday, and the sun has just gone down, leaving Washington in the gloom of a cold winter dusk. Roosevelt has before him a message from Winston Churchill, brought to him earlier that day, the implications of which he has been pondering. Australia's leaders, in near panic at the prospect of a Japanese invasion, have been demanding the return of three divisions sent to help the British fight the Germans in Africa. This is impossible, if the Germans are to be beaten. Churchill and Roosevelt had recently agreed that the United States would be responsible for Australia's defense, and now Churchill is informing his "good friend" Franklin that Australia is willing to rescind this demand if an American general were named supreme commander in the Pacific, with a promise that American troops would follow him.

Roosevelt knows which general Churchill has in mind. He is the only man qualified to be supreme commander in the Pacific. The outcome in Africa, Churchill's message makes clear, hangs in the balance. Without the Australian divisions, the British will lose the Suez Canal, and with that gone, perhaps the war.

On the desk at which Franklin Roosevelt sits, a huge desk cluttered with dispatches and reports spilling out of wire baskets, the can of Camel cigarettes and the forest of knickknacks, the lighters, paperweights, stuffed elephants and toy donkeys, small comic figurines, salt and pepper shakers, lay the message from Churchill. Roosevelt ponders it through wreaths of tobacco smoke, his long ivory cigarette holder at work; he likes to smoke as he thinks a matter through.

As dusk thickens outside, he reaches his decision.

***

The presidential order started coming in over the Corregidor radio at 11:23 a.m. on February 23, Manila time. Decoded, it was handed to MacArthur at 12:30 p.m. It directed him to proceed to the large southern island of

Mindanao, where he would determine the feasibility of a prolonged defense of that island, but after no more than a week there, he was to continue on to Melbourne, where he was to assume command of all United States troops.

Clark Lee saw him a few moments later, and was shocked at the change in him. He looked old, ill, and drained of the confidence he had always shown. After a long talk with his wife he met with his staff. He read the president's message to them. "I face an impossible dilemma," he said to them. If he disobeyed Roosevelt, he would be court martialed. If he obeyed, he would desert his men. Therefore he intended to resign his commission, cross to Bataan, and enlist as "a simple volunteer."

They protested, arguing with him. There was the rumor of a great relief expedition assembling in Australia, an almost audible buzz, heard over and over again for a week now. The Aid had finally arrived, it just didn't come to the Philippines, obviously because Washington meant for the General to lead it back to rescue the garrison. A direct order from the president to a commander in the field was extremely rare, so why else would Roosevelt issue such an order? Because MacArthur was the only man for the job. His value to the Allied cause was too great to sacrifice, even for honor's sake. Honor was the greatest virtue, duty an obligation almost as sacred, with the two always in a state of tension, and on this occasion, and as unpleasant as it was, duty trumped honor. Roosevelt knew he was ordering the captain to be the first to leave the sinking ship, and he was trying to soften the blow by giving MacArthur the opportunity to redeem his honor and save his men.

Most of the officers on MacArthur's staff were sycophants and perhaps they were only giving voice to thoughts they knew were already in his mind, but in any case this was a powerful argument. Still, MacArthur dictated a draft of his resignation. His chief of staff, the man who at this time was closest to him, General Richard Sutherland, persuaded him to sleep on it.

In the morning, possibly because the shock of Roosevelt's order was by now at least partially absorbed, the prospect of a great counteroffensive launched from Australia seemed more substantial and the arguments of his staff more potent. MacArthur radioed Roosevelt, agreeing to go but asking that he be allowed to choose the right time. "I know the situation here in the Philippines," he told the president, "and unless the right moment is chosen for so delicate an operation a sudden collapse might result."

The next day he was told that the decision was his, "the timing of your departure and details of method."

For thirteen days MacArthur hesitated. Decades later, when the scholars and historians really dug in and he was being reevaluated as an historical figure, as a military commander, and as a man, the suggestion would be made that this was a pose, that all along he'd had no intention of dying, by his own hand or while fighting with the troops on Bataan or in any other way that was avoidable, that with his dizzying ego he did not have to be convinced by others that he was too valuable for that ever to be allowed to happen to him, that he knew history would record his desire to die with his men and to make that believable (especially to his men) he would have to show hesitation, he couldn't immediately obey the order to jump ship, he had to show he didn't really want to go. And so thirteen days of wavering, and in the end having to be persuaded by the renewed arguments of his devoted staff that he *must* leave.

Carlos Romulo, a Filipino official who had become close to the General on Corregidor and who had the opportunity to observe him closely during those thirteen days, thought MacArthur felt he would be breaking, in his own mind, his pledge to die with his men. From where Romulo stood, it was no pose, it was a man torn in half by the often-conflicting virtues of honor and duty.

***

In the end he had to be nudged twice, first in a cable from George Marshall on March 6, and then by Roosevelt on March 9, telling him he was needed in Australia at the earliest possible date, and at last MacArthur turned the corner. On the morning of March 10 he radioed that he expected to depart on March 15 and reach Australia on March 18.

So much for the timing. As for "details of method," everyone expected that he would go out by submarine, running silent and deep, with Japanese aircraft and warships prowling the seas the safest way, the way President Quezon and High Commissioner Francis Sayre had slipped away. But for some time MacArthur had been toying with another idea. (Apparently, even as he was convincing himself that he had to die, he was making contingency plans to do otherwise. Some have cited this as another reason to believe he never intended to go down with the garrison, but it isn't surprising for a master of strategy whose ingrained habit of mind was to work out well ahead of time all the possibilities inherent in any situation.) The idea being toyed with, of course, was to go out by PT boat.

There is no question that John Bulkeley convinced him it could be done, but the General made his decision without knowing the terrible condition of the boats, which Bulkeley chose to conceal from him. And the arguments put forth in support of that decision, by Bulkeley, MacArthur, their biographers, would make any thinking person blush: in anticipation of a MacArthur breakout, the Japanese were increasing their sea and air patrols and it would be fatal to wait two extra days for a submarine to arrive (increased Japanese patrol activity, based solely on the often inaccurate reports of untrained Filipino coastwatchers, was largely imaginary); to use small surface craft instead of a submarine would take the Japanese by surprise (from an aircraft a PT boat's phosphorescent wake, as PT men found out to their horror later in the war, could be seen from fifty miles away, and the engines could be heard from a good ten miles away, which is why PT boats being out on the water rarely surprised anyone for long); the boats could get to Mindanao, jumping-off point for the flight to Australia, faster than a submarine (by perhaps a day, which was of no consequence whatsoever, since the departure from Mindanao could be arranged to suit the escape party).

That MacArthur was claustrophobic would seem to be confirmed by his aide, Sidney Huff, who confided as much to his diary. "As he talked about it, it was obvious that he preferred the PT boats to a submarine. It was almost as if he suffered from claustrophobia. He had shown the same attitude by refusing to sleep in the underground tunnel." And a submarine would only intensify any feeling of claustrophobia, however mild: a cigar-shaped space about the length of two subway cars in which every square inch on either side of a narrow central passageway was occupied by bunks, piping, crates, torpedoes, seabags, or some kind of machinery—giving the sense of there being no room at all. Diesel fumes, sweat, the stench of seasickness, toilet odors, and the pervasive smell of fried food from the galley only reinforces the fact that there is no fresh air because you are hundreds of feet beneath the surface of the sea.

To risk death on the open deck of a boat and not in a steel cylinder at the bottom of the ocean may have been the underlying reason for MacArthur choosing the PT boats, with all the other reasons, irrational and unfounded, marshalled in support of it. But that is impossible to say with certainty. What is certain is that MacArthur's decision condemned the squadron to destruction. The China trip—their last hope of seeing America and escaping death or a Japanese prison—was gone forever.

It's abundantly clear that Bulkeley saw the run to Mindanao as his opportunity for everlasting glory and fame beyond even his wildest dreams. But what about the men under him? They are no longer with us, not one of them, and nothing in their letters or future writing or in casual comments recorded by family and friends indicates how *they* felt about it. When finally they were told what was up, they knew what was going to happen to them, and they knew there were other, safer ways for MacArthur to get out. They had a right to feel resentful, even bitter, but they were aware of MacArthur's importance and perhaps they believed it was their fate to do what they could to save him, whatever the alternatives, whatever the risk. One thing is certain: they would not be deterred by risk. They had volunteered for the PT service knowing it was hazardous duty, and they had already proved themselves over and over again courageous to a man.

In the end, whatever they might have believed or thought or felt, and whatever the price they would have to pay for it, the simple fact remains that they were men who, in the earthly order of things, were fated to perpetrate the most daring sea rescue in American history.

CHAPTER 21

Cigars for a Starving Man

Ever since the first of March, when MacArthur invited Bulkeley to his cottage on Corregidor and told him he had been ordered out by the president, and had been assured that the PT boats could get him out, the planning had been going forward, in secret. Bulkeley went to Corregidor every day to meet with Sidney Huff and Admiral Rockwell's chief of staff, Herbert Ray. In Sisiman Cove, in stupefying heat and the kind of humidity that made cigarettes so damp they fell apart before they could be lit, they were scraping the sea moss off boat bottoms and reinforcing the decks to support the weight of the extra fuel that would be stored topside—twenty 55-gallon drums on each boat. They were overhauling struts and engines. They were giving the boats a fresh coat of dark green paint, and cleaning and oiling all the guns. Every man was issued a pair of army shoes, a canteen, a rifle, and a pack. They were going somewhere, that was clear, but they would be the last to know where. Bulkeley shared the secret only with Kelly, and they kept it even from the other officers—until March 11. On that morning, when Bulkeley went to Corregidor for the daily planning session, he was called into MacArthur's office and told that the departure date had been changed.

Back at Sisiman Cove, in the operations shack, Bulkeley called a meeting with the four boat captains—Anthony Akers, George Cox, Vincent Schumacher, and Bob Kelly.

"We're taking General MacArthur to Mindanao," he told them. "We leave this evening."

He pinned a map of the archipelago to the woven grass wall of the hut. "And here's how we're going to do it."

The boats would leave separately, from different locations on Bataan and Corregidor, meet at the entrance to Manila Bay, and run all night. "I expect to reach Tagauayan, at the north end of the Sulu Sea, by dawn tomorrow."

A finger was on the map, pointing to the tiny island.

"If we're attacked, the 41 boat, with General MacArthur aboard, will turn away and attempt to escape while the other three boats engage the enemy. Should the boats get separated, for that or any other reason, these are the alternate rendezvous points."

His finger moved to them, two tiny islands south of Tagauayan.

"We'll anchor all day Thursday and leave just before sunset, run down past Panay and Negros and into the Mindanao Sea and make our landfall at Cagayan, on the northern coast of Mindanao, at seven o'clock on Friday morning."

We can only guess what was going on in the minds of the four young boat captains. With no sextant to determine longitude and latitude they would never know exactly where they were. Two consecutive all-night runs at speed and over open seas where, with any kind of wind, they could expect to encounter waves fifteen to twenty feet high. The demands on the boats, all in a condition that normally would call for drydocking and a complete overhaul, would be extraordinary. Vince Schumacher, who was well aware of the condition of his own boat, running on only two engines and with her damaged struts not welded but taped together, thought it was like expecting a seventy-year-old man to run a five-minute mile.

Bulkeley then went through a set of explicit instructions of what to do in various circumstances, beginning with mechanical problems—almost certain to be encountered given the boats' worn-out engines and impure gasoline. "If any boat breaks down, she will transfer passengers and proceed independently or transfer all personnel and scuttle ship if necessary. The last boat in the column is designated to go alongside the disabled boat."

Passengers? Kelly knew, but it was a complete surprise to the others, who had assumed they were taking out only the General.

Bulkeley went on to disabuse that notion. Twenty-one people would be going out. "Eight on the 41, four on the 34, four on the 35, and five on the 32."

"We're not going to have room to take all our men," Tony Akers commented.

"That's right," Kelly said. "Some of us are going to be left behind."

Bulkeley already had the list. Seven men, all from the scuttled 33 boat, would be transferred to the Inshore Patrol on Corregidor. Ed DeLong and eight of his men from the 31 would also be staying—after the loss of the 31 they had been reassigned to the seagoing tug *Trabajador*.

The others listened in silence as Bulkeley read off the names. Sixteen men, severed from what had become a family, contentious at times, never in perfect harmony, but after what they had been through they were as close as any blood ties could possibly be. Sixteen names … it was a knell. Already, the attrition had begun.

***

Roosevelt had authorized the departure of MacArthur and no one else. George Marshall amended this to include the General's wife and son and his chief of staff. But MacArthur wasn't going to let Marshall or anyone else decide who would accompany him. If he was going to lead a great counteroffensive soon he would need his staff, and so he would take them all, and quite a few more besides, including his son's Chinese nanny, Ah Cheu. He would travel in state, like royalty, surrounded by his court. Marshall didn't learn that twenty people had gone out with the General until the trip was over. "I was astonished," he would say.

***

On the morning of March 10 MacArthur had met with his Bataan field commander, General Jonathan Wainwright, for the last time. He told Wainwright he would be leaving the next evening. And then, very forcefully, he said, "Jonathan, I want you to understand my position very plainly. I am leaving for Australia pursuant to repeated orders of the President. Things have reached such a point that I must comply with these orders or get out of the Army. I want you to make it known throughout all elements of your command that I'm leaving over my repeated protests."

It was a strange thing to say to a field commander, whose last duty, if indeed such a duty even existed, was to act as spokesman and apologist for his superior.

They were sitting in lounge chairs on the porch of the small cottage where MacArthur always stayed when he wasn't in the underground tunnel. The General was tired but dapper in a khaki bush jacket that had been made for him by a Chinese tailor. Sitting across from him, Wainwright was spectral, eyes sunk into an emaciated face and hardly any flesh on his bones, made that way by the three-eighths ration on Bataan.

"If I get through to Australia," MacArthur went on, "you know I'll come back as soon as I can with as much as I can. In the meantime, you've got to hold."

The reduced ration would last until July 1, by which time he expected to be back. This would seem far too optimistic, the logistics for retaking the Islands were enormous and the planning alone, which hadn't even begun, would take that long. But even if it could be done, that was four months away.

At top speed, PT boats created enormous wakes that extended for over a hundred yards and were visible from miles away. Judging from the wake, the boat shown here is at idling speed, yet the wake is still large and conspicuous. (National Archives [80-G-17401])

A PT boat at maximum speed: bow well above the water, stern down almost to the waterline, with only a small part of the hull in contact with the sea. Being "up on the step," bouncing from wave to wave, made for a punishing ride. (National Archives [80-G-17402])

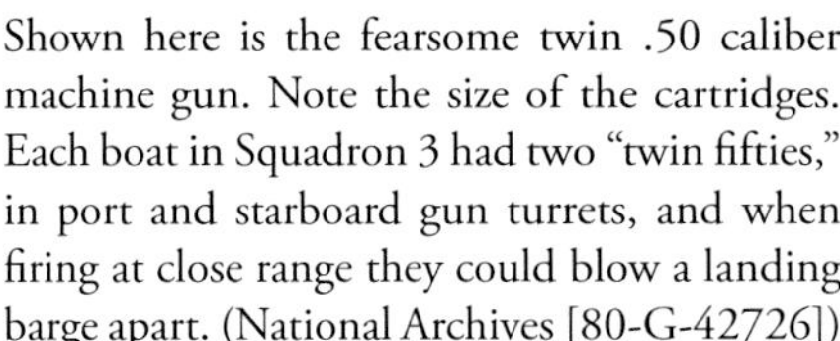

Shown here is the fearsome twin .50 caliber machine gun. Note the size of the cartridges. Each boat in Squadron 3 had two "twin fifties," in port and starboard gun turrets, and when firing at close range they could blow a landing barge apart. (National Archives [80-G-42726])

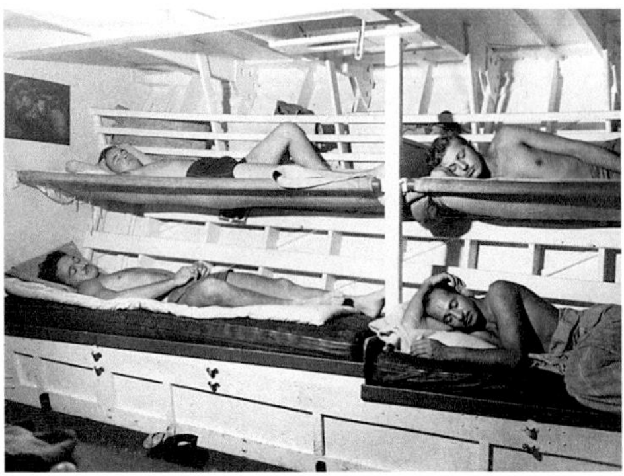

The crew's quarters in a PT boat were surprisingly roomy. Not shown is the adjoining dining table with its eight chairs. Despite the spacious bunks, in the tropical heat of the Philippines the men of Squadron 3 hardly ever slept below decks. (National Archives [80-G-258668])

In a PT boat the ship's cook had an adequate galley to feed the crew. For the men of Squadron 3, pancakes were standard fare for breakfast, until the powdered eggs and powdered milk ran out. (National Archives [80-G-258667])

PT boats carried four torpedoes, each weighing half a ton. It took a power winch and at least four men to load them into their tubes. After the destruction of Cavite power winches were in short supply and the men of Squadron 3 had to wrestle them into the tubes using rudimentary block and tackle and brute strength. (National Archives [80-G-17319])

PT 32 was one of the four boats that took MacArthur out of the Philippines, but it ran into trouble during the run to Mindanao and was scuttled by her captain, Lieutenant Vincent Schumacher. With some of his men, Schumacher was taken to Australia in a submarine. (Courtesy of PT Boats Inc. Museum and Archives, Germantown, TN [DOC094])

The Army and Navy Club, in Manila's Port Area, offered a standard of luxury for American servicemen unequaled anywhere in the world: tennis courts, an Olympic-sized swimming pool, a gymnasium, a library and Reading Room, a first-class restaurant, and a 1,000-square-foot dance floor. (National Archives [80-CF-7912-1])

The Manila waterfront in 1941, just before the outbreak of war. In the foreground is the Manila Hotel, where General Douglas MacArthur lived with his wife and young son. Behind the hotel, across the Pasig River, is Fort Santiago, where MacArthur had his headquarters. (National Archives [80-CF-7912-10])

The Cavite Navy Yard before the massive Japanese air raid on December 10, 1941. In the upper left corner are the wooden sheds where Squadron 3's six boats were moored and serviced during their first two months in the Philippines. (National Archives [80-CF-7914-11])

After the December 10 bombing of Cavite, hardly a building was left standing. The navy yard had no air raid shelters, and over a thousand people were killed, mostly Filipino yard workers. Most of Squadron 3's spare parts and supplies were lost. (National Archives [80-G-243705])

PT boats operating near the Manila docks shortly after their arrival in the Philippines. The six boats of Squadron 3 were initially based in Manila but were transferred to the Cavite Navy Yard, ten miles south of the city. (Courtesy of PT Boats Inc. Museum and Archives, Germantown, TN [DOC093])

Rear Admiral Francis Rockwell commanded the U.S. naval forces from his headquarters at Cavite. He survived the bombing and in its aftermath helped fight the fires and rescue the injured. He escaped from the Philippines with MacArthur. (National Archives [80-G-243709])

John Bulkeley speaks to workers at the Elco Shipyard in New York City in May 1942, shortly after his return from the Philippines. The boats of Squadron 3 were built at the Elco yards. Behind Bulkeley is a newly constructed PT boat ready for launching. (National Archives [80-G-17336])

MacArthur talks with Major General Jonathan Wainwright (in cavalryman's hat) during army maneuvers on Luzon two months before the outbreak of war. With MacArthur's departure Wainwright assumed command of all American and Filipino forces. After the surrender he spent three and a half years as a prisoner of war. (National Archives [111-SC-0128895])

MacArthur at the induction ceremonies in August 1941 that merged the Philippine Army into the U.S. Army, creating a single force under his command. (National Archives [111-SC-0128883])

MacArthur, not having gone to Bataan even once to visit them, and eating more than they were, seemed to have an incomplete sense of what the skimpy ration was doing to the troops. They were walking skeletons, all of them. Lining up to be fed, a man no longer needed his mess kit, all he had to do was hold out his hand, into the palm of which his entire day's ration would comfortably fit. Wainwright, who ate what his men ate (and looked it), knew it was a matter of weeks, not months, before it would end. The next hard push by the Japanese—and it was coming—could not be stopped by an army of walking skeletons.

MacArthur went on talking for a short time about Bataan before drifting into an explanation of why some officers were being evacuated and others left behind, striving to justify his choices, not something a field commander needed to hear. More than to Wainwright, he was talking to posterity.

Finally the two men got to their feet.

"Goodbye, Jonathan," MacArthur said. "When I get back I'll make you a lieutenant general." He then presented Wainwright with what quite possibly he needed least, two jars of shaving cream and a box of cigars.

***

It is the evening of March 11. The sun has just gone down and the light is fading as the 32 boat idles into Mariveles harbor. Waiting on the one undamaged pier are four brigadier generals and a lieutenant colonel, each man with a single piece of luggage, a bag or a suitcase, resting at his feet. They have been there since the afternoon, having come over from Corregidor on a launch as part of a coordinated movement carefully designed to appear random.

At about the same time, across the big grassy hill from Mariveles, in Sisiman Cove, at the long rickety coconut-log pier, the 34 and 35 sit waiting, one on each side of the pier, as a broad-bowed wooden launch chugs into the cove. Aboard are six army officers, Admiral Rockwell, and the only enlisted man among those chosen to go out. The launch ties up and one by one the passengers step onto the pier, each man with one piece of luggage. Except for the engineers below, everyone aboard the PT boats watches as this collection of army brass, led by the tall, white-uniformed Rockwell, makes its way along the pier. Each boat is to carry four of them, and as they approach they separate, four to the left and four to the right, and board the boats.

The 41 boat has already left Sisiman Cove, slipping across the channel to Corregidor's North Dock. She is tied up there, engines idling, as in the failing light several cars appear. The lead car is MacArthur's battered Chrysler, from which he had the four-star license plates taken off and added to the luggage. The cars stop a short distance from the boat and the passengers get out: the General, Jean MacArthur, four-year-old Arthur, Ah Cheu, General Sutherland, Navy Captain Herbert Ray, the devoted aide Sidney Huff, and Major Morehouse, an army doctor chosen by MacArthur to be his personal physician. Little Arthur, flanked by his mother and his nanny, clutches his stuffed panda.

Before stepping aboard, MacArthur pauses to have a word with General George Moore, who commands the harbor defenses. "George, keep the flag flying," MacArthur tells him. "I'm coming back." Everyone, it seems, must be assured of that.

There is no record of any response from General Moore, but there are a number of others with Moore who have come down to see the departure, and the men watching from the 41 can see the fear and the sense of abandonment on the faces of all of them.

With all the passengers aboard, MacArthur turns to John Bulkeley and says, "You may cast off, Buck, when you are ready."

George Cox is at the wheel. "Take us out to the turning buoy, George," Bulkeley tells him, and Cox signals the engine room and the boat moves slowly away from the dock at idling speed, away from the tunnels, the scorched rock, the bomb craters, the smoldering fires, the pervasive smell of cordite and dust, which has become the stench of defeat.

CHAPTER 22

The Great Escape (1)

At exactly 8 p.m. the four boats met at the turning buoy just inside the mine channel at the mouth of Manila Bay. The sky was clear and dense with stars. In single file the boats crept through the minefields. When they reached the open sea they assumed a diamond formation: the 41 in the lead, the 32 and 35 some thirty yards behind and off to port and starboard, the 34 sixty yards directly behind the 41.

It was up to Bulkeley to keep the boats on course, and at twenty-minute intervals he would turn the wheel over to Cox and take a compass bearing and an rpm reading before going below to the dayroom, where he would use these, along with an estimate of windage, to check his location on the chart. With no other navigational aids this was at best a guess, and his guesses were far enough off to bring them within a mile of Cabra Island, when they should have been at least five miles from it.

Lights suddenly sprouted all over the island, signal fires, which could not have come as a surprise. So close together and running hard, the four boats were making a stupendous roar that many of the men only half-jokingly thought could be heard in Manila. They were only fifty miles into their desperate endeavor, but any hope of surprising the Japanese was already gone.

Skirting Cabra Island, Bulkeley set a course for the next checkpoint, tiny Apo Island, at the head of Mindoro Strait, through which they would then run due south to Tagauayan. But the weather began to deteriorate alarmingly. The wind had come up and great foaming waves twenty feet high slammed against the boats. Most of the men were wearing oilskins in anticipation of dirty weather but the flying spray drove against their faces like stinging pellets of birdshot. Walls of water fell across the decks, solid as stone. Every man held on to whatever he could—piping, a ladder rung, the handle on a hatch cover. The boats would fall off into a trough, then climb the steep slope of the next wave, hang there for a moment, as if floating in space, then plunge down the other side. Going through the peaks and troughs the boats were violently tossed around, shaking as if the wooden hulls were about to come apart.

On the 32 Ned Cobb clawed his way to the cockpit, where Cone Johnson was at the wheel, struggling to keep control of the boat, a drenched Schumacher standing next to him, his binoculars full of water and his eyes burning so badly with salt spray that he couldn't see. The wind was howling and so were the engines and Cobb had to yell to be heard.

"Skipper, the drums are working loose!"

"Secure them, then!" Schumacher told him.

"We'll have to slow down a little," Cobb advised, "or we'll lose somebody. They'll be pitched right over the side."

"We can't slow down without losing station."

But then Schumacher thought the better of it and told Johnson to cut their speed a little. Cobb went back and in the howling tempest, on the bucking, pitching deck, water washing over them, he and three other men managed to tighten the lashings on every one of the twenty drums of gas.

The sailors might have been miserable but their passengers were in indescribable agony. Every one of the army officers got seasick fast. Anyone who has been violently seasick would probably agree that it is as close to wanting to die as you might possibly get. Everything falls away. It is as if you are already beyond the inhabited world and that nothing is of any consequence. On the 34, Iliff Richardson made his way into the galley for a shot of cold coffee. When he turned the galley light on, he saw the most wretched-looking general in the United States Army. "Get me a bucket," the man called in a weak voice. Richardson had hardly set the coffee mug down when the man yelled "Get a bucket!" Richardson found one, but it arrived too late.

Buckets were the order of the day. When Arthur and Ah Cheu both became violently ill, Jean MacArthur moved them to the two officers' bunks below, providing each with a bucket. On the floor beside them MacArthur lay sprawled on a mattress, his face white as a corpse and his eyes dark-circled and red-rimmed, as if he were staring into the Inferno. He kept retching, though he had already brought up everything, and his limbs were so rigid that he was unable to move them. Jean, diminutive and not very tough-looking, proved to be the opposite. Of all the passengers, she suffered the least. Wearing a light dress, a coat over the dress, and little straw shoes, she stayed at her husband's side, rubbing his hands hour after hour.

***

By midnight the boat captains were struggling to keep track of each other. The 34, at the rear of the diamond formation, began to fall behind. Fifty yards, a hundred. In the cockpit, Kelly lost sight of the flagship. Standing beside him, Admiral Rockwell was silent. They kept falling behind. Kelly knew what the problem was. He was filled with anxiety, but not showing it.

At last, Rockwell began to lose patience.

"Don't you think we're getting a little far apart?" he asked.

"We'll close in gradually," Kelly told him, without believing it.

"Damn it, let's close up!"

Custom and respect for a ship's commanding officer limited any other officer on the bridge, even an admiral, to giving advice. But this was not advice, it was a direct order.

Kelly's mind raced. The 34 was the only boat that hadn't been fully overhauled, and was so full of carbon that she couldn't make much speed until the carbon was burned out. He didn't bother to explain this. Kelly was a product of the Naval Academy, where from the first day you are taught that excuses were for weaklings, for the unfit, the bumblers, the incompetent. Forget about the carbon. He needed to get more speed out of the engines. He had been giving her all the throttle he had for the past hour and more.

Then it burst upon him like a sunrise.

Al Ross, the boat's quartermaster, was standing just below the cockpit, holding on to the piping at the base of the port gun turret. Kelly turned the wheel over to Iliff Richardson and stepped down so he could talk to Ross without the Admiral hearing him. Ross nodded and made his perilous way astern.

In the engine room, Velt Hunter, sitting on his perch above the starboard engine, the control panel before him, was thinking that this must be what it was like to take a trip in a concrete mixer. His fellow engineer, Paul Eichelberger, must surely have been thinking the same thing. There was the constant sensation that they were revolving in almost a complete circle and that at any moment they would turn upside down, the engine room canopy suddenly below them and the floor above their heads.

Suddenly, Al Ross popped down the hatch, oilskins dripping.

"Listen up, you two," he said in his penetrating Maine twang, "the skipper says to disconnect the throttles and push the carburetor levers as far up as they'll go."

Ross disappeared up the hatch. Hunter knew that Kelly was asking for more turns. When you pushed the throttles as far as they will go, there was a gap, very small, about a sixty-fourth of an inch, that would never quite close. The only way to close it was to disconnect the throttles and push the carburetor levers up by hand. Hunter knew this, but he had never expected to be given such an order. By disconnecting the throttles, Kelly no longer had control of the engines. They were now literally in the hands of the engineers. And the engineers too had no control over them except for holding them with their bare hands at maximum rpms. In an action this would be suicidal, but Bob Kelly was hardly that, he was extremely competent, in fact, and Hunter figured that something had to be going on topside that required it.

In the cockpit, they felt the boat jump as it increased speed. Rockwell didn't ask how that had been accomplished. Peering into the spray, the night black as pitch, he still wasn't satisfied.

"We're closing pretty slowly," he complained.

One sixty-fourth of an inch wasn't giving them a great deal more speed, and Kelly doubted they were closing at all. He thought they must be at least two hundred yards behind the 41 by now.

But he said, "No use pushing her too hard, sir."

"Why not?" Rockwell demanded.

"Yes, sir."

In minutes, though, Kelly realized they really were closing—and fast. Unknown to him, up in the 41 Bulkeley had noticed that the 34 had fallen behind and had reduced speed.

Kelly was alarmed but calm. With his throttles disconnected, he couldn't reduce *his* speed. Al Ross, standing on the cockpit step, attentive as ever, saw Kelly look at him.

No words were necessary. Ross made his way back to the engine room as fast as the rolling, pitching deck allowed, and yelled down the hatch: "Reconnect!"

In the time it took Ross to get back the 34 not only gained on the 41, but overtook it and went roaring past.

In the darkness Kelly saw Rockwell give him a look that said, "I'm sailing with a madman."

Just then they happened to be passing an island, its outline visible against the stars. Rockwell was peering at it.

"How far are we from that island?" he wanted to know.

"About four miles, sir," Kelly said.

"You're guessing, aren't you?"

"Yes, sir," Kelly admitted.

"Looks farther than that to me. Take a bow and beam bearing."

"Aye aye, sir," Kelly said. He had no instruments of any kind. Making a forty-five-degree angle with two fingers, he sighted along them to a point ahead. When he came abeam of that point, since he knew his speed, it would give him, very roughly, their distance from the island.

Rockwell was staring at this performance.

"Don't you have a pelorus?"

Kelly admitted that he didn't.

"And no sextant."

"No, sir."

"How in hell do you navigate?"

Kelly told the simple truth: "By guess and by God, sir."

Rockwell seemed to collapse into himself.

"My God!" he burst out. Then, angrily, "How can we even hope to get where we're going?"

***

Even before the tempest the boats had been having trouble. On the 32 the deck over the engine room, patched up after the explosion back in January, was cracked and leaking badly. The bolts holding the center shaft tail strut were sheared off, causing another leak. The bilge pump couldn't keep up with the flooding and in the engine room Herb Grizzard and Dale Guyot were using a bucket to scoop the water out. Once the heavy weather hit, the leaks grew worse, and seawater would pour down the engine room hatch every time either of them went up with the bucket. It was unnerving, more water would come down the hatch than was in the little canvas bucket, but other than give up, there was nothing else they could do.

The 35 boat too was straining the nerves of everyone aboard. The engines would quit, start again, then conk out, the boat coming to a dead stop and then roaring ahead as Akers restarted the engines and jammed his throttles to the wall to catch up.

All the boats had trouble with the engine magnetos. The engines would sputter, a sign that the magneto points were wet, and the boat would have to stop until they could be dried off. The stops were the worst, the sailors tensing up, the passengers choking down their terror. With the motors turned off, the boats bobbed violently in the towering seas, pitching sideways so steeply they seemed certain to capsize at any moment.

By 3:30 a.m. the four boats had lost contact with each other. Each boat captain now had to make his way to the rendezvous on his own.

Half an hour later, at 4 a.m., all three engines on the 34 suddenly stopped.

"Now what?" Admiral Rockwell said crankily.

Kelly knew instantly what it was: the gas strainers were clogged with wax and rust. Briefly, he explained the problem.

"How long to clean them?"

"Half an hour," Kelly said, with blind trust that his two experienced engineers, Hunter and Eichelberger, would vindicate him—though it had taken longer than that to clean them when they were in the calm, sheltered waters of Sisiman Cove.

They waited, bobbing crazily on the heaving sea.

Meanwhile, off in the black night, alone and struggling, the 32 also came to a complete stop. Seawater had shorted out the ignition system. All along, the 32 had been running on only two engines. One wouldn't restart, and the boat burbled along on one engine, groping its way toward the rendezvous, hopelessly behind the others, or so everyone thought.

CHAPTER 23

The Great Escape (2)

Day was rising, a pale Pacific dawn. The 32 was rolling in the heavy swells. It was the end of a sleepless night for Vince Schumacher. He felt certain he was miles from the other boats. After an entire night in the open cockpit both he and his exec, Cone Johnson, were exhausted, cold, and sopping wet. They stood there now with two of the passengers, Generals Spencer Akin and Hugh Casey, a fierce wind blowing in their faces.

Up in the starboard gun turret, more a lookout than a gunner, Clem Langston suddenly shouted, "Dead astern! See it? A ship!"

It had the jolt of electric current. In these waters, any ship could only be Japanese.

Schumacher found it in his binoculars. The morning light was not yet fully developed and he could make out only a pale image in the distance. But it seemed to have a superstructure that rose above its deck, and he quickly decided that it was a destroyer. He might have handed the glasses to Johnson, to get a second opinion, as it were, but he wasn't as calm as he should have been.

"Jap destroyer," he exclaimed. "She has five-inch guns. If we resist it means the lives of all the men in the boat."

"We're damned well going to resist," Casey said bluntly. Hugh Casey was MacArthur's chief engineer and quite possibly the second most important man being taken out, next to the General himself. Trim, silver-haired, handsome as a movie idol, Casey had worked an engineering miracle on Bataan and he knew his talent and expertise would be desperately needed in the planning for the coming invasion, and he wasn't going to allow himself to be captured without a fight. Beyond that, he was Irish and by nature pugnacious.

Casey's resolve seemed to rally Schumacher. "General quarters!" he shouted, but as the men moved quickly to man the guns and ready the torpedoes for firing he thought again about trying to outrun the ship. It was what he had meant in the first place, by not resisting.

"We could try making a run for it," he explained.

"That might be a good idea," Casey allowed. "I thought you meant you were going to surrender."

"We'll have to lighten ship," Schumacher said. "That means dumping all the drums of gas."

He didn't have to explain that if they did that there would be no possibility of the boat making it to Mindanao. Neither Casey nor Akin objected. Slugging it out with a warship thirty times their size, with a thousand gallons of high-octane gasoline on the open deck, waiting for the bullet that would incinerate them, was a less appealing prospect than running from a fight.

Schumacher gave the order to cut the lashings. Cone Johnson jumped down from the cockpit and met up with Ned Cobb, who had an axe in one hand and a knife taken from the galley in the other. He handed the knife to Johnson and one by one they cut the heavy drums loose and rolled them over the side, the drums sinking out of sight for a moment and then bobbing like corks to the surface.

The moment the last drum was over the side Schumacher shoved up the throttles. During the night they had gotten the second engine to start, but with only two engines they didn't have enough speed to outrun a destroyer, even with the few extra knots a lightened ship gave them. In his mind every sailor aboard knew this, Schumacher included, even before he decided to try it, but in his unthinking heart every man was hoping that somehow they could, for they were under no illusions about the outcome of a fight with a destroyer in broad daylight. Even Bulkeley had changed his mind about that, having made it PT doctrine to attack a large warship only at night.

Except for the engineers below, all eyes were on the enemy warship as it steadily closed the distance.

"We'll have to turn and fight," Schumacher decided finally. No one overruled him, or had any right to. He was in command. It was his decision to make, and his alone.

He turned hard over and headed straight for the destroyer—and all over the boat hearts sought to beat their way through rib cages.

Schumacher took another look through the binoculars—and what he saw now, with the benefit of better light and a closer image, flew like a dart into his brain. At the same moment Casey, even without binoculars, could see it.

"That's one of our boats!" he shouted.

***

On the 41 it was one of the passengers, the navy man, Captain Ray, who first saw the 32. He was only a moment ahead of Bulkeley, who was at the wheel, with George Cox standing by, a pair of binoculars hanging from a strap around his neck. (Bulkeley had spent three hours trying to find the other boats in the darkness, and meanwhile the 32 had gotten ahead of him.)

"Looks like she's attacking us," Ray said unbelievingly.

Cox found the 32 in the glasses. "She's uncovered her fifty calibers and her torpedo tubes are out," he confirmed.

That was overheard, and it made the rounds in an instant. Everyone topside began yelling and waving, but it had no effect. Bulkeley swung the boat broadside to the approaching 32, to present a more familiar silhouette. It worked. They all watched, the tension leaving them in a rush as the 32's wake subsided and her bow settled into the sea.

As the 41 came close aboard the men on the 32 saw MacArthur appear on deck. It was the first time any of them had seen him up close. He was a shocking sight, unshaven, his eyes bloodshot, his face lined and sagging from the night's ordeal. Cone Johnson, from the perspective of his twenty-three years, thought he looked incredibly old, hardly resembling the man whose photograph he had seen in *Life* magazine less than six months before.

The 41 pulled up alongside the 32, with Cox now at the wheel, and Bulkeley hopped aboard. Always high-strung and temperamental, and now with his nerves scraped raw by the difficulties and constant tension of the previous night's run, he piled into Schumacher, shouting at the young boat captain, and at times even at the crew, until he was hoarse. Schumacher's incredibly poor judgment had jeopardized the entire rescue mission and put General MacArthur's life in danger. It might have occurred to the recipient of this tirade that it was Bulkeley himself who had done just that, when, as he well knew, there was a safer and much less arduous way for MacArthur to leave. The General may have made the choice, but his decision was based on faulty information, about the condition of the boats and about what they were capable of. In his recklessness and impetuosity, ingrained and therefore inescapable, it was John Bulkeley who had put everyone's life in danger, and who had subjected his acknowledged hero to unimaginable misery.

But Schumacher bore his cross in silence. Only decades later, talking to a historian, would he have the opportunity to explain himself. Two lookouts were standing high on each side of the 41's bridge. The lookouts added a "superstructure" that was uncharacteristic of the usual low, smooth silhouette of a PT boat. He mistook two men for substantial parts of a warship's superstructure. The distance of the initial sighting, condition of the sea, and dim light also had to be factored in.

Perhaps. But between Bulkeley and Schumacher something shifted. For Bulkeley, it was as if a question mark was now perpetually hanging over

Schumacher's head, and between them nothing would ever be quite the same again.

When he finished blistering Schumacher, he ordered him to recover the gas drums. It was a slow and cumbersome process, and Bulkeley finally decided it was too risky to stay long on open water in broad daylight. He ordered his gunners to sink the drums. As they were firing, the bullets punching holes in the drums and the gas leaking out and putting a greasy shine on the surface of the sea, Bulkeley plotted a course that, since he couldn't know exactly where he was, he could only hope would take them to the Cuyo Islands and the rendezvous at Tagauayan. He did know that they weren't even close to Tagauayan, but the Cuyos were full of tiny inlets and coral reefs and he intended to find shelter at the first one he encountered, and then work things out from there.

***

Slowly the sun appeared, flooding across the water and turning it white. Hundreds of small islands dotted the sea, some high and rocky and almost bare of vegetation, some low and palm-fringed with small white-sand beaches. These were the Cuyo Islands, and as the sun rose out of the sea the 34 boat was already threading its way among them, through little shoaly channels and past enormous coral heads, scattering the small, colorful reef fish that congregated there.

They had come in sight of the first ones at dawn. It had taken Hunter and Eichelberger thirty-five minutes to clean the gas strainers and fuel pumps, only five minutes longer than the half hour Kelly had hopefully predicted. All three engines immediately restarted, and they had pushed on through the night, over the rough seas, alone but underway again. Admiral Rockwell was on the bridge all night and into the new day. Kelly had two other officers aboard, Iliff Richardson and Henry Brantingham, either of whom could have taken the wheel for a spell, as could Al Ross, his quartermaster, but Kelly, at the wheel since the beginning of the journey, stayed there. It was as if he and Rockwell were each subconsciously thinking, *If he can stay here, so can I.*

Now, moving ever deeper among these flyspecks of islands, with bright daylight upon them and the accompanying fear of being seen from the air, they were trying to find Tagauayan, the agreed-upon rendezvous. The 41 had the only detailed chart of the Cuyos. All Kelly had was a large-size map of the Philippines, on which the Cuyos were but a cluster of small dots, indistinguishable from each other.

Rockwell had been silent for some time, but as they made their slow way through the maze of little islands he was moved again to complain.

"Without any navigation instruments or even a decent chart, how on God's earth do you expect to make a proper landfall?"

Kelly dug a piece of paper from his pocket. For a long moment Rockwell stared at the pencil sketch.

"What *is* this?"

"That's Tagauayan, sir. I made a sketch of it from Lieutenant Bulkeley's chart."

"This is impossible," Rockwell said, meaning, apparently, the situation they were in. He had long since given up hope they would ever find the place.

A short time later, shortly after eight o'clock, it came into view. As they got nearer, Rockwell agreed that the hills and cove looked exactly like Kelly's sketch. But when they entered the cove, an hour after the agreed-upon time for the rendezvous, it was empty.

Kelly circled the island. There was no sign of the other three boats.

"My God, we've lost the General," Rockwell concluded.

Kelly felt certain that with the General and his family aboard Bulkeley would take no chances and with daylight would make for the nearest island and wait there all day before moving down to the rendezvous site. He shared his theory with Rockwell, whose pessimism would not allow him to fully accept it.

They dropped anchor in the cove. A low cliff threw its shadow over the boat. Beyond the cliff there was a hill, intensely green and about 500 feet high. Cramped and stiff from the long cold night, the men were looking forward to stretching their legs.

But it was not to be.

"Ross, I want you and Goodman on that hill with the signal flags," Kelly ordered. "Report any vessels or airplanes sighted. No one else leaves the boat."

Richardson and Brantingham unlashed the punt from the forecastle and got it into the water. Al Ross and Dave Goodman, the radioman, climbed in and the two officers rowed them to the beach. Meanwhile, the three army officers emerged from below deck, woozy but filled with blissful relief. They even had an appetite, and one of them asked about breakfast.

Kelly ignored them. He had more important things on his mind. He set the crew to refueling. The drums were unlashed and rolled up to the gas tank openings and emptied one at a time. It took four men, grunting and sweating, to lift each drum and hold it over the funnel. The empty drums were thrown into the water and in the punt Willard Reynolds and John Martino held the openings in the drums underwater until they filled completely and sank.

Unlike Bulkeley, Kelly did not have his gunners shoot holes in them as they bobbed on the surface. With even a small bit of air left in them the drums would partially sink and then float for months before finally sinking to the bottom. And floating drums, easily seen from an airplane or ship, would have the Japanese on them like hounds fastened on a scent.

***

At four o'clock, with the sun lowering, Kelly made his decision. Any spotting planes would now be heading for home, and he was about to pull his lookouts off the hill and head for Mindanao on his own when someone yelled, "Hey, Skipper, they're signaling!"

Standing in the high grass, Goodman artfully worked the two red flags. One letter at a time, he spelled out the message: SHIP APPROACHING, POSSIBLE MTB.

Kelly quickly found it in his binoculars.

It was the 32 boat. No sooner had it tied up alongside the 34 when there was a rising roar to seaward and the 41 came around the point and into the cove.

There were more life and death decisions to be made, and minutes after her anchor was down, Rockwell, Akin, and Casey boarded the 41. Six wicker chairs had been rounded up and set in a semicircle on the forward deck, and MacArthur, Bulkeley, and Richard Sutherland, MacArthur's chief of staff, took the other three. All those not involved in the conference did not have to be told to keep their distance.

They were halfway to Mindanao, one more night to go, but MacArthur had had enough. He was thinking it might be a good idea to wait for the *Permit.* This was the submarine that would have taken him out had he not opted for the PT boats, and it was now backing up the operation. It was scheduled to arrive at Tagauayan at daylight the next morning—an irony not lost on anyone.

Rockwell was nervous about staying in the cove and was anxious to get going. MacArthur's concerns were not his. He seemed unaffected by all they had gone through. He had slept for two hours that afternoon, which was all the sleep he'd had in over forty-eight hours.

"I think we should get the hell out of here—now! We're already out on a limb, and if we hang around long enough we're just asking for trouble," he said to the others.

Sutherland agreed.

MacArthur was undecided.

"This next lap might be even rougher than the first," Bulkeley warned.

Rockwell got to his feet and studied the sky for a moment. The sun was low on the horizon and had turned the banks of high clouds in the west a deep, glowing red, like fire in the sky. *Red sky at night, sailor's delight* ...

Rockwell sat down. "We'll have good weather tomorrow, and calm seas," he assured the others.

MacArthur was thoughtful for a moment. Then, with his customary decisiveness, he said, "We will proceed as planned." He leaned close to Sutherland then, and said, "Dick, I can't do anything to Rockwell, but if it's rough tonight, I'll boil you in oil."

There was the question of what to do about the 32 boat. The passengers were divided among the other two boats and Schumacher was told to wait for the *Permit*, inform her captain that the other boats had left as planned, and then proceed to Iloilo on the island of Panay, 125 miles away and reachable with the gas he had left. He was to refuel there and make his way to Mindanao.

There followed an incredible suggestion by one of the army generals, and heard by everyone, that the crews on the two departing boats be reduced to better accommodate the increased number of passengers—in other words, to make things more comfortable for the army. Any sailors left behind would be stranded on the tiny island. With this expedition Bulkeley might have needlessly taken his men into harm's way, but he wasn't *that* callous, and he argued the general out of it.

That same general was one of those transferred to the 34. He hadn't had supper yet, and he told Al Ross to tell the cook to bring up some food. Ross yelled down to Willard Reynolds, "He wants you to bring him some food," the *he* saying everything.

Reynolds's reply was immediate and loud enough for all to hear. "Tell him to come down and get it or I'll throw the goddamned stuff overboard."

This is probably the only case on record where an enlisted man told a general what to do, and got away with it, but any harm done to Reynolds would have sparked a mutiny. Willard was well-liked by all hands because he was efficient and king of his domain—the galley. Even with little to work with, the food he prepared was always hot and tasty. He was also the boat's medic, and in that capacity a man of demonstrated valor.

Perhaps the general sensed the hostility radiating all around him like gamma rays. In any case, he went down to the galley and took his plate in silence.

CHAPTER 24

The Great Escape (3)

Departure was set for 6 p.m.. There was still no sign of the 35 boat, with four army men aboard, and they left without her.

The 34 boat was now in the lead. At the conference Rockwell had made the claim that though MacArthur was the supreme commander in the Far East (or about to be, if he managed to get to Australia), he was the ranking naval officer, and that put him in charge of the boats—a technicality that was militarily unassailable. And he wanted the 34 to be the guide boat. They were navigating in the crudest way imaginable—mostly by dead reckoning, which is almost pure instinct, not much above the level of guesswork—and it was his own instincts that he trusted most. Bulkeley could not object, in fact he thought it was a good idea, but for a different reason. The 41 could search out the smoothest part of the 34's wake, so that the General could ride more comfortably.

Comfort was not to be had. As soon as the boats were out in the open a westerly wind sprang up and the surface of the sea began to heave with fifteen-foot swells, the wind whipping spray off the whitecaps and sending it into the faces of the men on the boats.

In the cockpit of the 34, Rockwell squinted into it. "The General's going to give me hell for this in the morning," he said to Kelly.

A bit later he said, "It would be best to wear a little to the west of our proposed course. It's still daylight and we'll be crossing the sea lanes, and they're sure to be patrolled by enemy vessels."

Obediently, Kelly ticked the wheel a few degrees to the right.

Just then, Brantingham, also in the cockpit as Officer of the Deck, sighted what he thought was a ship through his binoculars. "Three points on our port bow. Distance about five miles."

With his own binoculars, Rockwell looked in that direction, but like rain on a windshield, the spray blurred his vision. He handed the glasses to

Iliff Richardson, who was off watch but who preferred being knocked about in the cockpit to being knocked about below. "Do you see a vessel there?" Rockwell wanted to know.

Shielding the lenses with one hand, Richardson brought the ocean up close to him—and the long low outline of a gray destroyer appeared and then almost disappeared as it rose and fell with the swells.

"It's a destroyer," he announced calmly.

"Come hard right," Rockwell ordered without consulting Kelly, a breach of naval etiquette and certainly not respectful of the commanding officer, though it was exactly what Kelly had been about to do. By now most of the crew could see the ship without the aid of binoculars, and hearts beat faster and throats went dry. A Japanese destroyer could make thirty-five knots, almost forty with all her steam up.

Kelly had the 34 at full speed—all of eighteen knots. Behind them, the 41 wasn't able to do any better.

If they were seen, it was over. And so darkness was their only hope.

John Martino, on watch near the aft port torpedo tube, was holding on to a deck cleat to keep from being tossed overboard. "Come on, come on, get down there, you bastard," he muttered. The "bastard" was the sun, and he was urging it to hurry up and set. But it seemed to hang there above the horizon for weeks.

Relentlessly, heartbeat by heartbeat, the tension ticked up, everyone waiting for the dreadful moment when the destroyer would alter course and come for them.

On the 41, MacArthur was lying in his cabin with his eyes closed, Jean MacArthur rubbing her husband's hands, though she was seasick herself, little Arthur prostrate, Ah Cheu throwing up again. They could hear the rush of activity above, and the crew talking about an enemy warship, but they, like the other passengers who lay wet and insensible on the heaving deck above, were seemingly beyond caring.

Then, up in one of the gun turrets, with the lower rim of the sun at last touching the sea, Dave Harris was moved to optimism. "She's holding course," he shouted to his shipmates. "She can't have spotted us."

The sun went down. The danger had passed. Amazingly, despite their huge foaming white wakes, the boats had not been seen.

***

Darkness fell in its sudden way. On the 34, Kelly came back to the old course, compensating for the short westerly run. Ahead, lightning flashes could be seen, and the sea became even more wicked. The compass on the 34 spun wildly as the boat was tossed about. Kelly was trying to find the narrow passage into the Mindanao Sea, but he could only estimate a course—there was no way to stay on an exact heading. He was plowing through the darkness entirely on dead reckoning and could only hope he was heading due south. Rockwell made no attempt to correct him, his own sense of direction apparently in agreement with Kelly's.

When the glowing dials of his watch came together at midnight, Kelly thought they might be off the strait, and with no disagreement from Rockwell he turned left. Though he couldn't see it, he knew he had been running along the long coastline of Negros Island, close enough at times to hear the pounding of the surf—to his left. If he had guessed wrong he would be driving the boat onto the reefs. But they didn't hit anything. He had no charts, he had never been here before, he could see absolutely nothing, but since he didn't crash into a beach, he kept going—until at last he knew they were through the passage and safely into the Mindanao Sea.

It was as if any success, however modest, had to be paid for. In the open waters of the Mindanao Sea the two boats experienced the worst hours of the entire trip. There were times when even Bulkeley, in whom there had always been enough confidence for all of them, thought they might not make it. Big foaming waves twenty feet high slammed and jolted the boats, thundering over the cockpits and drenching everybody topside. Heavy salt spray lashed faces like hail. Burningly, chokingly, it went into the nose and mouth and down the throat. Every man held on to whatever he could, standing with bent legs, like a skier taking the bumps. The passengers were tossed about like bean bags, and those lying down below were thrown clear of the bunks. On the 34, one general was draped over a torpedo tube. Al Ross offered to help get him below, but he waved Ross off. "Let me die here," he moaned.

With the speed, the water, and the wind, it got so cold that everyone was shivering. Binoculars filled with water, eyes too. No one could see, in addition to which it was pitch-black. The men had had little or no sleep for more than two days, and it was a struggle to stay awake. George Shepard was crouched against one of the torpedo tubes, using it as a brace, when his eyes closed and he sagged onto the deck. He was sound asleep, and with no brace against the violent pitching and bucking, he was lifted into the air. John Martino happened to be close by and with the reflexes of a cat he reached out and grabbed Shepard an instant before he would have gone overboard. Shepard still didn't wake up, and Martino stuffed him against the tube and held him there with the weight of his body, but Martino wasn't sure *he* could stay awake and he wondered if both of them might not end up being pitched over the side.

Then Willard Reynolds went into action. Somehow, he managed to brew coffee in the galley without spilling a drop. He passed the word and one by one the men clawed their way down for a shot of caffeine. By the time Kelly sent Brantingham below for the thermos jug, what was left of the coffee was stone cold. But it was strong, and it took the taste of salt water from their mouths.

In the cockpit, Rockwell was shivering as if standing naked in a cold wind, but he would not leave his topside post. But he was wrought up. This was a seagoing nightmare, beyond anything he could ever have imagined. "I've sailed every type of ship in the navy except one of these MTBs," he shouted at Kelly above the wind, "and this is the worst bridge I've ever been on. I wouldn't do duty on one of these for anything in the world!" Rockwell had commanded the battleship USS *Nevada*, which could plow effortlessly through the heaviest of seas, her bridge ninety feet above the water, where only in a typhoon would salt spray reach it, and there was a time, not long past, when he had seen in the dashing little boats something of the old romance of the seas, like a modern-day jet pilot longing for the open cockpit, but like a lot of men who were destined to serve on PT boats, intimacy with them taught him otherwise.

***

On the 41 boat, conditions were similar. The boat captain, George Cox, passed out at the wheel. Then, with Chief Morris Hancock at the helm, the 41 started to veer slowly off course. Hancock was dozing while standing up in a howling gale. Bulkeley, half asleep himself, noticed in time to step up and grab the wheel. As he steered, he had a rare moment of self-doubt. He began to think that the boats were not going to make it through the night, and he wondered not if, but when he would hear the splintering sound of cracking wood that would signal the end.

Meanwhile, below decks, there was a strange occurrence.

Sidney Huff had settled himself on the lower steps of the officers' cabin. In the dim blue light he could see MacArthur lying below him on the mattress. Jean seemed to be asleep. MacArthur's seasickness was as severe as ever, almost a paralysis, a stiffness and rigidity of the limbs that made it almost impossible for him to move. There had been moments when Huff thought he was going to die. Huff had just fallen asleep when a voice came to him as if in a dream: "Sid? Sid?"

It took a moment for Huff to realize it was MacArthur. In the same moment he came groggily awake—and was astonished to see MacArthur sitting up.

"Sir?" he said mechanically as he tried to gather his wits.

"I can't sleep," MacArthur said.

"I'm sorry, sir."

"I want to talk."

"About what, sir?"

"Oh, anything. I just want to talk."

Thus began the strangest episode of Huff's life, a bizarre monologue by the General that was to last two hours—though, as Huff perceived, he wasn't really talking to anyone, he was thinking out loud, reviewing the events that had led to his humiliating defeat and trying to analyze it. He talked about what he had gone through in the last six years, since the day he arrived in the Philippines to become field marshal of a nonexistent army, and about the program he had drawn up for preparing the Philippines to defend itself by 1946. He remembered how difficult it had been to persuade the legislature to provide enough money, and how the defense budget had been steadily whittled down to the point where it was almost meaningless. He recalled his differences with Washington and how orders had been prepared for his recall, and how he had, more or less, been forced into retirement in 1937.

MacArthur, as always, had a highly selective memory. He remembered the strong points in his plans for Philippine defense and conveniently forgot his tragic decision to fight on the beaches. He remembered the parsimony of President Quezon's military budgets and left out the negligence at Clark Field that deprived him of much of his air force. He remembered his differences with Washington and omitted his failure to store adequate food on Bataan. As he was wont to do, he was reconstructing a personal history that most suited him and that he had no trouble believing. It's what makes his memoir, *Reminiscences*, so unreliable, more a record of his terrors and complaints than the kind of unstintingly honest account we find in the memoirs of that other great general, Ulysses S. Grant. On the other hand, and for that very reason, the book says a lot about the real Douglas MacArthur.

Huff thought the performance bitterly dramatic, and gravely sad. On this bouncing voyage to Mindanao, this hellish passage that brought them not only mental but physical wretchedness, MacArthur had been thrust downward from the crest as far as a man could go.

Finally, like a seance—though in this case it was a man communicating with his own spirit—the General's murmurings ended as abruptly as they began.

"Good night, Sid," he said, and lay back on the mattress and closed his eyes.

***

The two boats were plunging through strange waters with islands all around them. On the 34, Kelly could occasionally see the outlines of the big ones—Negros and Mindanao—through the storm. Invisible were dozens of small ones and hundreds of reefs. In the stern, the men stood one-hour watches, keeping a lookout for the 41 so they wouldn't lose it. Three good waves in a row and it would be out of sight. Every half hour Kelly would send one of the crewmen over the boat for inspection, to see how the hull was standing the strain. No one liked moving about, with the very real risk of being tossed overboard by the wildly pitching deck, and a man subconsciously cringed when he heard Kelly call his name and he was handed the flashlight.

Kelly knew from a study of Bulkeley's chart that out there somewhere in the howling tempest was Silino Island, a tiny thing, only half a mile square, where he had to make the turn into the narrow channel between Silino and the shoals off Mindanao's Tagolo Point. He was wrestling with the wheel, it was all he could do to keep within twenty degrees on either side of the compass course, which meant a possible error of forty degrees, an enormous variance. But they had come this far mostly on dead reckoning, a great deal of which is luck, and it was not unreasonable to think their luck would hold; that was the hope, desperately clung to.

In the dark they missed the little island entirely. From then on until dawn, with Rockwell not saying a word, Kelly would change course as he thought necessary.

At first light they saw land dead ahead.

It was the peninsula just west of Cagayan. The wind died then and the sea became smoother, and with the vastly lightened gasoline load the boats were able to put on some speed. Everyone aboard, especially the passengers, began to show a renewed interest in life. Half an hour later, at six-thirty, the light on the point at Cagayan's entrance was sighted. As he approached the pier, Kelly throttled down to idling speed to allow the 41 to dock first, as a military courtesy to the 41's most illustrious passenger, who was now on deck, his gold-braided cap glistening in the sunlight of a new day.

All through the perilous passage from Corregidor to Mindanao we have seen it. During the first night there was not a single encounter with a Japanese warship. Despite the frequent stops, as the boats wallowed helplessly in towering seas for up to thirty minutes at a time, not one shipped a rogue wave that would have sent it to the bottom. North of the Cuyo Islands Bulkeley left twenty gas drums floating in a big oily sheen—the drums that didn't sink after his gunners shot holes in them—something Japanese pilots, even had they been as myopic as the buck-toothed, bespectacled wartime American caricatures portrayed them, could have failed to see, but there seemed to have been no air patrols to report what would have set the Japanese on their trail like hounds on a scent. The 41 boat, lying exposed for almost a full day in a tiny coral inlet, was not seen. The destroyer they encountered had—incredibly—failed to see their foaming hundred-yard-long wakes. During the passage along the coast of Negros, and again after passing unseen Silino Island in the dark, running blind, neither boat ran aground among the hundreds reefs in the area—another miraculous stroke of good fortune.

It must be acknowledged, the seamanship was superb, and indeed, as the boats docked there were congratulations all around, with Rockwell warmly complimenting Kelly on his navigation, not undeservedly. But if truth had been transmuted into a virus that morning, circulating in the air, to be breathed in by all, everyone would have jumped off the boats and danced manically on the dock in celebration of what had really gotten them through.

CHAPTER 25

To What End

It was a moment of great drama and great style. His feet on solid ground at last, MacArthur was rejuvenated, suddenly his old self again, the hangdog look gone, his jaw thrust out, the hawk's visage recaptured. It was as if he had gotten very old very fast and then suddenly younger again. Even before he stepped ashore, standing in the bow of the 41 as it idled up to the pier, his hands on his hips, the army colonel who was waiting for him with a guard of American infantry thought he looked like Washington crossing the Delaware—notwithstanding his unshaven face and wrinkled uniform.

MacArthur returned the salute of General William Sharp, the commander of the Mindanao garrison, who informed him that the clubhouse and guest lodges of the Del Monte pineapple plantation had been prepared for the General and his party. They would be flying to Darwin from the Del Monte airstrip. Before getting into one of the waiting cars, there was an emotional farewell between the General and the bearded, exhausted navy lieutenant. "You've taken me out of the jaws of death, and I won't forget it," the General told Bulkeley. They exchanged a warm handshake, and then MacArthur promised that he would get Bulkeley out, along with his officers and men.

It was a promise only partly kept, and for those few officers it would mark the beginning of a new life, of medals and awards and publicity tours, the adulation of the nation heaped upon them, but for everyone else in the squadron, those who had been left behind on Bataan and Corregidor and those who had manned the boats during the run to Mindanao, it was the beginning of the end.

***

Just before MacArthur stepped into the waiting car, Bulkeley thought to ask him about his orders. MacArthur thought for a moment.

"You are to conduct offensive operations in these waters," he said. "I'll have Sutherland draw up the orders in detail, and you'll get them before I leave. But until I do leave, hide the boats. No use in attracting unwanted attention."

The men on the boats, avid spectators to all this, watched the half dozen cars pull away from the pier. Then the orders came, lines were cast off, and Bulkeley led the way to a small cove about five miles from Cagayan. The boats were anchored about sixty yards from a coral reef and tidied up, and the crews were put on holiday routine—the navy's phrase for a relaxation of duties. In this instance, relaxation meant sleep, and except for a one-man watch on each boat, in minutes there were men draped like corpses all over the decks, so deep in sleep that both George Cox on the 41 and Henry Brantingham on the 34, the officers who had volunteered to take the watch, seriously wondered if they could awakened if the boats were attacked.

They needn't have worried. Around noon the sound of PT engines reached them, and as the word went around, as quickly as they had fallen asleep every man was on his feet.

It was the 35 boat, long missing and thought to be lost.

***

The 35 anchored close to the other two boats and the four passengers, three army officers and Paul Rogers, the enlisted man, were taken ashore to await transportation to Del Monte. Tony Akers went aboard the 41 to report to Bulkeley. George Cox joined them. Akers had quite a story to tell.

On the first night, plagued by repeated engine failures, they found themselves alone in the dawn. Akers thought he was close to Tagauayan, the rendezvous point, but he couldn't be sure, it might be many miles away, and worried about being spotted by Japanese air and sea patrols, he laid up all the next day in the lee of a tiny island.

In the middle of the afternoon they had a bad scare. William Konko, the boat's radioman, was on watch in the port gun turret when in the eye-splintering sunlight he caught sight of a two-masted sailing vessel. She was running a course that would bring her across the 35's stern. He shouted the alarm and Akers, dozing in the cockpit, sprang up and grabbed his binoculars. Bond Murray, his exec, was right beside him.

"I can't make out any colors," Akers said. "But they could be Japs. Or they could be brown Japs." (Filipinos whose loyalty did not lie with the Americans.)

"She's big enough to have a radio," Murray observed. "If they report seeing us, we've had it."

"Sound general quarters," Akers ordered.

Murray turned around, took a couple of steps out of the cockpit and yelled, "General quarters!" Most of the men were asleep, but with the edgy instincts that months of combat instill in a man they were on their feet in an instant and moving to their battle stations. Akers got the boat underway and swung out of the little cove. As he crossed the bow of the approaching ship, with the intention of swinging in broadside and raking her with his guns, a Filipino on board frantically began waving a small American flag.

Akers drew alongside, hull to hull, and Murray with a .45 automatic and Konko with a rifle, boarded. It was a fishing vessel, or so the captain claimed. Konko thought he was telling the truth; the ship reeked of fish that might have been too long in the sun. Murray and Konko retreated to the 35, and with much smiling and waving the two vessels parted company.

"I'll bet they have a Jap flag too," Murray commented dryly.

Late in the day Akers decided to proceed to Tagauayan. He found it without much trouble—and to everyone's surprise they also found the 32 boat there.

Akers and Schumacher had a word. Schumacher explained that the 34 and 41 had already left for Mindanao and that he was to wait for the *Permit* and deliver the same message before making a run to Panay, where he hoped to refuel. The two boat captains shook hands and wished each other luck, and Akers set off for Cagayan. During the night run the 35 ran into the same heavy seas and driving rainstorms that had pummeled the other two boats, and daylight found Akers considerably off course. Luckily, Negros Island was still visible on the horizon—he was actually heading away from it—and this allowed Akers to reorient himself. In daylight the run into the Mindanao Sea and down to Cagayan was much easier than at night, though it was nerve-racking nonetheless, with the constant fear of being sighted by enemy aircraft. But despite the belief, fervently held by both Bulkeley and MacArthur, that the Japanese had increased their sea and air patrols in anticipation of a breakout, during the six hours the 35 ran in broad daylight, along coastlines and through channels that anyone looking at a map could see were obvious escape routes, not a single enemy plane or warship was seen.

***

The day after the 35 boat joined them, Bulkeley had his written orders. He was to attack hostile shipping in Visayan waters (the Visayan Islands were in the middle of the archipelago: Panay, Cebu, Negros, and Leyte, all quite large) and in the waters north of Mindanao. Sutherland clearly foresaw the end.

"Upon completion of the offensive mission," he wrote, "due to destruction of material" (the boats) "or lack of essential supplies" (ammunition, gasoline, and torpedoes), "you will proceed to Mindanao, reporting on arrival to the commanding general, Mindanao Force" (for duty with the army).

Something else arrived with the written orders: mimeographed copies—one for every officer and man who had made the trip—awarding them the army Silver Star for uncommon valor in the line of duty. The letter was signed *Douglas MacArthur*.

No doubt this was appreciated, but inflaming their hopes was another letter, promising that at such time as the boats should be destroyed or become valueless, all of the officers and crews would have first priority in getting passage to Australia by plane.

***

As the days passed, Bulkeley fretted about the absence of the 32 boat. By now Schumacher should have refueled at Iloilo and joined them on Mindanao. He took several trips in a light plane over the rendezvous point around Tagauayan and off the coast of Negros, but saw nothing. The mystery of the missing 32 boat wouldn't be solved until much later, and would end in acrimony and lasting bitterness between Bulkeley and Schumacher.

***

For the first time in months, the men on the boats ate the kind of food they had once taken for granted but had almost forgotten even existed: fresh vegetables, eggs, fruit, fresh bread, and meat, trucked down from Del Monte by the army. The cooking was done on the shore and the hot meals brought aboard the boats. Army officials even arranged for the PT squadron to have dinner with the air crews of the 28th Bombardment Squadron. Buses took the sailors to the Del Monte plantation in shifts, over the course of two evenings.

On the second evening, Brantingham took the starboard section of the 34 to dinner. When he returned with them to the boat, Kelly and Richardson went with the port section, returning after dark. The last to ride out in the punt from shore, the two had just stepped aboard when Jesse Clark, who had the gangway watch, shouted "We're dragging anchor!"

Kelly went to the forecastle and grabbed the anchor line—and felt it come loose in his hands. The tide was pushing the boat toward shore, and the coral reef was no longer sixty yards away but more like sixteen.

"Fire 'em up!" Kelly yelled and Velt Hunter hurried down the hatch to the engine room, but as he was starting the engines there was a shuddering, grinding scrape—one propeller had sliced deep into the coral.

Up in the cockpit, Kelly put the engines in gear, ahead. The boat started to shake like a dog shedding water, a terrific vibration—the propellers digging deeper into the coral. The engines couldn't move the boat. Unable to stand the strain, they stopped.

Every man went over the side. Their shoes were cut open by the razor-sharp coral as they tried to push the boat off. It was like pushing against a concrete wall. The boat wouldn't move an inch.

Kelly had a flaming temper and it burst out of him now in a string of vivid expletives. He was expressing the feelings of every man on the boat, some of whom joined in with curses of their own. From ship's cook to commanding officer, a sailor feels only disgust when his ship runs aground, and also a bit naked, like a turtle without its protective shell.

Bulkeley was at a conference with army officials. Kelly shouted to George Cox on the 41 to get underway and give them a tow, but by the time the bridles and towing cables were connected the tide was ebbing and the 34 couldn't be pulled off without ripping out her bottom. They would have to wait until morning to see what could be done.

***

In the morning, Bulkeley returned to find the 34 high and dry. Stripped down to skivvy shorts, the men from both the 34 and 41 were working with a couple of axes and their hands to clear away the coral and carve a channel to deep water, some twenty-five yards away. A big crowd of Filipinos, men, women and children, had gathered nearby, squatting on their heels to watch, vastly amused.

Bulkeley was not. He went directly up to Kelly.

"What the hell?" He was angry, and disappointed in his second officer.

"Look at this."

Kelly showed him the anchor line. The anchor had held but the anchor shackle pin had fallen out, the threads stripped. The old story—continuous usage and no replacement parts. It was an exoneration of sorts.

"You'll have a hell of time getting her off," Bulkeley said. "If you can't, we'll have to burn her. I've got to go to Del Monte. How you proceed is up to you."

For a long minute Kelly watched the men chopping and digging with their hands at the coral, and he decided they weren't going to free the boat without help. He went ashore and found an army sergeant in charge of a small diesel tug, the *Misamis*, and asked for a tow. The sergeant agreed to help.

The 34 wouldn't budge. The little tugboat kept pulling, until her steel towing post broke off, putting an end to the operation.

Kelly refused to give up. He sent Iliff Richardson ashore to get help from the army. A persuasive young man meeting with sympathetic army officers produced a bounty—laborers, picks, crowbars, fire axes, shovels ... and dynamite, which made all the difference. Using half sticks of dynamite, the big rocks were cracked so that they could be removed, and piece by jagged piece the coral was excavated from beneath the boat.

By sunset they had a channel from the 34's bow to deep water, though the boat itself was still firmly embedded. That evening a second tugboat, half again as large as the *Misamis*, happened onto the scene. The two tugs lined up side by side for one final effort. With the tow post of the *Misamis* gone, sailors wrapped the towing cable around her wheelhouse. Everyone stood clear and watched as the two tugboats, orange sparks flying from their smokestacks, propellers churning the water into froth, pulled mightily. The tow lines were taut as fiddle strings but nothing moved, neither the tugs nor the 34 boat. A minute went by, then another, then a third, the two tugboats straining at the tow lines like dogs on a leash, belching smoke and sparks but going nowhere. More minutes went by, the men watching in silence, tensed for the moment when something would break, as surely it must: the towing post on the larger tug, the sponson on the 34, the tow lines themselves.

Then someone yelled, "She moved! I saw her move!"

It was true. Almost imperceptibly, literally an inch at a time, the 34 began to move. Then others saw it. Faster and faster, the 34 was sliding through the channel to deep water as a thundering cheer went up.

An inspection of the boat revealed serious damage below the waterline, propellers, struts, and rudders all badly mangled. But the hull was intact, there was no danger of the boat sinking. The larger tug towed the 34 to a dock at Bugo, on the opposite side of the inlet from Cagayan, where the 35 was already moored. Bugo had a refueling station but no repair facilities. Bulkeley had heard of a small machine shop farther up the coast near the village of Anakan, and the next morning the 34 was under tow, slowly moving northeast along the Mindanao coast towards Gingoog Bay, seventy miles away.

CHAPTER 26

Kidnapping the President

To Bulkeley's surprise, it was MacArthur who had summoned him to Del Monte. He thought the General would be gone by now. So did MacArthur. Upon his arrival he had been expecting to see four B-17 bombers waiting to take him and his party to Australia. There was only one. Four had taken off from an airbase in Australia but two experienced engine trouble and turned back, and a third went down in a storm. So he would have to wait.

Only hours after arriving at Del Monte the General had received a troubling report. Manuel Quezon was on Negros Island. Back in February, the Philippine president and his family had left Corregidor on a submarine. They had gone only as far as Panay, and shortly after had moved to neighboring Negros. It was intended that Quezon go to Australia to form a Philippine government in exile, but he changed his mind. He didn't want to be seen as deserting his people. More to the point, he was an embittered man.

In the early days of the war Quezon, like MacArthur himself, had believed the promises that came from Washington (they were never overt, more like hints, really) that help was on the way. When nothing came, he began to suspect the truth: that Europe was the first priority. The Pacific could wait. As he saw more and more signs of this—news reports of convoys going to Ireland and Great Britain—his mounting bitterness, never far from the surface, turned into unconcealed rage. There was the moment in the tunnel on Corregidor when he shouted for all within earshot to hear: "*Que demonio!* How typical of America to writhe over the fate of a distant cousin, Europe, while a daughter is being raped in the back room!"

Then, with the Japanese on the verge of conquering the Philippines, came their promise of independence for the Islands. This had a profound effect on Quezon. He told Carlos Romulo, a trusted aide: "We must look to our own survival, and to hell with the United States. The war between Japan and America is not our fight."

MacArthur had been aware that Quezon was wavering, but he couldn't be sure he had talked his former boss out of any rash acts. Now, with Quezon not in Australia but holed up on Negros, and with reports of Japanese warships approaching the island, he suspected treachery.

***

They sat across from each other on the porch of the clubhouse, in padded wicker chairs, the General still unshaven and in his wrinkled khakis, Bulkeley still in his piratical incarnation, which he clearly relished: the fierce black beard, the red bandana around his head, the double holsters, the Bowie knife tucked menacingly in his belt. He was also carrying a Tommy gun around with him now, a Thompson submachine gun, the weapon favored by Al Capone's Chicago gangsters.

"Buck, I have another job for you." MacArthur's voice was calm but strained. He was stuck on Mindanao, the Japanese had landed on the island's southern coast, and now there was Quezon to deal with. The pressures were mounting. "I want you to go to Negros, find Quezon, and bring him to Del Monte," he told Bulkeley

"Sir?" Bulkeley was understandably confused. He knew nothing about the activities of the Philippine president. To him, Manuel Quezon was only a name.

MacArthur told him what had transpired between himself, Quezon, and the U.S. government, and that he thought Quezon might actually go over to the enemy. Bulkeley had witnessed Japanese atrocities in China, he had actually seen their soldiers use Chinese prisoners, their arms bound, for bayonet practice, and with the attack on Pearl Harbor he had formed a hatred of the Japanese—not just as the enemy but as a race—that allowed for no other emotion. Now that hatred spilled over to include Quezon.

"That bastard," he muttered.

"I don't care how you get him here, just do it," MacArthur went on. "We're sending him to Australia whether he likes it or not."

"Don't worry," Bulkeley said. "I'll bring the son of a bitch back—one way or the other."

***

Only the 41 and the 35 were available for the mission. Perhaps because time was needed to ready the boats for the 200-mile round trip, they didn't leave until the evening of March 18, several days after the meeting between MacArthur and Bulkeley, and the day after MacArthur left for Australia.

The two boats ran all out for a hundred miles, across the Mindanao Sea to the little town of Dumaguete, on the southern tip of Negros, where Quezon was said to be staying. Somehow the General had gotten word to Quezon that PT boats were coming to take him and his family to Mindanao.

It was one in the morning when the two boats arrived, pitch dark, the town and the harbor blacked out. The 35 stood out to sea, to keep watch for enemy warships, as the 41, idled into the harbor and edged up to the pier.

No one was there. Bulkeley waited, on a hunch, which played out when Andres Soriano, an aide to Quezon, walked onto the pier. No one had known when the boats would be arriving, and it was his job to watch for them.

He had a message from Quezon: "He is not interested in leaving Negros."

"Where is he?" Bulkeley had jumped off the boat with his Tommy gun, double holsters, and Bowie knife. One look at him and Soriano apparently decided that cooperation was called for.

"He is not here," he confessed. "He is in Bais."

It was a town twenty-five miles up the coast. Soriano had a car. Bulkeley called for backup and DeWitt Glover and Carl Richardson each grabbed a Springfield rifle and joined Bulkeley and Soriano in a mad dash to Bais, Bulkeley urging ever greater speed over the narrow little road until they were up to seventy miles an hour, the car seeming almost to be outrunning the headlights. Sitting in the back, Glover was sure they were going to end up flattened against a palm tree, and he kept thinking, *What a stupid way to die.*

Then Bais at last, dark and seemingly deserted at two in the morning, the shutters on the houses closed against the evil night fairies and all the dogs barking. They found the house where Quezon was staying. Summoned by Soriano, he came to the door in pajamas and a silk bathrobe, bringing with him his racking, tubercular cough.

"I'm taking you to Mindanao," Bulkeley informed him bluntly, like a constable making an arrest.

"I am not going," Quezon said.

"Yes, you are. You are going back to Mindanao and then on to Australia under direct orders from General MacArthur."

"I am not leaving."

"Look at me. Look at them ..."

Bulkeley pointed to Glover and Richardson, who, with their hard, set expressions and rifles at the ready looked almost as menacing. "Do you really think I'm going to take no for an answer?"

Quezon said nothing.

"I have no more time to waste," Bulkeley told him. "You and your family have fifteen minutes to get your things together, or we'll drag you onto the goddamn boat, Mr. President. You have my word on that."

Bulkeley noticed that Quezon's hands were shaking. He was quite frail and it might have been his illness. Or perhaps not. In any case, after a long moment of consideration, he said, "I am ready to go."

They had to round up three more cars. Coming with Quezon—he insisted on this and Bulkeley didn't feel like getting into another argument, he just wanted to get going—was Quezon's wife, son, and two daughters, and Vice President Sergio Osmena, a general, and nine cabinet members. Plus, of course, their luggage.

Back they went to Dumaguete, with such a valuable passenger not quite as fast as before. At the pier they found the 41 boat where they had left it, but to Bulkeley's consternation, also waiting for them was Tony Akers and the entire crew of the 35 boat—but without the boat.

***

The beginning of the end had come with sickening suddenness—the boat patrolling at a slow idle in the quiet night, the stars out, the sea calm, and then the jarring *thud* and the soul-crushing, splintering sound of her hull being ripped open. They had run into a submerged fish trap and it had ripped a twenty-foot strip out of the bow. Water came pouring in. No one had to be told what to do. The bilge pump was put in play and Joe Chalker, John Houlihan, Bill Konko, and Bond Murray, the exec, formed a bucket brigade, but they were losing the race with the water. When Akers saw the lights of the cars approaching the pier he angled in next to it and ran the boat into the surf near the beach. Everyone jumped off, taking with them their ditty bags and a change of clothes and leaving the 35 to beach herself by slowly drifting to shore.

***

On the pier the 35's crew made their way through a noisy, confused scene and boarded the 41. No one else seemed ready to go aboard. Some members of Quezon's entourage were hotly debating the best place to sit. There was more luggage than available space and much bickering about what to take. Quezon's wife was terrified by the prospect of sailing a hundred miles over the open sea in so small a boat (as she would learn, not without justification), and she began imploring Quezon not to go.

It was all too much for Bulkeley.

"That's it!" he boomed, waving the Tommy gun. "Everyone get aboard and forget the goddamn suitcases!"

To the Filipinos he was a truly fearsome sight, like some bearded, wrathful figure out of the Old Testament, and everyone got aboard without the suitcases—though seven bulging mail sacks also made it aboard. Bulkeley would claim that they contained fifteen million dollars in United States currency, the total assets of the "free Philippine government in exile," but there is no evidence that anyone, and certainly not Quezon, told him this. It is safe to assume, however, that the mail sacks did not contain mail.

Less than an hour into the return voyage they ran into heavy seas, as heavy as any they had encountered on the run from Tagauayan. Every passenger crumbled under it, especially Quezon's wife and two young daughters, who became so seasick they lay below deck holding hands, and at one point were heard to be praying for death. Quezon himself stayed on deck, and so he was a frightened witness to what happened when a rogue wave, huge and froth-flecked, rose out of the night and slammed into the boat.

Houlihan also saw it, and immediately made his way to the cockpit. "Two torpedoes are loose," he told Bulkeley. "The retaining pins have broken."

Hanging part way out of their tubes, the two torpedoes instantly started a hot run—a terrific hissing of compressed air, the propellers spinning, the motors turning first pink and then red hot with no water to act as a coolant. Quezon saw a flame shoot out from one of the tubes and thought: *This is our end.* The other passengers, pushing and shoving, trying to get away from the tubes, piled onto the other side of the boat. Bulkeley had George Cox take the wheel and stepping down from the cockpit he tried to calm the panic-stricken Filipinos. They were right to feel terrified: the two torpedoes were now armed, and a slap from another wave would set off the warheads and blow them all to glory.

By now two torpedomen, Jim Light and John Houlihan, had crawled out on the tubes. With the boat rearing and plunging in the huge seas it was like riding a bucking horse in a rodeo. With incredible agility, the waves washing over them and blinding them, they held on to the wet, slippery tubes with only their hands while trying to kick the torpedoes free. It didn't work, but Quezon was so impressed by their daring that he would later award them the Distinguished Conduct Star of the Philippines. Finally an impulse charge was set in the back end of each tube—there had been some difficulty getting it ready—and the two torpedoes were sent scooting.

The 41 made her landfall at Oroquieta, a town on the northern coast of Mindanao sixty miles from Cagayan. Bulkeley had radioed ahead to alert the authorities there of his arrival, and soldiers were on hand to greet the president. Quezon went directly to the church where he gave thanks to God in his gratitude at being alive. After thanking Him, Quezon shook hands with every sailor on the boat, passed out some money, and then he and his entourage got into cars for the drive to Del Monte, where they would wait for the next plane from Australia.

Meanwhile, the men, with Quezon's money in their pockets, went ashore and bought up all the liquor, bread, and candy they could find. Ever since the move to Sisiman Cove their diet had had a lot of holes in it, but it would seem those were the three items they missed the most.

CHAPTER 27

Respite

What Bulkeley had called a machine shop was an oversized garage sitting in the thin shade of an acacia tree that housed the office and workshop of the Anakan Lumber Company. The manager and the only white man there, Cecil Walter, a small, wiry, sun-browned man in a battered fedora, long in the tropics, was aboard the small tug that met the 34 boat as she was being towed into Gingoog Bay. Walter hailed the 34 and said he would take the tow line.

Instead of the Anakan pier, the 34 ended up at a lumber corral across the little bay from Anakan, moored to a buoy at the bow and to pilings astern. When she was secured, Walter went aboard and explained to Kelly that Japanese planes flew over almost every day and if they attacked the 34 at the company's pier they might also destroy that, which, understandably, was as important to him as the 34 was to the sailors. In fact, so was the lumber corral, filled as it was with valuable hardwoods, the huge logs of mahogany and teak that by now were selling for near-exorbitant prices. Walter would prove to be unfailingly helpful, but he regarded his visitors with mixed emotions.

Work started the next morning and proceeded in the most primitive manner. The stern of the 34 was in shallow water, deliberately, so as not to make things too difficult for the native divers. Like the pearl divers of legend, they could hold their breath for an astonishing amount of time as they worked underwater, removing the mangled struts and shafts of the propellers and rudders. Some of the crew, and even Kelly, took turns trying to pound the propellers back into shape with hammers on palm logs while Walter did his best to straighten the rest in his workshop.

There was a lot of work to do on the boat itself—the auxiliary generator, the engines, the guns, the torpedoes, the electrical system, all needed servicing—while lack of equipment and spare parts delayed progress on every hand. But in Gingoog Bay life aboard the 34 was pleasant. Conscious of the importance of high morale, Kelly put the crew on the peacetime tropical routine: work to end at noon, then a short siesta, and in the afternoon half the crew to go ashore on liberty. Accompanied by either Henry Brantingham or Iliff Richardson, Kelly would often go ashore for an evening of poker with two army officers who showed up after hearing about the PT's arrival. Significantly, no one on the boat, officer or enlisted, was to go ashore with a weapon.

In giving that order, Kelly had in mind the recent tragedy in Cagayan. A few days after their arrival there, half the crew on both the 34 and 41 had gone ashore on liberty. Ten men went in a boisterous group to a small native store where drinks were sold and where, even more enticingly, girls could be seen hanging about. Before the arrival of the PT boats Americans were not a common sight in Cagayan and in their fascination with these exotic strangers the girls were a bit more than friendly, which was more than lively, impulsive Bill Posey needed. As his shipmates had seen in Manila, he had a way with women not a few of them envied. He made it look so easy, and in no time he had a pretty Filipina sitting in his lap, sharing his drink, though some of the other men weren't doing so bad either.

Suddenly the lights went out, and an instant later there was a blinding flash and the ear-splitting explosion of a .45 caliber pistol fired in a small room. Boys and girls all dove to the floor in the dark and amid the shouts and screams there was a scurry of feet, someone running from the room, and then Posey's voice yelling, "For God's sake, turn a light on!"

Someone finally turned on the lights, and there for all to see was Posey's late girlfriend still in his arms but with the entire top of her head blown off. Posey's hair and face were singed by powder burns from a gun fired at very close range, and his shirt, neck, and face were covered with blood and brain matter.

In the investigation that followed, conducted by the local authorities, it was learned that one of the men had his .45 yanked from his holster just after the lights went out. The gun was found just outside the store. Among the several young Filipinos who had been with the girls was the boyfriend of the girl who had so blithely transferred her affections to Posey. A crime of passion, then, and no doubt made even more unendurable by the white skin of the transgressor. All PT sailors were issued sidearms and they were, after all, in a war, but after that no one, for any reason, was allowed to take a weapon ashore.

***

With the 34 under repair and the 35 abandoned on Negros with a gaping hole in her hull, only the 41 boat was fully operational, a situation galling to Bulkeley. He was as eager as ever to take the fight to the enemy but he needed more boats to do it.

He ran back up to Negros only to find that the 35 was not where Akers had left her. Against the logic of wind and tide, she had not beached herself near the pier at Dumaguete. After a long search she was found on a reef near the southern tip of the island, her forward compartments full of water, but otherwise intact.

On the neighboring island of Cebu was the second largest city in the Philippines, and doing business in Cebu City was the Opan Shipbuilding and Slipway Corporation, whose facilities were almost as grand as its name, boasting as it did a modern machine shop and a marine railway (with tracks going down to the beach and into the sea). That was the place for the 35, and a real tugboat arrived from Cebu City the next day with a working party of both navy and army personnel from the American garrison there. It took a full day, but the 35 was pulled off the reef, given a temporary patch job, and towed to the Opan works, where she was loaded onto a train car and pulled ashore by a winch.

Next was the 34. When the work at the crude Anakan facility was done, Kelly put the boat through a trial run, with all hands aboard. Predictably, with bent propellers and the struts still out of alignment, she could make only a fraction of her normal speed, and the vibration was so severe it seemed to rattle their teeth.

Then Bulkeley showed up.

"Do you think you can get her to Cebu?" he said to Kelly. "There's a real machine shop there."

"I think so," Kelly said, "but it's going to be the slowest trip in a PT boat anybody ever made."

It was done at ten knots, slower than some sailboats, and other than a storm it was through the worst of conditions, a bright, moonlit night in which, from the bridge of an enemy warship, the two boats could be seen from many miles away. Nerve-racking work, but there was no end of that. On the 41 the crew had Tojo, their pet monkey, to distract them, along with Carl Richardson, a natural mimic whose perfect imitations of its mannerisms and vocal sounds so disturbed the obviously intelligent little creature that it would run up onto to the roof of the charthouse and hold its hands over its ears.

The 35 boat had had her bottom repaired, scraped, and repainted and was just coming down the ways on the morning the other two boats arrived. With the 35 back in the water, the 34 was winched up. Upon his return from the Quezon mission, when the 35 boat's future was uncertain, Bulkeley had detached her entire crew and transferred them to land duty. Not exactly land duty—they were sent to a huge inland lake to work with the army in setting up a small flotilla of gunboats to prevent Japanese seaplanes from landing on the lake. Which meant that the 35 now had no crew. Bulkeley decided that Henry Brantingham would be her new captain, and with him went a number of men from both the 34 and the 41.

The Opan shipyard was owned and operated by Morrison "Dad" Cleland, an almost mythical figure, seventy-one years old but looking fifty, big, hulking, a resident of the Philippines for twenty-six years, having arrived on a tramp steamer in 1914, a fugitive from a safe life, though not quite a soldier of fortune. He settled down and became prosperous. He was naturally gregarious and something of a gourmet. One night he took Bulkeley and Bob Kelly out to dinner, where they had bottled beer (a great rarity at that time), a crab-meat salad, lobster Newburg followed by roast duck with a tart citrus relish, with sides of asparagus, corn, and sweet potatoes, and ending with a dessert of chilled mangoes and coffee. It was a dinner that both Bulkeley and Kelly would remember for the rest of their days.

There was a sizable army garrison in Cebu City, with its attendant paymaster. The PT men had not been paid since the war began and had accumulated a total of over two thousand dollars in back pay. Saving any of it was out of the question. There was a satisfying number of waterholes in the city and, granted liberty, without exception the men went from bar to bar and spent it as if given a deadline to be rid of all their cash. After three days everyone was broke and digging for nickels to buy a cup of coffee ashore. As predictable as a sunrise, next came poker games with the army.

Then came a night when no liberty was granted. In an air of mystery, a skeleton crew was left aboard each boat and everyone else piled aboard the 41 to be taken to Shell Island, about half a mile from Cebu City's harbor.

"Listen," Carl Richardson said. He was in the bow with DeWitt Glover, lowering the anchor, and coming to them across the dark water was a faint humming that grew louder to become the steady throbbing of large diesel engines.

"That's a submarine," Glover declared.

Just then George Cox called all hands forward, and Bulkeley addressed them.

"You are to say absolutely nothing about what you see or do tonight," he warned. "Nothing—to anybody."

The submarine was the *Seadragon*. She had come up from Australia with torpedoes for the PT boats and ammunition for the Cebu garrison, and she was to take on thirty tons of food and deliver it to Corregidor. It took a large working party of soldiers and sailors two nights working nonstop to get the loading and unloading done, and on the third night the submarine *Snapper* came in with the same mission. By the time *Snapper* left, arms and backs were aching. But for the boat crews there was the compensation of getting news of the war outside the Islands and a pile of American magazines, even if they were two months old. We will never know if it crossed anyone's mind to wonder, after what they had seen and done, why MacArthur had chosen to risk his life and the lives of everyone with him by choosing the PT boats over a submarine, for as was clearly demonstrated at Cebu, submarines continued to slip in and out of Philippine waters almost at will. Not one was even detected, let alone sunk.

CHAPTER 28

The Last Action

On the afternoon of April 7 the 34 boat slid down the ways and into the water, but the 35 was leaking and had to be hauled out again. On the following day at one o'clock, liberty began for the starboard section of the 34 and that half of the crew went ashore. An hour later, Bulkeley boarded the 34 with some charts. He was on fire.

"Are you ready for some action?" he said to Kelly, when they were alone in the charthouse. "Army planes spotted two Jap ships, a cruiser and a destroyer, off the west coast of Cebu. We're going out tonight and knocking off one or both of those ships!"

He spread the charts on the table. Cebu was narrow and 140 miles long north to south. Cebu City, and the PT boats, were on the east side of the island. On the west side, between Cebu and Negros, was Tanon Strait, not very wide anywhere, but narrowest at its southern end, Tanon Point, where the channel between the two islands was less than four miles wide.

Bulkeley tapped the chart with his finger. "Tanon Point is a perfect set up for an ambush. The estimated speed of those ships is eight knots, so that should put them there at around midnight. I want the 41 and 34 ready to go by 1900 hours"—seven in the evening.

Half of Kelly's crew was ashore. He sent Iliff Richardson to round them up, but Richardson could find only two of them. At least eight men were needed to fill battle stations. With the 35 in drydock, Velt Hunter and Dave Harris, who had only recently been shifted to the 35, were brought back to the 34, both happy to be rejoining their old shipmates—and to be going out on the mission, though it be a dangerous one. The men manning the boats had not volunteered for PT duty to avoid combat. That the enemy had actually been sighted meant a great deal; on routine patrols there was always the gnawing, underlying tension of waiting for something to happen, at best an unpleasant feeling, and emotionally draining. Knowing you were definitely going into action brought on a different kind of tension, a fusing of excitement and fear that brought on the adrenaline and could be almost heady.

***

A light breeze was blowing, the sea calm, and no moon until 2 a.m. The 41 was leading, with George Cox at the wheel. In her wake was the 34, with Kelly and Richardson in the cockpit. With the three consecutive nights of hard labor followed by a long afternoon running around Cebu City looking for his men, Richardson was tired, and admitted it. Kelly took the watch and sent him below for some rest.

Two hours later, though it seemed only minutes after he had fallen asleep, Richardson felt a hand touch his shoulder. He was awake in an instant.

"General quarters, sir," Willard Reynolds said to him, and Richardson rolled out of his bunk and was at the wheel as the other battle stations were being manned. He could see the dark shape of the 41, about a hundred yards off his starboard quarter—and, dead ahead, something that made his heart skip.

Just before he had been awakened, DeWitt Glover, at the wheel of the 41, had been the first to see it—the dark silhouette of a ship coming round Tanon Point, some four thousand yards away.

"There she is!" he shouted. As more of it became visible—the long, distinctive outline of a very large warship—he added, "Jumping Jesus, there she *is!*"

It was the cruiser, but she was alone. If there was only one target, the plan was for the 41 to lead the attack. The 34 was to follow.

Now, on the 41, Bulkeley takes the wheel. At idling speed he makes a hard right turn, curving into firing position. Cox is sighting through the torpedo director. As they close to five hundred yards he unlocks the torpedo firing keys. The cruiser looms before them, gliding almost silently by, dark and massive behind a phosphorescent bow wave. "Fire!" Bulkeley says and Cox presses two chest-high buttons on the cockpit panel. Two torpedoes leap into the sea. They stream toward the cruiser, their wakes white as string. Anger rises in Bulkeley and Cox's heart sinks as they watch the torpedoes straddle the cruiser, missing at the bow and stern.

But she gives no sign that she has seen anything.

As Bulkeley makes a wide arc to get into position for another attack the 34 approaches broad on the cruiser's bow. Richardson is at the wheel, Kelly at the torpedo director. Al Ross is crouched at the gun on the forward deck. Willard Reynolds and Dave Harris are up in the port and starboard turrets.

Below the turrets, Dave Goodman stands ready to pass ammunition belts to each turret from the open ammo boxes before him.

As the 34 closes to a thousand yards all on board hear the *zing-pingg* of torpedoes being fired from the 41—and then the thunderous blast of her engines as she retreats as full speed. Kelly fires two torpedoes. At almost the same instant the cruiser suddenly increases speed and the torpedoes pass well behind her. Then, like a lighthouse beacon, the cruiser's searchlight snaps on. It touches the retreating 41 before settling on the 34.

It is like standing in an empty parking lot at night under the glare of enormous lights. There is no place to hide. Up in the port turret, Reynolds has his fists clenched on the machine guns, his heart pounding. He is acutely aware of the Miraculous Medal suspended from a chain around his neck, a present from his mother. But he doesn't pray. He hasn't prayed since he was a child and he decides it would be cowardly to pray now, when he had not been to church in years, when all God was during those years was a word to swear with.

The cruiser opens fire. There is an orange flash, the scream of the shell, then the explosion that sends up a geyser of water two hundred yards behind the 34, which is now at full speed.

"Port turret, commence firing!" Kelly yells as Richardson cranks the wheel clockwise, turning right so that the port turret will bear on the target.

Reynolds squeezes the trigger bar and feels the heavy jolts as orange tracers pour out in a twin stream. There is a loud *swoosh* as a shell goes by a foot from his head and then a scooped-up crump as it explodes in the water astern. He can see his tracers plunging dotted lines into the darkness and hitting the water and flinging high into the air. He is firing too low, but the searchlight is full on them and it's worse than staring into the sun.

As if in reply to Reynold's guns, the cruiser opens fire with all she has, and now, mixed in with the deep booming of her heavy guns is the rapid *poomp poomp poomp* of her antiaircraft batteries and the woodpecker chatterings of her many machine guns. There are match flares flickering along the entire length of the cruiser from all the guns that are shooting at them. The bullets and shells, dense as bees, are going right over their heads.

It is during an attack like this that the individual daring of the boat captain is put to its supreme test. The time he shall fire his torpedoes is determined only by him. The closer he approaches the target, the greater his chances of a hit—and the greater the chance the boat will be hit by enemy fire.

Within Kelly, and surmounting all other emotions, is anger that his first two torpedoes had missed. Like the tiger, the lion, its every nerve and fiber focused on its victim, Kelly bores in.

The fire from the port turret ceases abruptly.

"Reynolds is hit!" Dave Goodman screams. He is spattered with Reynolds's blood.

"Right a touch," Kelly says calmly.

Richardson repeats the order and ticks the wheel to the right.

"Steady."

"Steady."

A deafening explosion directly overhead knocks Richardson to his knees. Fear almost keeps him there. He sees Kelly still on his feet and realizes the boat is still in one piece, and so is he.

"Come right!" Kelly yells and Richardson jumps up and repeats the order as he grabs the wheel and spins the rudder over.

"Steady."

"Steady."

The 34 is heading directly for the cruiser's midships. Six hundred yards. Five hundred. There is a huge explosion and geyser of water just alongside. The 34 lurches sideways but stays on course.

She is now four hundred yards from the cruiser. It looms before them like an enormous building filled with blinking lights. Every gun on the ship seems to be firing at them. Richardson almost loses his nerve. At three hundred yards he yells, "We're going aboard, Mr. Kelly!"

His agony is relieved when he hears the pinging of two torpedoes being fired. He sees their wakes hesitate, wiggle, and then straighten out on the target line.

Kelly orders a hard right and they peel away from the cruiser. Except for their machine guns, they are defenseless now.

***

As Kelly was pressing his attack, Bulkeley had run the 41 across the cruiser's stern, firing off the last of his ammunition in an attempt to distract the enemy gunners. It had no effect, and he set a course for Cebu. He soon found himself blocked by an enemy destroyer and he turned south toward Mindanao. His radio was out and so he couldn't tell Kelly where he was going. This would soon be the source of much anxiety for both men.

***

Reynolds was slumped in the port turret. With a series of hard right turns Kelly had managed to lose the cruiser, but they were still at battle stations. John Martino, with no torpedoes to tend to, felt free to go over and help

Dave Goodman get Reynolds down. He had been shot in the throat and shoulder and was still bleeding, but he was conscious. Kelly told them to take Reynolds below and see what they could do for him. Gently, they laid him on a bunk in the crew's quarters. Reynolds was not only ship's cook but also her medic, and he knew better than they did what they could do for him—a shot of morphine, the wounds to be sprinkled with sulfa powder, then gauze compresses to help stop the bleeding, and a cigarette, which they didn't want to give him.

"The smoke is going to come out the hole in your neck," Goodman said to him, only half in jest.

"As long as it comes out," Reynolds told him.

Kelly set a course for Cebu, anxious to get Reynolds to a doctor, but like Bulkeley he ran into what he thought was a destroyer—in fact, everyone thought so. Directly ahead, and less than a mile away, a searchlight came on. The vessel was heading directly for the 34 at full speed. The 34 was at about the same speed—thirty knots. At a relative speed of sixty knots they were past each other before Kelly had time to maneuver and before the enemy could get off a shot. The vessel turned, and a stern chase ensued—the 34 running like a hare before the fox, zigging, zagging, the wand of light finding the boat, losing it, finding it again, the vessel firing steadily, the water trees rising all around the 34, some less than fifty feet away, the shrapnel buzzing over the cockpit and thunking into the hull and superstructure. For a full twenty minutes it went on like that, in heart-pounding suspense as everyone waited for the fatal hit that never came.

The 34 outran her pursuer. Far behind them the searchlight was waving around, searching the water, and was soon out of sight. As if in reward, at that moment the moon came up in full splendor over the hills of Bohol, lighting the whole coast of the island with a lunar brilliance that rivaled the sun—one of nature's most beautiful moments.

With the danger passed, all hands were secured from general quarters and the regular watch set. Kelly went on a tour of the boat. He found countless bullet holes. The main mast was shot away, rendering the radio useless. The boat's victory emblem—a mounted Japanese bayonet—was shot away. He dropped down into the engine room, where George Shepard was standing among the engines, casually touching the manifolds to make sure they weren't getting too hot and regulating the scoop controls. "Well done, Shepard," Kelly said to him, which was the highest compliment that existed in the navy of that time, and which almost never passed Kelly's lips. The man at the wheel develops a sense of timing with the engineer who is following the signals on his panel—this is true of all boat captains and all engineers—but during the night's action Shepard's timing had been such that there hadn't been even the usual two-second delay between Kelly's throttle signals and the engine room's response, so that Kelly had felt as if he'd had direct control of the engines. It was almost as if Shepard had been able to hear Kelly thinking.

Except for Reynolds and those on watch, the men gathered near the cockpit to rehash the battle, excitedly exchanging stories of what each had seen and heard and felt, like fighter pilots back from a dogfight. But their impressions of the fight, as well as those of the officers on both boats, officers who would write the after-action reports, does not match the reality.

Richardson would write not long after that at first he didn't hear or see the explosions as their torpedoes hit the cruiser but then caught a glimpse of white splashes alongside her rising into the beam of the searchlight. Much later he would later tell a journalist that he saw big black chunks of torn cruiser debris flying through the searchlight beam, and that as they passed astern of the cruiser she was dead in the water and completely dark. Bulkeley would claim that he saw the cruiser's searchlight fade out, and heavy yellow smoke rise up, and when an accompanying destroyer put a searchlight on her decks (though Richardson saw her as completely dark) "Japs were all running around, not knowing where to go. Her stern was under in three minutes, and she had sunk in twenty." Kelly would report seeing two large splashes amidships at the cruiser's waterline. John Martino also claimed to have seen what he took to be two hits.

Japanese records confirm that the light cruiser *Kuma* did encounter PT boats on the night in question but was only hit near the bow with a single torpedo that failed to explode (which is entirely in keeping with the faulty, obsolete, Mark VIII torpedoes carried by the PT boats, many of which were duds—and, unknown to the sailors, they would usually run deeper than what they were set for, passing underneath the hulls of the enemy ships). There is no reason to doubt the Japanese report; the *Kuma* was in action for well over another year, until she was sunk by a British submarine off the west coast of Malaya on January 11, 1944. And the vessel which Kelly and others on the 34 took to be a destroyer was actually the torpedo boat *Kiji*, somewhat larger than a PT boat but nowhere near the size of a destroyer.

This in no way demeans the men who fought the action. It was a daring attack, at times verging on the suicidal, during which not one man failed in his duty, and more than a few performed with great valor. But how do we account for the enormous discrepancy between what these men saw and what actually happened? It would be ridiculous to say they were delusional. And yet …

The human mind. It is unfathomable.

CHAPTER 29

The Dead and the Dying

The full moon turned the sea into moving silver, with the sky like velvet, a soft, beguiling night that made it easy to imagine there was no war. Midnight had come and gone, it was now the ninth of April, a couple of hours before dawn, and Iliff Richardson, still at the wheel of the 34, suddenly remembered it was his birthday. He was twenty-four years old. He began to think of the night's action as his birthday party, surely one of the most remarkable anyone could have. He kept thinking about it, the action itself, the beautiful scene before him now, fixing it in his mind so that when he had his thirtieth birthday and fortieth and seventieth, he could look back and remember how it had been, the strange elation as he stood at the wheel of a big speedboat that had been shot full of holes, running at thirty-two knots through the silvery brilliance of a tropical night.

His revery was broken when Kelly took the wheel. They were approaching the channel leading into Cebu City—narrow, bordered by shoals, without charts difficult to navigate even in daylight and extremely risky at night, even with the moonlight. But with a wounded man aboard Kelly had decided to take that risk rather than wait for daybreak

He throttled down to a slow idle and was gliding forward on soundings—Al Ross in the bow tossing out the weighted sounding line and calling out the changing depths, when there was the unmistakable grating sound of the hull encountering solid rock.

Kelly came to a full stop. He was nettled. Ross had just called out twenty feet. How could they be aground?

The flashlight beams told them. The water *was* twenty feet deep, but there were coral pinnacles all around them, like a petrified forest, spiraling up to within five feet of the surface. On one of them they were stuck fast.

Everyone but Kelly, the engineer on duty, and the wounded Reynolds went over the side to try rocking the boat loose, but flailing about in twenty feet of water, there was only a limited amount of rocking they could do. It wasn't enough.

Dawn was near, and with it would come the danger of attack from the air.

"Take the punt ashore and send an army doctor and an ambulance out from Cebu City," Kelly told Richardson. "And a tugboat."

***

Cebu City was nine miles away. Only a mile away was the village of Minglanilia, where there was a train station with a telephone that worked, more or less. Richardson managed to get through to army headquarters and arrange for an ambulance to be on the pier in Cebu City at 5 a.m. to pick up a wounded man and to have a tugboat sent to Minglanilia.

"What's going on?" the officer on the other end wanted to know.

"I'm off a PT boat," Richardson told him, "and we just sank a Jap cruiser."

He would remember for a long time how good it felt to say that. He walked back to the beach, but the punt and the two men who had rowed him ashore were gone.

And so was the 34.

***

The tide had started to come in and the men had again gone over the side. This time, helped by the engines, they had managed to roll the boat off the coral. The center propeller and strut were bent but there was no other damage. Kelly went back the way he had come, *very* slowly, flashlight beams playing on the water, until the coral pinnacles could no longer be seen. He had missed the entrance to the channel, but in the dark he would only be guessing again, and he might miss it again, and so he decided to wait until dawn.

Dawn came, but with a thick low fog. Finding the channel would be no easier than in the dark, and Kelly decided to wait until the sun burned it away. Two crucial decisions that had to be made, but taken together they sealed the fate of the 34.

Shortly before eight o'clock, in the clear morning air, the 34 in the channel now and moving at fifteen knots, a fat yellow bomb falls unseen and lands ten feet off her bow. It blows a hole in the crew's quarters you can walk through, tears the port Lewis gun off its mount, blows the windshield in, and covers everyone with water and mud.

No one has seen them. Four Japanese float planes are diving at them out of the sun, unheard in the sound of the 34's engines.

The men scramble to their battle stations. The channel is too narrow to maneuver in and it's up to the gunners now—Dave Harris in the starboard turret, John Martino in the port turret, Al Ross at the Lewis gun in the bow. The second plane dives and drops its bomb, missing by thirty feet. The guns are firing, the firm, heavy tracers arcing through the air like Roman candles. The planes have two bombs each. Eight altogether, and each time one comes down Kelly waits with iron control, watching it until the very last moment before kicking the boat over, hard right, hard left, the bombs missing by twenty or thirty feet. Despite streams of bullets from the 34 no plane is hit, and when they finish their bomb runs they circle and come in again, one by one, to strafe. Kelly does his best but bullets are not as easily dodged. Harris is hit in the throat and falls to the deck. Bullets disable the guns Martino is firing, somehow not hitting him, and when he sees Harris fall he climbs into the starboard turret only to find that gun too has been hit. Then one of the planes visibly wobbles and starts streaming smoke. "I got him!" Al Ross yells as another is making its run. The bullets literally knock the gun out of Ross's hands and send it clattering to the deck, one of them opening Ross's thigh. Like a can opener, a stream of bullets slices through the canopy of the crew's quarters where Willard Reynolds is lying wounded. He is hit again, this time in the lower abdomen, unbelievable pain.

The planes continue to strafe, raking the boat with fire she cannot return. The engine room is taking water and the boat is sinking. There are injured men aboard.

Kelly makes his decision: there is nothing to do but beach her.

***

Kawit Island, a green hump of land rising out of the harbor, was within sight of Cebu City and encircled by a coral reef. Not until he ran the boat aground did Kelly realize that the reef extended a thousand yards from the beach. Relentlessly, as if they would settle for nothing less than complete extermination, the three remaining planes kept up their strafing runs, circling over the stricken and now motionless boat, one after the other peeling off into a dive, over and over.

Having given the order to abandon ship, Kelly hurried below to tell the engineer on duty, Velt Hunter, and there he came upon a ghastly sight: Hunter was covered with blood, his right arm practically blown off. He was hit during the first strafings, when bullets had ripped open the engine room canopy, and for some twenty minutes the right-handed Hunter had stayed at his post, working the throttle levers with his left hand, responding to the signals on his panel with his usual precision, so that Kelly had had no inkling anything was wrong.

He went into the crew's quarters and found Reynolds lying with his hands over his belly, blood oozing between his fingers as he tried to keep his intestines from falling out. He was white-faced with the pain.

"Leave me here," he told Kelly. "I'm done for. I'll be all right here. Just get the others out."

"The hell with that," Kelly said to him.

A thousand yards, four feet of water, over an uneven bottom of coral and sand, dodging bullets, the four unwounded men struggled with their burdens. Dave Goodman and George Shepard half carried Hunter, who was too weak to walk that far. Lurching and stumbling over the treacherous bottom, Kelly and John Martino carried Reynolds, whose intestines refused to stay in. Despite the wound in his thigh, Al Ross made it to shore on his own. Kelly and Goodman went back for Dave Harris's body. To them, he wasn't just a corpse. He was David Harris, Torpedoman second class, United States Navy, a shipmate and a friend, and they felt it was worth risking their lives to recover the body and give him a decent burial.

Kawit Island was garrisoned by a company of Filipino soldiers. They didn't have a doctor with them, but they did have some stretchers, and Kelly had them carry the wounded to the other side of the island, facing Cebu City, and onto the small launch they employed for their supply runs. He put Shepard in charge, with orders to get the wounded to the hospital in Cebu City.

The three planes had finally departed, no doubt out of ammunition, and Richardson had just arrived, distraught. He had been standing on the pier in Cebu City, watching helplessly as his boat was being savaged, and finally, not able to stand it any longer, he had the American civilian who was watching with him drive him to a spot opposite Kawit Island, where he stole a dugout canoe and paddled it across to the 34. He boarded from the stern and found bullet holes in every square foot of the boat and blood and empty cartridge cases all over the deck. Kelly came aboard and together they loaded the canoe with ship's papers, binoculars, and some personal belongings and paddled all the way to Cebu City.

There they parted company. Kelly went directly to army headquarters to report the previous night's action to the proper authorities, but uppermost in his mind was the fate of John Bulkeley and the 41 boat. They hadn't returned to Cebu. Where were they? Were they still alive?

In Cebu City, nobody knew. There had been no word of the 41. Always a hard-minded man, Kelly stopped thinking about it, the way you always stopped thinking about someone who is killed in action, especially a friend. That person was gone, never to be seen or heard from again, and if you kept thinking about it you could become as incapacitated as if you had taken a bullet. Better to take a bullet than suffer that disgrace.

***

Richardson rounded up two small pilot boats to get the 34 to the Opan works. He agreed with Kelly that the boat could be patched up and floated to Dad Cleland's dockyard to be refitted and rearmed. He was directing the work of the Filipino soldiers who had come with him, clearing debris and sealing the hull, when the three floatplanes interrupted them. In panic, the soldiers piled back aboard the pilot boats. Wisely, Richardson waded ashore. He watched from the beach on Kawit Island as the planes made short work of both boats, chopping one in half with machine gun bullets and riddling the other and forcing it to run aground. Several men were killed, the survivors jumping off the boats only to be strafed in the water. Then the planes turned their attention to the 34. First the bombs, six of them, dropped one at a time. They made a shattering noise, like a load of glass hitting pavement, and sent up tall geysers of mud and water, but every one of them missed. Then came the strafing. Pass after pass, until the 34's gas tanks exploded and flames shot up, barely visible in the bright sunlight.

Far above, the planes droned off.

***

Kelly was at Opan shipyard, talking with Henry Brantingham and the crew of the 35. The boat was still under repair. The men listened to Kelly's account of the night action with avidity, and with pangs of regret.

In the office, the phone rang, and someone came out to tell Kelly the call was for him.

It was Richardson. After making his way back to Cebu City he had gone to the hospital to visit Willard Reynolds. Reynolds had just come out of the operating room. Lying there on the bed he was barely conscious, but he gripped Richarson's arm with surprising force and said, "I'm going to be pretty sick, ain't I?" Then, still looking up at Richardson, his grip slackened as he entered a new dimension, the life draining from his eyes until they were as flat and blank as the head of a nail. It was not so much his passing but the suddenness of it that shook Richardson.

On the phone, he said, "Reynolds is dead. They're burying him and Harris in the American cemetery with a priest and a military escort, at four o'clock. Can you come?"

"Of course I'll come," Kelly told him. "I'll meet you at the bar of the American Club and we'll go over together."

Richardson never showed up. He sent a Filipino soldier to tell Kelly that the funeral had been postponed until ten o'clock the following morning.

Richardson had met a soldier, Tom Jurika, about his age, who had been born and raised in the Philippines and who offered him the use of an apartment in Cebu City. Richardson was exhausted from the varying emotions of the day and it was a place to get some food and rest. It was in the apartment that he heard about the surrender of Bataan, while listening to the Voice of Freedom, the radio station on Corregidor. He was too tired to think much about it. He went into the bedroom and sat on the edge of the bed to take his shoes off, but he was too tired to unlace them, and he lay back with his feet on the floor and fell asleep with his soggy, muddy, blood-stained shoes still on his feet.

CHAPTER 30

Flight

The explosions started at four-thirty in the morning. Richardson drowsed through them for a long time, wondering what they were. Then there was a very big one that shook the building and brought him completely awake.

Outside the window, it was still dark. He went down into the street. The city was burning, fires everywhere. There was an eerie light, red as watered blood, the sky hanging black and quiet over it.

He headed for the waterfront and there he found Tom Jurika.

"The Japs are here," Jurika said calmly, as if he were commenting on the weather.

"Already?" Richardson looked with alarm out into the harbor.

"No," Jurika said. "They're landing about ten kilometers down. We're burning the town for them."

He meant the army, which had demolition parties out destroying supply dumps and anything else, warehouses, even office buildings, that might be of use to the enemy. It was arson sanctioned by the authorities, and it had a heady effect on the two young men, reducing them for a short while to children excitedly playing with matches. Most of the downtown buildings had been abandoned, the population fleeing to hills, and they set fire to several garages, a warehouse, and a big office building, on the premise that it contained files that had to be destroyed. The black sky, the flames reaching up from the burning building, the long red sparks rising above the flames and floating up into the blackness. Richardson stood in its heat and watched his handiwork with a strange feeling, half righteous, half criminal. Perhaps Jurika was feeling the same way; after that one, they threw away their matches and went back to the apartment

Jurika had a car, also multiple pairs of shoes in his closet. He gave a pair to Richardson. Not a perfect fit, but they were better than his soggy, blood-stained navy shoes. Taking some canned food with them, they drove to Busay Heights to watch the Japanese come in.

***

Kelly too had been awakened by the early morning explosions. An American businessman who owned a large house in the hills above Cebu City had invited him to dinner and had put him up for the night. Downstairs, he found his host on the phone, gathering information. It was a bleak picture: the Japanese invasion had begun and the Americans were blowing up the town.

The previous afternoon, with the 34 destroyed and all his men in one way or another accounted for, he had given the three unwounded men some money and told them to go have a drink and try, for a short time at least, to enjoy themselves, because what was coming might even be worse. With those three men on his mind he tried to get back into the city but was stopped by armed sentries: no one was allowed back in, everyone must get out. And indeed, along the road he was on masses of people were streaming out—mostly Filipinos, a few Americans, some navy and army people from the Cebu garrison—and from them, over the course of the next few hours, Kelly picked up bits of information. It was like the pieces of a puzzle being fitted together: the 41 had escaped and was in Mindanao; Brantingham had burned the 35 boat and along with his men had headed into the hills; Richardson had been seen in the city helping with the demolition. But there was no word of Dave Goodman, George Shepard, or John Martino, or of the two wounded men, Al Ross and Velt Hunter, who, presumably, were still in the hospital.

He sat it out for a while in the house of the American businessman, watching as the Japanese landed in the harbor of Cebu City far below, almost without opposition.

It was time to go. Soldiers passing the house had told them of a camp deep in the hills where food and other supplies had been stocked, a hideout, but Kelly was skeptical. The Japanese were relentless, there would be no hiding from them, and besides, the very idea of hiding from the enemy was abhorrent to him. He decided that the thing to do was to get down to Mindanao, somehow, and find Bulkeley and the 41 boat.

***

Henry Brantingham had the same idea. That is, to get to Mindanao. He hadn't heard about the 41 and thought she was lost, but mindful of MacArthur's promise, he was hoping to get to Australia. He talked it over with the men he had with him. No one objected, for them too there was the hope of getting out, but there was disagreement on how to get to Mindanao. Brantingham wanted to hike through the hills to the west coast of Cebu, to get out of the way of the Japanese, and then see about getting a boat of some kind. Dick Regan thought they should circle around to the east and cross the narrow straight to Leyte. "A lot less walking, and we'd be closer to Mindanao." But they would be closer to the Japanese, someone pointed out. We'll travel only at night, and hole up during the day, Regan countered. A debate ensued, about half the men agreeing with Brantingham and the rest with Regan. Running out of patience, Brantingham finally put a stop to it.

"I'm going west, and there will be no splitting up," he told them. Acquiescence was quick and unanimous. They had confidence in Brantingham. They were in no position not to have.

They still had the rifles and army field packs they had been issued, salvaged from the 35. The packs were stuffed with extra clothes and personal items to which they now added canned goods, pots and pans, and sundry other items suitable, they thought, for a long camping trip. Within hours, struggling over steep trails, through dense undergrowth, in suffocating heat, they had thrown away their packs, keeping only their sidearms, rifles, and canteens, which were soon empty.

Ahead of them, as some already began to suspect, lay a nightmarish test of their endurance.

***

Through the same rolling hills and rugged mountains Richardson moved, astonished by what he was seeing. Back trails that normally saw little human traffic were filled with Filipino families, long lines of men, women and children, none knowing where they were going, an entire population in flight, such was the fear of the Japanese. Richardson too was being moved by fear, though of a different variety: captivity. He could not imagine himself as anyone's prisoner. Had he been on Bataan when the garrison surrendered, he knew he would not have gone with them into the prison camps. He would have slipped away, up into the hills, anywhere.

Tom Jurika had gone his own way, looking for the mysterious Camp X they had heard about. Richardson had paused for a couple of days, helping out at an army motor pool until the Japanese got so close that, along with the Filipino soldiers, he had run off through a hail of bullets. That had been enough to convince him that resistance of any sort was hopeless. Hanging around on Cebu, he would be captured. There was no shame now in trying to get out, and he decided to try to get over to Leyte and so perhaps make Mindanao and a plane to Australia.

***

By now, the eleven sailors were so used to the endless monotony of wet and damp and skid and tangle and insect song that it seemed to them that life was nothing else. Over narrow trails, uphill and down, on and on, each step a wrench and pull, at once beset by leeches, surrounded by biting insects, slashed by briar vines, through a green, alien world in which effort quickly produces that exhaustion that makes further effort seem as ridiculous as it is frighteningly necessary.

Fortunately, it was not all jungle through which Brantingham and his men made their way. At one point they encountered a hillside farmer, who gave them a meal of boiled cornmeal and chicken. Occasionally they would come upon a *sitio*, a settlement too small to be called a village, three or four nipa huts in a banana grove, or in the dappled shade of palm trees. But on most days they saw no one, and were near nothing but each other. In the tropical forest the little wounds the leeches make don't heal. Scratches don't heal. The air is damp and there is no way to keep the wounds dry; there is no sun to help the healing. The little wounds grow larger, and rotten. They become tropical ulcers and the flesh in time rots away to expose the shiny white bone which quickly yellows with lymph and blood and ooze. So with Paul Owen and Jesse Clark, both of them limping along now, slowing the group down even more, misery added to misery. Dick Regan, the advocate of the eastern route, the shorter one, might be excused for saying, "I told you so." There is no evidence he said it, but surely he must have had the thought.

Trying to maintain a sense of direction, the trails not taking them directly west but meandering, alarmingly at times, living on green coconuts and bananas, they worried on. On the seventh day, or perhaps the eighth, or ninth, depending on whose count it was, Brantingham, who was in the lead, saw through a break in the foliage a most welcome sight: the sea shimmering far below, deep blue in the sun and flecked with whitecaps.

Coming out of the forest, they entered a small town. There was the dusty plaza, the two-story stone municipal building, the church of pink adobe across from it, the statue of Jose Rizal, an open cement building filled with wooden stalls that was the town market, the gasoline station with its single

Cal-Tex pump, long unused under a layer of dust. The little column had not gotten quite as far as the plaza when a small, slightly built man in tan pants and a white shirt came hurrying up to them. He was the mayor, though he didn't introduce himself as such. Alarm showed clearly on his face. Making frantic shooing motions with his hands as he approached, he said, "Go back! Go! Go! You go!"

"Hell, we just got here," Brantingham said to him. He was hoping there would be a doctor in town to treat Owens and Clark, before their ulcers became infected.

"Hapons!" the mayor explained.

Brantingham drew his pistol, looking warily toward the plaza. Behind him, also watching the plaza, the men kept their rifles at the ready.

"How many?" Brantingham asked.

The mayor thought for a moment, then raised both hands, palms outward, as if in surrender.

"Ten? That's it?" Brantingham said.

"Ten," the mayor repeated.

Just then a Japanese soldier appeared in the plaza and saw them.

"Let's go," Brantingham said, and the sailors headed off, back the way they had come. Once outside the town they could see they were being followed at a distance by four soldiers. They didn't appear to be looking for a fight. The little garrison was outnumbered and it was as if they wanted to be sure the Americans were leaving.

Brantingham had no intention of leaving. The town was on the seacoast and he was sure they could find a boat in it somewhere. And he'd had more than enough of the jungle. All of them had, and they found a good spot to lay down an ambush. With those four killed, there would be only six left, and they would go in and liberate the town and get themselves a boat.

They waited for what seemed a very long time, but the enemy never came. They kept waiting, until dark, and passed through the town unnoticed by the Japanese. On the wide, slanting beach they came upon three outrigger canoes, one with a sail. As if inviting theft, all three boats had paddles in them.

Brantingham and four men took the sailboat, the largest of the three, the other six men the two remaining two boats. The sailboat led, towing the other two, which were helped along by two men paddling in each. All that night and into the next day they snaked along in tandem. Luckily, the sea was calm and they made the east coast of Negros without incident. There, Brantingham brought out his Texaco road map and found the main road to Dumaguete.

There were no Japanese on Negros, and plenty of boats in Dumaguete, so it wasn't necessary to steal one. The men's wallets were empty, but Brantingham had had the foresight to take all his money out of the bank before Manila fell and foreign bank accounts were frozen by the Japanese. His wallet was stuffed with paper pesos, and he was able to hire two fishing boats whose owners were willing to take them to Mindanao. They spent the rest of the day resting and making up for lost meals, Owens and Clark were treated by a doctor, and after dark they set off, their fate now in the hands of men who, though familiar with the sea, had never been to Mindanao, and had never, in fact, ventured very far from their fishing grounds off Negros.

CHAPTER 31

Glory Road

On Mindanao we see John Bulkeley, just returned from the night action off Cebu and anxious to report the sinking of a Japanese cruiser, anxious too about the fate of the 34 boat, Bob Kelly and all those men. He makes his way to General William Sharp's headquarters, looking for the first time in a long time like an American naval officer—clean shaven, wearing khakis, navy shoes, officer's cap. He wants to make a good impression. He is there to beg for gasoline. He tells Sharp that he intends to go back to Cebu to look for the 34 boat, pick up torpedoes, and carry on the fight. Sharp hands him a radiogram: the Japanese had landed on Cebu and taken Cebu City. And he could not let Bulkeley have any gas. What little was left was needed for the planes coming in from Australia.

So it was over at last. The 41 was not going anywhere, and neither was Bulkeley. He was out of a job, and was now attached to the army. While waiting for orders, beset with visions of himself and the 41's crew fighting it out on Mindanao with rifles to the end, he was summoned by Sharp.

"I've just gotten an order from General MacArthur," he informed Bulkeley. "You're to go out on the plane that's leaving tonight."

"Just me?"

"That's the order."

Mixed emotions hardly describes it; within Bulkeley they clashed violently. From the very start, his ideal had always matched what he was truly, an officer whose life was joined with that of his men. Now he was walking out on them. On the other hand, fighting as a guerrilla (there was not the slightest chance he would surrender) would not be the best use of his talents. And there was, undiminished, his evangelistic vision of the role and effectiveness of PT boats, with which his name was now synonymous. After the night actions in the Philippines he had absolutely no doubt of their effectiveness against large enemy warships, and he believed fervently that with enough of them the Japanese navy could be demolished. Stateside, he would be their champion.

As he waited for his flight, back and forth it went: the impulse to disobey the order and stay on, rally what was left of his squadron, and do what he could here; the seductive, magnetic pull of that larger vision. Perhaps it was never really in doubt. In any case, Bulkeley sent word to George Cox, who would be in command in his absence, that he would push hard in Australia to get the rest of them out as soon as possible.

***

Cox was lying in the shade of a canvas shelter half he had rigged up on the deck of the 41, half dozing through the siesta hour, when he saw an old, dilapidated stake truck approaching the dock where the 41 was moored, in the little town of Iligan. The truck came to a halt and a man stepped out of the cab. A tall blond man in well-worn khakis, unshaven, gaunt.

Cox suddenly hitched himself up. He thought: *It can't be.*

"We heard you were dead!" he exclaimed to Bob Kelly, by way of greeting.

"Where did you hear that?" Kelly said, perhaps with amusement, it was hard to tell.

"A pilot showed up here from Cebu and said he talked with a priest who did the funeral service for you and another sailor," Cox told him.

"He got it wrong. That was Harris and Reynolds."

The entire crew gathered around to shake his hand and hear his story—the dramatic end of the 34 boat, the burning city, getting separated from Richardson and the rest of the crew and his flight into the hills. There followed a series of adventures he would just as soon forget, wandering from island to island, often just ahead of the Japanese, begging for rides in cars, ox carts, anything that moved, looking for a boat that would take him to Mindanao. For an exorbitant price, a smuggler with cases of beer and whiskey aboard finally did, leaving him in a deserted village through which passed the truck that had brought him here.

During all this, one man was conspicuously missing.

"Where's Bulkeley?" Kelly asked.

"Gone south," Cox said.

"I'll be damned. How does it look for the rest of us?'

"Pretty grim," Cox admitted. "There aren't many planes coming in. And the old 41 is finished. No torpedoes and no gas. We're just waiting for the army to take her up to Lake Lanao to use as a gunboat, and then we're going to see about getting a flight out."

As if reading Kelly's mind, Cox added, "You're free to go, Mr. Kelly. The skipper thought you were dead and before he left he made me squadron commander."

No crew, no boat, and for the time being, no job. Unlike Bulkeley, Kelly felt no pangs about leaving. He knew his own worth, and that it was highly valued by others. He went directly to Del Monte to see General Sharp about a flight out.

Sharp was amazed to see him. Bulkeley had reported him killed in action.

"There's not much hope of getting out," Sharp warned. "There's hardly any gas left to refuel the planes on this end, so I doubt they'll send any more."

Kelly had no use for that kind of pessimism. MacArthur had told Bulkeley he would get his people out. In the village near the airstrip where he was sent to wait, Kelly found another pessimist, the local army commander, who flatly told him not to get his hopes up. He seemed resentful of Kelly's first-priority status, the navy favored over the army, and a lowly lieutenant at that. Kelly didn't bother to explain, even when the colonel put him in charge of a pack train to Lake Lanao he was then in the process of organizing. They were still cutting the trail, and he had a man rounding up fifty carabao and drivers, and when he had them Kelly was to lead it to the lake. Kelly had no intention of missing a plane by being off herding a bunch of water buffalo through a jungle, but he saw no need for an immediate showdown. Fifty carabao was a lot to round up. It would take days, he told himself.

The days went by—eight of them, during which no planes arrived. The dam he had constructed against the insidious, infectious pessimism all around him began to leak. When the colonel called him to his headquarters and ordered him to inspect the jungle path up to Lake Lanao there was no showdown. Kelly simply went back to his quarters to pack his kit.

He had just finished when the phone rang.

"Get to the landing field, right away," General Sharp's aide told him.

There, the agonizing wait began. In the darkness over a hundred men had gathered. Each man had a number, assigned to him in Australia. A plane would not hold more than thirty, but perhaps two or even three planes might come. Or someone whose name was called might not show up and the next man on the list could claim his seat. They were all young technicians and pilots, survivors from the fighter and bomber squadrons that had been in the Islands before the surrender of Bataan. And there was George Cox, Tony Akers, and Kelly. Sharp had called Cox and Akers and told them to be at the field, but neither man was there.

"Listen!" came a shout. A silence like death fell over everyone. There it was, a faint droning sound that as they listened grew into the deep steady pulsing of aircraft engines. It soon became apparent that there was only one plane. It circled the field in the moonlight and landed.

A man with a clipboard appeared. Holding a flashlight, he called off thirty names in the order of priority numbers—including Kelly, Cox, and Akers.

Kelly answered, "Present." He had a feeling in his stomach heavy as lead as two men stepped up to take the place of Cox and Akers. One can only imagine how they felt when, just as they were about to board, the two young naval officers came running up, breathless but overjoyed.

***

At Allied headquarters in Melbourne, Bulkeley was waiting for them. But to their amazement so was Vincent Schumacher and six other men from the 32 boat: Cone Johnson, George Barlett, Ned Cobb, Leroy Conn, Watson Sims, and Densil Stroud. They had come on the submarine *Permit* after Schumacher had abandoned the 32 at Tagauayan, back in March. Before returning to Australia *Permit* had gone to Corregidor to deliver supplies and pick up more passengers, and it's not clear why the eight other men from the 32 had been left there. Neither Schumacher nor Bulkeley, in their official reports of the incident, mentions them, and the men themselves—Joseph Boudolf, Robert Burnett, John Clift, Herb Grizzard, Dale Guyot, Harry Keath, Clem Langston and James McEvoy—left no record of the decision, if that's what it was.

Bulkeley enjoyed a convivial reunion with his three just-returned officers but his encounter with Schumacher had not been a happy one. Arriving in Australia only to find Schumacher already there, Bulkeley was livid. Schumacher explained—two engines out of commission, the third unreliable with seawater leaking into the engine room, the bolts holding the center tail strut sheared off, only one spare magneto (an old one) that didn't work, only a thousand gallons of fuel, an easterly wind and rough sea, put it all together and he wasn't going to make Panay, where Bulkeley had told him to go. To safeguard the lives of the crew, he destroyed the boat and everyone got aboard the *Permit*. Bulkeley listened to this, and then, to Schumacher's face and later in his official report, he took it apart. When he last saw her, on March 12, the condition of the boat was good. Replacement bolts were aboard the 32 and the center strut should have been repaired, stopping the leak into the engine room. Even without repairs, the 32 was able to make twenty knots. There wasn't a thousand gallons of gas left, there was close to 1,900 gallons, enough for three hundred miles at twenty knots, with Panay sixty miles away. Schumacher said that his orders were to meet the submarine, deliver the message that MacArthur had gone on to Australia, then to use his judgment and "make out as best you can." Bulkeley said no orders to "make out as best you can" were given.

There was an investigation, of course. With no hard evidence at hand, it was largely one man's word against another, and in that Schumacher never had a chance, not against a senior officer whose reputation was soaring. The young boat captain was reprimanded for the loss of his boat and cited for poor naval judgment—the kiss of death. Schumacher's time in the PT service was at an end.

***

For John Bulkeley it was in a sense only beginning. Awaiting him at home were the accolades bestowed only on a national hero. He was a reincarnated Lindburgh, the ticker tape parade in New York City, countless banquets and speeches (not only by him, but in praise of him), a triumphal visit to the White House, where the President of the United States, with Bulkeley leaning low over the wheelchair, placed around his neck the loop of ribbon from which hung the Congressional Medal of Honor.

There was more. An appearance in the pages of *Time* magazine. Cheering crowds wherever he went. Reporters. Press photographers. The sight of him excited people much as a movie idol does, though it was not as mindless, he wasn't a celluloid hero but genuine. He was assigned to the new Motor Torpedo Boat Squadron Training Center in Rhode Island, but try finding him there. He was in far too much demand. War bond drives. Ribbon cutting ceremonies. Pep talks to factory workers. And most of all, recruitment drives. His appearance in college auditoriums brought them in by the thousands, young men eager to hear of his exploits and more than eager, after hearing him speak, to volunteer as officers in the PT service. (There was the famous occasion at the naval officers school in Chicago when he asked for fifty volunteers and was practically swept off his feet as all 1,024 attendees mobbed him to ask for the job.)

He was making the most absurd claims, though of course they weren't absurd to him. He told the class at Tower Hall in Chicago: "The PT boat is a great weapon. The enemy has not yet won a brush with one. Our little half squadron sank one Jap cruiser, one plane tender, one transport, badly damaged another cruiser, set a tanker on fire, and shot down four planes," when in fact no ships were sunk. "Five hundred PT boats would give the United States mastery over all the Pacific," he went on, a truly incredible statement that seems not to take into account the vastness of that ocean and the size, proven ability, and fighting spirit of the Japanese Imperial Navy, destroyed only, in the end, by overwhelming carrier air fleets. But comradeship, action, glory, relative independence—those were not false promises, and he made those too.

In all of this, though, the war bond rallies, the public appearances, the press conferences, the interviews, the dinners at which he was always the guest of honor, something was missing. Not once did he mention the men who were left behind.

CHAPTER 32

Last Flight from Mindanao

On the afternoon of April 27, as Bulkeley and his three equally fortunate officers were getting ready for their return to the United States, two ponderous, lightly armed PBY seaplanes rose from the harbor at Darwin and headed northwest on a mission so daring it is difficult to imagine anyone agreeing to undertake it. They were to fly 1,200 miles through skies controlled by the Japanese, deliver food and medical supplies to besieged Corregidor, and take out a select group of passengers, 2,400 miles in all, with Lake Lanao as a refueling stop both coming and going.

At the lake, DeWitt Glover and Bill Konko were waiting for them. Along with the rest of the original crew of the 35 and the men from the abandoned 41, they had been working for the army in the area around the lake, evacuating American missionaries, driving trucks, running the motor pool, preparing a flotilla of small armed boats to prevent Japanese seaplanes from using the lake, helping out in whatever way they could while biding their time in the hopes of escape. It was Tony Akers who had told Konko about the two seaplanes coming in, giving him the job of acting as signalman. Akers and George Cox were the officers in charge. Apparently no one saw them leave, and it was an especially low moment when word came that they had left for Australia from Del Monte, leaving them almost leaderless, with Bond Murray the only officer left out of the four from the 35 and 41. It seemed an ill omen that only officers were being summoned.

About an hour after midnight, Glover and Konko were waiting near the landing area in a speed banca—an outrigger canoe with an outboard motor on it and a small machine gun amidships—of which Glover was in command. In the stern sat the Filipino who operated the motor. An army airman was at the gun, and Konko and Glover were in the bow, Konko holding a small searchlight.

The first plane came in and dropped down—all sound, it couldn't be seen in the darkness—and Konko flashed the recognition signal, but got no reply. Then the second plane came in, but much farther off, too far for them to go out to it.

They approached the first plane, but still no recognition signal.

"Load the gun," Glover told the airman. With no signal, and with one of the planes landing so far off, it wasn't beyond the realm of possibility that they were Japanese.

"Get ready to fire," Glover added, as Konko swept the light along the plane's fuselage, looking for some insignia. Back and forth went the beam of light. No insignia, and Glover was about to tell the airman to open fire when Konko shouted, "Wait. I see something."

It was a small star, about four inches across, way up on the bow of the plane.

***

The two seaplanes were immediately refueled by hand from 55-gallon drums brought out from shore in bancas, in the dim light of hooded flashlights. There wasn't a minute to spare. They had to make Corregidor and get back before daybreak.

On Corregidor, waiting for them, was Ed DeLong. Back in February, after the loss of the 31 boat, he and most of his crew had been reassigned to the seagoing tug *Trabajador*, which had been converted into a PT boat tender, with DeLong in command. In the middle of March, no boats had shown up for several days running, and DeLong and his men had been puzzled by their absence, until they heard the astonishing news that the boats had taken MacArthur out. By that time it was apparent that no help was coming, and the boats were not coming back, and they tried to reconcile themselves to the fact that there was nothing left to them but a silent, darkening world. When the Bataan garrison surrendered they were already on Corregidor, but they knew it was only delaying the inevitable.

Then, at the last moment, DeLong was told to pack a small bag and be ready to leave—and to say nothing to anyone about it. Because of his priority status as a PT sailor he had been put on the list of evacuees scheduled to fly out on two seaplanes. He was buoyed up and weighed down at the same time. None of his men were on the list. He was leaving all of them behind—Robert Caudell, William Cook, James Culp, Robert Langer, Charles Dimaio, Robert Monroe, Theodore Morgan, Doyle Smart—men he had shared much with, the danger and hardship of their narrow escape at Binanga Bay, their time aboard the *Trabajador*. He couldn't even tell them he was leaving. He was slipping away like a thief in the dark.

Just inside the west portal of Malinta Tunnel a crowd had gathered, evacuees mixed with well wishers. There were fifty people going out, including twenty army nurses.

A small convoy of trucks took them to South Dock. The bombardment had gotten heavier but it was targeting Topside and Middleside, where the island's big guns were located, and the pier lay undisturbed. Four motor launches were waiting. The boats went out half a mile into South Channel and hove to, rising and falling on the swell. It wasn't long before people were being sick over the side. At last, DeLong heard them. The engine exhausts looked like little flares in the night sky. Both planes landed less than a hundred yards away. Two boats headed for each. It was tricky boarding, pitching boat to pitching plane, engines roaring overhead. Delong followed the others in through the port gun blister. There were no seats. Everyone sat along the catwalk with their knees drawn up and their backs against the hull. There was a window in the hatch and through it DeLong could see Corregidor under bombardment, a black shape glowing and flaring. The takeoff was smooth and as the plane lifted into the air his spirits lifted with it.

***

The planes landed on the lake at daybreak. Two open-sided buses were waiting to take the passengers to a hotel in Dansalan, at the upper end of the lake, to wait for dark and the all-night flight to Darwin. Konko, Glover, and another man from the 41, John Balog, helping the passengers get from the planes to the beach in dugout canoes, were surprised, and pleased, to see Ed DeLong step from one of the planes. He was a conscientious officer, unaffected and personable, and the men had always been fond of him. They told him about all the senior officers taking off for the south—Bulkeley, Kelly, Akers, Cox—and asked if he knew who else was on "the list," two words that had become as sacred as prayer. DeLong told them honestly that he didn't know, hadn't even known *he* was on the list, but that was not the whole truth, and DeLong felt compelled to tell them about the men he had left behind, who obviously were *not* on the list.

"Well," Glover said, "it never did look too good for the rest of us," fatalism being something he had never had much use for but was learning to accept.

That afternoon, at the hotel in Dansalan, DeLong was sitting on the veranda in a wicker chair, watching the Moros walk past on the dirt streets of the town, just beyond the big tree-shaded lawn, when Bond Murray came up the steps and took the chair next to him. Murray had been informed that he was to go out on one of the seaplanes and he'd arrived at the hotel around noon to join the other passengers.

"Just think," he said to DeLong, "tomorrow morning we'll be having breakfast in Australia."

DeLong smiled but said nothing. He could not seem to shake the sense of guilt he felt about leaving.

The buses left late in the afternoon for the lake. When they got there, Konko stood watching as Bond Murray got off one of the buses, obviously a passenger. Accepting their likely fate, the two of them had talked about heading into the hills together, where they might go, what they would need to survive. Murray walked up to Konko, who had been his radioman on the 35, and said, "I don't like leaving you behind, but I've got orders." He gave Konko his pistol and a few packs of cigarettes. DeLong gave his pistol to Glover, but in silence.

By the time all the passengers were back aboard it was getting dark. DeLong watched from the blister as a motorized banca towed the first plane from the brushy shoreline where it had been hidden out into open water. Then the long takeoff run, the lumbering flying boat sending up a great rooster tail of spray and finally rising like a big pale insect from the flat surface of the lake.

His own plane was being towed out when there was a jarring crunch. A moment later, someone cried out, "Hey, there's water coming in!"

Each passenger had been given a heavy wool blanket and several of the nurses began stuffing theirs into a hole in the hull. A crewman came back, took a look at the damage, and returned to the flight deck. For a few minutes the plane was motionless. Then one of the pilots appeared at the head of the cabin. They had hit something in the water, he told them, a rock or a submerged log, and it looked bad, but he had radioed Australia and two Flying Fortresses were coming to take them out. The Del Monte plantation had the only airstrip that could handle a B-17, and they would be taken there to meet the bombers.

***

All day they worked frantically on the plane, the crewmen joining the small group of soldiers and sailors who had been assigned to help out at the landing site, Konko and Glover among them. At first the plane was thought to be too damaged to fly again, but the hole was eventually repaired to the satisfaction of the pilot, who now thought he could get the plane airborne.

As the plane was being refueled, a car approached the landing site. In it was Henry Brantingham. No one had told him about the seaplanes. He happened to be on a tour of the lake being conducted by Commander Ryland Tisdale, the ranking naval officer in the area and the man to whom he and his men had reported for duty after their long and perilous escape—the two fishing boats they had hired on Negros had made it to the west coast of Mindanao and from there they rode a rickety open-sided bus, trussed chickens and baby pigs in bamboo cages sharing the seats with the passengers, seventy potholed miles to Del Monte. There is no record of what transpired there, but though their names were eventually added to the long list of evacuees they were told they would not be given any special priority as members of the PT squadron—which sent their spirits as low as their names were on the list—at the very bottom.

The car stopped along the shoreline where the plane was being refueled. Brantingham and Tisdale got out and soon found out that the plane was about to leave for Australia—empty. Like the rest of the world, the aircrew knew all about the spectacular MacArthur rescue and when the pilot learned that a PT man had just arrived, he let it be known that he intended to take out all PT sailors.

Tisdale told Konko and Glover to get all the PT men they could find and send them out to the plane. This meant going all the way back to the camp that had been set up for the men assigned to work at the seaplane site. Once there, it took time to go around and look for people. Adding to the urgency, news came that the Japanese were approaching the lake from the south.

Glover was able to find only a few men and by the time they got back to the refueling site the plane had taxied out onto the lake and was warming up its engines.

Konko was there. He and Glover had split up, but Konko hadn't been able to find anyone and had returned alone, knowing, with the Japanese approaching, that once it was refueled the plane would not wait.

There was only that stretch of water between them and freedom, easily crossed by the bancas used for the refueling—but the bancas were already out at the plane.

"Some army guys grabbed them and went out to see if they could get aboard," Konko explained with considerable bitterness.

The five of them stood helplessly on the shore and watched the plane take off. When the bancas returned the army men were still in them. They were disgusted. They were army, with no orders to leave, and the pilot had refused to take them.

CHAPTER 33

Decision

They were all sitting around in the camp—Glover, Francis Napolillo, John Balog, John Lewis, Ben Licodo, Otis Noel, Paul Owen, George Winget, Charles Beckner, and Bill Posey—not saying much as they waited for Commander Tisdale to arrive. With the seaplanes gone, they no longer had a job to do, and Tisdale had told them he would be there at seven in the morning with new orders.

It was almost eight o'clock when a bell began ringing in the part of the camp that was occupied by Filipino soldiers, a frantic, ominous clanging. The sailors got to their feet and stood watching as a stampede ensued, the young, untrained soldiers in blue denim running wildly through the camp in all directions, most without their rifles. It was over in less than a minute, and when the men looked around, there was no one left.

Then, through the silence, came a faint clanking sound.

Tanks?

"Boys," Glover decided, "it's time to go."

They took the road many of the soldiers were on, but Japanese planes had passed over during the morning and it came to them that all those blue denim uniforms were an invitation to a strafing, and they headed across country. Along footpaths that wound through scrub forest and alongside fields of ramie and corn they traveled for six hours, through the worst heat of the day, when the sun begins to feel like some malignant, living thing that is trying to kill you, with no idea where they were going, intent only on getting away from the Japanese, until at last, with their water long gone, they stumbled into a small army camp. The men there were fugitives, like themselves, and had only boiled rice to offer, gluey and unsalted, but as someone once said, Hunger is the best sauce, and the sailors thought it tasted pretty good.

Here the men separated, it's unclear why. A few stayed in the camp, where there was food and water, others left but in different directions, depending on which rumor they chose to trust their luck with. Glover went his own way, not following any particular urge, and was the first to come upon old, crusty, hard-bitten Jacob Dreiser, a man cast in the same mold as Cecil Walter and Dad Cleland, a man who had long ago made the Philippines his home, who hadn't seen his native land in decades and who didn't seem to miss it—and a man who knew what he was doing. He owned two sawmills and five mines on Mindanao, but the Japanese were coming and he was preparing an evacuation camp, a jungle hideout for himself and his family. He had seen enough in his long life to know that wars are never short, and he had gathered enough provisions to last for two years. He needed help moving some of his supplies, and Glover volunteered his services, deciding that he could do worse than hook up with a man who obviously knew how to survive.

***

When the bell had sounded the alarm Bill Konko happened to be off with a few army men, and after some discussion they agreed it would be best to head for Del Monte, where General Sharp had his headquarters and where they might be of some use. They walked for a while along the road the panicked Filipino soldiers had taken and came to a small town. There they met a man who owned a large farm. Half the town was already empty, its residents fleeing ahead of the approaching horde, and so was this man, but not on foot or in an ox cart. He was that rarity, a car owner, and he offered to take Konko and the others to the farm before going to his own hideout.

Their stay was a short one. The Filipinos living at the farm begged the men to leave. They didn't want to be caught helping Americans when the Japanese arrived. Women and children were there. Konko felt the same way, he didn't want any harm to come to them. When it was suggested that the Americans go deeper into the interior, to a small, out of the way barrio where the people were friendly and where they could hide, Konko and the others readily agreed.

***

The Japanese were soon in Dansalan, which put them in control of Lake Lanao. The Del Monte plantation was up on the Bukidnon plateau, only twenty miles from the lake in a straight line, but no road led directly from the lake to the plantation. It was twenty miles of steep hills and jungle. The passengers from the seaplane who were sent there to wait for another flight were staying at a ranch house surrounded by rolling fields of pineapples, as endless as the sea. The airstrip was a mile away, and the ranch house had been converted into a dormitory, with cots and bunks in all the rooms. The men were on the ground floor and the nurses upstairs.

In the middle of the night Ed DeLong woke to what might well have been thunder. He went out on the porch and looked north, toward the coast, and saw the pale flashes, like sheet lightning.

Others came out. Bond Murray, standing just behind DeLong, said calmly, "Naval gunfire."

DeLong nodded. "They'll be landing at dawn."

One of the nurses was standing near them. "Do you think there's still time for the planes to come in?" she asked.

The bombers weren't due to arrive until the following night.

DeLong shrugged slightly. "The beaches are only fifteen miles away."

"Maybe our boys will stop them," the nurse said hopefully.

Early the next morning two buses came to take them to army headquarters for breakfast. They were eating in a tense silence when a young officer came into the mess tent.

"The Japs are ashore," he announced.

"Are the planes still coming?" someone asked.

"There's been no word otherwise."

The officer suggested they wait in the mess tent instead of going back to the ranch house. It was a long, tense day, with no further news. They were sitting down to an early supper when a different officer came and told them the army was pulling back to a new line, and that they were giving up Del Monte.

In the tent, there was a heavy silence. The lake and the Del Monte airstrip were the only places a plane could reach them. They had no choice now except to stay with the army.

As they were walking to the buses DeLong and Murray exchanged a look.

"I see a surrender coming," DeLong said.

"Yeah," Murray agreed. "It's going to be the Japs or the jungle, and I'm not sure which scares me the most."

***

Iliff Richardson had managed to get from Cebu over to Leyte, as he hoped to do. In Tacloban, where the island's garrison had its headquarters, he found a launch that was headed for Mindanao. It put in at Surigao, on the north coast, where there was an army detachment, and there Richardson met an army captain named MacGregor. He explained who he was and that he had a priority from General MacArthur to fly to Australia.

"You're one day too late," MacGregor told him. "The Japs took Del Monte this afternoon. All you're in time for is the surrender." MacGregor grinned at him. He spoke in a very quiet and easy way. "There's going to be a party, and we'll all drink barbed wire."

"Is there an alternative?" Richardson asked.

"There is, for you. We're under orders here, but you're unattached, so your alternative is to get off the island if you can."

Luckily, the launch Richardson had arrived in was still at the dock, though barely. It was just pulling out for its return trip to Leyte when he jumped aboard. With him was Ernest Pierson, who on a day long past had heroically waded through a barrage of rifle fire to get a company of Filipino soldiers to stop shooting at his boat. Pierson had come to Mindanao with the crew of the 35 and had gotten away from Del Monte in a Wrigley Spearmint Gum wagon with some air corps men. As the only sailor in Surigao, he had felt a bit lonely and out of place, and the sudden appearance of Iliff Richardson had been, for him, like a vision bordering on the miraculous.

"If they're surrendering here, they'll be surrendering on Leyte too," Pierson observed as the launch chugged away from the dock.

"That's probably true," Richardson said, "but I'm not staying on Leyte. I'm going to find a boat and sail to Australia."

"Jesus," Pierson murmured. It was breathtaking. *Suicidal* was another word for it.

After a moment's thought Pierson said, "Can I go with you?"

***

They had been manning the makeshift gunboats on the lake and doing various chores for the army—John Tuggle, Joe Chalker, Marvin DeVries, Morris Hancock, John Houlihan, Henry Rooke, Carl Richardson, and John Lawless. Three enormous trees, each with a massive, gnarled trunk, shaded their camp. It was a cool, quiet place, restful, with cots, an army field stove, water from a nearby stream, which they were always careful to boil. About fifty yards away there was a road, with a trail leading to it.

On the morning of May 7 they were all there, just finishing breakfast, when a man they had never seen before walked in on them. He was wearing sergeant's stripes, and he said, without preamble, "The officer wants to talk to you. He's out on the road."

He was a major in clean suntans sitting in a battered, dust-covered Ford command car. A strip of bedsheet was hanging from a stick lashed to the front bumper.

"General Wainwright surrendered yesterday," he told them. "All the garrisons, on every island. Who's in charge here?"

"I'm the senior man," John Tuggle said.

"Take your men down to Dansalan and stack arms."

"Is that an order?"

The major looked at him. "You've been surrendered," he said. "That's the order."

Tuggle's face hardened. "Well, to hell with your order. We're not surrendering."

The sergeant was sitting behind the wheel. Without replying, the major signed him to go, and the car sped away.

Tuggle had not spoken out of turn. He knew every man there felt as he did. They had given the Japanese a hard time with their PT boats and they didn't want to be captured. That is not to say they weren't scared. They'd heard a rumor about a camp being set up in the jungle by an American civilian, Filipino gossip, but it was persistent enough to be true, and as they set off to find it every man threw away his dogtags.

***

On that same day, in the barrio where Konko and his friends were hiding, a woman returned from a visit to town in a kind of excited agitation, and the news she brought made the rounds with the speed of light. The Americans could tell immediately that something was up, and they didn't have to wait long to find out. Anyone who spoke any English at all was eager to tell them, perhaps in the hope they would leave, that the American forces had surrendered.

"I don't believe it," one of the men said, but something stronger than instinct told Konko it was true.

The others decided to stick to their original plan and try to reach Del Monte, even though they had heard that the road leading up to the airfield was blocked by the Japanese. They intended to surrender, but with the garrison. There were only four of them and they were afraid that if they gave themselves up, isolated as they were, they would be executed on the spot.

Konko also thought about giving himself up, but not for long. In his mind the jungle was a frightening place, dark, malarial, and unforgiving, but he had heard about the Japanese atrocities in China, prisoners tortured, shot, bayoneted, and he decided to take his chances in the hills.

CHAPTER 34

Surrender

Bataan had gone under on April 9 and now it was Corregidor's turn. On May 5, at 8:30 in the evening, more than 400 artillery pieces, lined up hub to hub in the Bataan hills, opened up with a sound almost indescribable, shattering the eardrums of some of the men firing the guns and heard deep in the underground tunnels like unbroken thunder. The furious barrage completely covered the little island, triggering landslides on the slopes of the hills, cutting landlines, blowing apart beach defense guns and searchlights, setting off land mines, and killing and wounding a large number of the men manning the beach defenses. Dust rose and hung in the air like a heavy fog, so thick that the searchlights that hadn't been hit couldn't penetrate it. On and on, the shells falling like rain. The noise was terrific, obliterating. No thunder could be so deafening. The earth trembled and shook in continuous upheaval. The shells fell so fast that individual explosions could not be heard. They made one continuous roar.

After three hours of this, at 11:30, the first wave of Japanese troops landed near North Point, then a second wave, 12,000 in all. Every battery on Corregidor that could bear on the landing site began firing, a continuous stream of red tracers pouring into the landing barges, the dazed defenders on the beach engaging the Japanese with rifle and machine gun fire and even bayonets, and for a while at least, holding their own. Then came another Japanese landing, this one behind the line of resistance, forcing the defenders at North Point to withdraw toward Malinta Hill.

Dawn on May 6 found the Japanese halfway between North Point and Malinta—and the main tunnel, General Wainwright's headquarters. Wainwright ordered a counterattack with the last of his reserves. It pushed the Japanese back but bogged down under the incessant shelling and continuous bombing and strafing from the enemy planes that were now in the air. Most of the men were pinned to the ground, and some were driven back into the tunnel.

Shortly after 10 a.m. word came that the Japanese had landed tanks and were massing at Kindley Field, at the extreme tip of the island. Knowing that a tank attack against Malinta Tunnel, with its hospital and hundreds of wounded, would bring on a bloody massacre, Wainwright made the most painful decision of his life. He ordered his commanders to lay down their arms at noon, at which time the Stars and Stripes, still flying from the tall wooden flagpole on the parade ground above the cliffs, would be lowered and replaced with the white flag of surrender.

***

By four in the afternoon almost everyone had left the tunnel to wait outside for the Japanese to come and take them into captivity. Wainwright was returning from a meeting with the victors and was on his way to the headquarters lateral, walking through the garish blue light to the sound of his own echoing footsteps, past the hospital lateral and then the silent wounded men on their hospital cots that had spilled out into the main tunnel, when Barron Chandler saw him. Chandler was still recovering from being shot through the ankles in the night action at the end of January, and as the haggard, almost painfully emaciated Wainwright walked past him Chandler saw that his eyes were wet with tears.

Chandler wasn't the only PT sailor on Corregidor at the time of the surrender. Twenty-three men had been left there: eight from Ed DeLong's *Trabajador*, the eight from the 32 boat who had been taken there by the submarine *Permit* but had not gone on to Australia with Vince Schumacher and the other seven men in his crew, and the seven men from the 33 who had been reassigned to the Naval Battalion and the Inshore Patrol. Two days before the surrender twenty-five people, nurses and army and navy officers, chosen by Wainwright, had been taken aboard the submarine *Spearfish,* bound for Australia, the last to escape. Not a single man from the PT squadron was with them; all had been assigned to beach defense. Incredibly, none had been killed or seriously wounded in the fighting, and they were all there, among the many others standing outside the tunnel entrance, hands over their heads, still wearing the steel helmets they had been issued, as the diminutive Japanese soldiers approached with their bayonet-tipped rifles. It seems only proper that we should know their names: Joseph Budolf, Robert Burnett, John Clift, Herb Grizzard, Dale Guyot, Harry Keith, Clem Langston, James McEvoy, James Culp, Robert Caudell, William Cook, Robert Langer, Theodore Morgan, Charles Dimaio, Robert Monroe, Doyle Smart, Clayton Beliveau,

Howard Fisher, Herbert Hough, Ed Morey, Hayward Miller, Arthur Waters, and Bill Stambaugh.

The Japanese had their own unique view of soldiers who would rather surrender than fight to the death, as they did. After the fall of Bataan, 75,000 prisoners were marched sixty-five miles to Camp O'Donnell in central Luzon—no food or water, stragglers beaten, bayoneted, shot, buried alive—and upon arrival the survivors were formed up on the parade ground to be addressed by the commander of the prison camp, who made it absolutely clear what the Imperial Japanese Army thought about them. He spoke from a small wooden platform at the front of the formation, through an interpreter, and it was a tirade. They were not prisoners of war, they were captives. They were nothing. They were a defeated army of cowards. They should not think of themselves as the lucky ones. The men who had died fighting on Bataan were the lucky ones. They were going to wish they had died there too. They did not deserve to live. A soldier who surrendered to the enemy was beneath contempt.

And so, in a sense, it was policy: what the victors had behind their barbed wire was not quite human but a subspecies of humanity, perhaps not lower than a dog but almost. The Japanese took good care of their dogs.

Off they went then, the unlucky ones from Corregidor, into the Japanese gulag.

***

Bilibid Prison is in Manila. It takes up an entire city block and looks like a medieval fortress with its stone turrets and high wall, the huge double gates of thick wooden slats with their massive iron ringbolts. All it needs is a moat and drawbridge to complete the illusion. Chilling to look at, much worse than that to be inside. Like everyone who surrendered on Corregidor, Barron Chandler and the other twenty-three men from the squadron were taken there, but only Chandler and Jim McEvoy stayed, perhaps because of their injuries. They would be there for the next two and a half years, in a stone cell, on a near-starvation diet, never seeing the sun, finding strength in prayer and in the blind faith that their country would not forget them, a faith that never wavered and that was vindicated at last when two American soldiers, carrying weapons and wearing helmets and uniforms strange to them, came into the cell and helped them to their feet, one of them saying, "Come on, fellas, we're going to get you out of here."

The rest of them were kept there for only a few days. Each day groups of 500 men at a time were being lined up and marched out the gate. Some of the men thought they were going off to be shot but Jim Culp settled them down with some solid reasoning: way too many going out for that.

Their turn came to line up. The group marched out the gate and along streets lined with silent, staring Filipinos, men, women and children watching with pity, many with tears in their eyes. At the Manila railroad station the prisoners were packed into boxcars filled with the excrement of the men who had gone before them and taken a hundred miles north to Cabanatuan, where there was an old Philippine Army camp—dozens of nipa-thatch, sawali-sided barracks, each sixty feet long and built to accommodate forty soldiers. As prisoners' barracks they housed 120 men and were encircled by an eight-foot-high barbed wire fence and, at even intervals, four-story wooden guard towers. There was a wooden hospital building, but it was a hospital in name only, a place where men went to die.

And die they did, the sickest and weakest first. At the end of May, when all the gathering up and shipping of prisoners from Bataan and Corregidor was completed, there were almost 14,000 men in Cab, as it came to be called, a three-letter word like no other. In the month of June nearly 800 men died. By the end of that year 2,200 more men died. In 1943, another thousand or so, the record is not exact. If one does the math, in June 1942 they were dying at the rate of almost thirty a day. Over the next six months the average falls to twelve a day. Only by the middle of 1943, when only the hardiest of them remained, men who knew what it took to survive and who had the will—yes, the will: death was easier than life, all a man had to do was lay back and die, as easy as letting go of a rope—did a day pass when there wasn't a single death.

Illness took most of them—diphtheria, malaria, dysentery, beriberi, typhoid, yellow jaundice, dengue fever, more often than not a combination of these—but the root cause was a skimpy daily ration of watery rice gruel almost entirely devoid of essential nutrients that over time reduced even the biggest and strongest men to walking skeletons, skin hanging on the bones, heads like skulls. There were no medicines, when you got sick you either recovered or you died. There was nothing except the will to live, though that can be potent enough.

Eventually five of the six men captured on Cebu—Al Ross, Dave Goodman, John Martino, George Shepard and Paul Eichelberger, were brought to Cabanatuan. Velt Hunter, who had been lying helpless in the hospital at Cebu City when the Japanese arrived, ended up in Bilibid with Ed DeLong and Jim McEvoy, though he didn't know the other two were there until they were liberated when Manila was finally retaken in February 1945. Like the twenty-three men from Corregidor, the six from Cebu would survive long enough to face an even worse hell, though as a descriptive that word is much too mild really.

***

In July 1944, as American forces approached the Philippines, the Japanese decided to ship the American prisoners to Japan before they could be liberated, to be used in the home islands as slave labor. They did not have enough freighters, and tried to make do with what they had. That meant putting too many prisoners on too few ships.

How does one describe a packed, hot, airless, filthy ship's hold where the passengers sit hip to hip as urine and excrement puddle beneath them, some collapsing face first into the stinking slop as they pass out, where men would start screaming, not like a woman but more like the howl of a dog, as they slowly go mad?

It was a world without mercy. On one particular ship, when the Japanese cut off the water— a favorite trick of theirs, like children who will set a cat's tail on fire simply to see it go crazy with terror—the howling and screaming got so bad that a Japanese officer threatened to seal the hatch if the noise didn't stop. This had no effect on those who were doing the screaming. In that heat, if the hatch was sealed, all of them would die. Without a word passing between them, men took action. You could kill a man with a full canteen swung by the chain, or strangle him with the small sweat towels the men wore around their necks or foreheads. Those making all the noise were told once to shut up, and when they didn't, they were killed, one after the other, perhaps half a dozen, until it became clear even to men half out of their minds that if they kept up the bedlam they would die. The screaming stopped.

By this time in the war American submarines roamed the western Pacific at will, prowling the shipping lanes, eager for kills. The hell ships sailed in convoy with other Japanese shipping and were not marked to indicate they were carrying prisoners. The result was a tragedy almost beyond comprehension. A rough count gives us more than 5,000 American prisoners who died when their ships were torpedoed, more than the total number of deaths at Cabanatuan. It was on one such ship, the *Shinyo Maru*, that Paul Eichelberger, Floyd Giaccani, and Jim Light perished when the ship was struck by a torpedo on September 7, 1944, a sinking which Arthur Waters somehow survived. Less than two months later, on October 24, 1944, the *Arisan Maru* went down, taking with her Dick Regan and Jim Stambaugh. On January 9, 1945, on one of the last prison ships sailing for Japan, Bill Plant, who had been in Bilibid ever since he was captured back in January, lost his life when the *Enoura Maru* was sent to the bottom.

***

The prisoners who reached Japan were sent to various camps, most of them in the home islands though some were in Manchuria and Korea, and immediately put to work—in coal, lead, and nickel mines, rolling mills and foundries, steel plants, railroad yards, lumber mills, drydocks and piers. They worked in rain and snow, in furnace heat and when it was below zero. They were given only enough food to guarantee they would work another day. To their hunger and despair was added the knowledge, galling and inescapable, that they were helping Japan's war effort against their own country, and all of it together began to work on their minds and spirits. Those things which had precariously bound them together in the Philippine camps, individual pride, loyalty to friends, the sense of being an American, began to lose their importance, until these slender connecting threads disappeared entirely and it became every man for himself, the human spirit reduced to enduring and hoping only to survive.

Where is the dividing line? What makes the difference between surviving and perishing?

Luck, you could say, and be right. Some guards were not abusive, while others would beat the prisoners at every opportunity. Food could be stolen, guards bribed to bring in medicines, ways found to rest while on the job. It all depended on which camp you were in, and what kind of work you did there. All other things being equal, it could come down to simply not getting sick to the point where there was no recovering.

Herb Grizzard died in a camp in Manchuria, while Ed Morey, Harry Keith, Clayton Beliveau and John Martino, also at camps in Manchuria, survived. Bill Cook and Ralph Brendlinger died in camps in Japan, while Bob Caudell, Jim Culp, Charles Dimaio, Bob Langer, Ted Morgan, Doyle Smart, Joe Boudolf, Bob Burnett, John Clift, Dale Guyot, Clem Langston, Howard Fisher, Herb Hough, Hayward Miller, Jesse Clark, Dave Goodman, Al Ross, George Shepard, John Shambora, Stewart Williver, and Harry Tripp, also at camps in Japan, survived.

***

On Mindanao, the formal surrender took place on May 10. Most of General William Sharp's forces were put into a prison camp in Malaybalay, some in

Camp Keithly, an old Constabulary camp near Lake Lanao. At Keithly, on July 1, four men escaped. In reprisal, the Japanese were going to shoot ten men for every one who got away. They executed three men: two officers and a sergeant, before the senior officer there, Colonel Mitchell, arguing and pleading, talked them out of it.

The Japanese had another idea. They were moving the prisoners at Keithly to Malaybalay, and they chose the Fourth of July to do so. The first stage of the move was from Keithly to the little port town of Iligan, and they staged a Fourth of July parade. Down through the hills along a narrow cobblestone road they came, a long column of men, their hands wired together behind them and all of them wired to each other. The well and the sick, all mixed together. They hopped and faltered and jerked in their telephone wires as they picked their way over the hot stones of the road. The soldiers guarding them clomped across the cobblestones in their hobnailed boots, lightly jabbing their bayonets into the buttocks of the trussed captives to keep them moving down the road.

One of the prisoners lurches and falls. When he does not get up three guards rush in from the sides of the column and cut him loose and half carry, half hurl him off the road. Two of them hold the prisoner up, his head lolling above them, while a third sets himself and lunges. The young American screams as the bayonet goes in. The guard puts his foot up against the man's belly and kicks the bayonet loose. The two guards release him and the man falls. Then all three guards stab at the twitching figure at their feet before hurrying to rejoin the parade.

It is not known for certain if Ed Delong, Bond Murray, Bill Posey, and Ernest Pierson were among the prisoners at Keithly or on the death march to Iligan. What is known is that both DeLong and Murray, listed in the records as prisoners of war, attempted to escape and were executed, while Posey and Pierson, not listed on the prisoner rolls, simply disappeared on Mindanao, never to be heard from again. After the war, in December 1945, their names were placed on the Tablets of the Missing in the Manila American Cemetery.

CHAPTER 35

Guerrilleros

Mindanao in 1942 still held great swaths of unexplored territory, most of it jungle. There were wild black bees in the forest, bees that can sting a horse to death. There were cobras, fifteen-foot pythons said to prey on humans, naked spearmen who hunted through the hills, Moros who would kill a wandering soldier simply because he was a Christian. There were leeches, crocodiles in the streams, there was malaria and a thousand other diseases. Few white men ventured far into the interior; none, certainly, without a native guide, though the guides too often got lost. Even before the war most men carried pistols in open holsters, like gunfighters in the Old West.

It was a forbidding, unforgiving land, and in it, for the time being, the only thing an American could do was hide. Resistance to the Japanese seemed out of the question. Even the simple act of hiding was complicated by the fact that outside the jungle the Japanese owned everything, and had proclaimed that all Americans who failed to surrender would be shot on sight. To John Tuggle and the seven men with him, the solution seemed to be to find some healthful place in which to live, doing some kind of work—and this is what spurred them on, following the rumors that would lead, hopefully, to Jacob Dreiser's camp and the young Americans reported to be there. If they turned out to be armed soldiers, perhaps all of them together could set up a fortified camp in the hills and maintain themselves by farming and hunting, and eventually, if an opportunity presented itself, hit back at the Japanese.

It proved to be more than a rumor. There *was* a Jacob Dreiser and he *had* established a camp, but what Tuggle and the others found there, with one exception, was not at all to their liking. The thirty-some American fugitives wanted only to be left alone. They were soldiers but they intended to do nothing except sit there and freeload off the food stocks Dreiser had stockpiled. None of them wanted anything to do with the war.

The sole exception was DeWitt Glover, who was overjoyed at seeing his old shipmates again. Glover had had his fill of indolence and timidity and had already made up his mind to leave. He too was eating the old man's food but was bothered by the fact that he wasn't doing anything to earn his keep. And he was simply restless. He preferred action, even danger; it would seem all PT men were natured that way.

Tuggle and the others ran their idea past him, about establishing a fortified camp somewhere in the hills, but Glover had another idea.

"There's a rumor that an American general is here to organize a guerrilla army. A submarine brought him from Australia."

"Where did you hear that one?" he was asked.

"The old man has friends who come in and tell him things."

More native gossip. But the rumor was persistent, as the Dreiser rumor had been, and, it was decided, worth following.

Laboriously they tracked it down, across cogon grass plateaus, through jungle and along all the trails, suffering from infected leech bites, hunger, thirst, occasional alarms as Japanese patrols were sighted, what was left of their uniforms disintegrating and their shoes rotting off, but their rifles and pistols were clean and they had ammunition for them, and more important to them than anything else in this world, they were free.

The man they found was not a general, nor was he from Australia, but he was destined to unite the Mindanao guerrilla and turn it into a true fighting force. He was a tall, straight, sandy-haired man in starched khakis, on the shoulder tabs of which he wore the silver stars of a brigadier general, hammered out of coins by a Moro silversmith. His hair was cut short and his red goatee, touched with gray, was neatly trimmed. There was power in his posture, and in his gray eyes, and perhaps this is what persuaded the nine PT sailors that their own destiny lay with him. His name was Wendell Fertig, a mining engineer living in the Philippines who had been called up from the army reserves as a major.

"Unified resistance is the key to success," he told them, and the nine fugitives, now at the end of their wanderings, couldn't have agreed more.

***

After weeks of aimless drifting, staying in little barrios, never too long in each, so as not to be a burden, Bill Konko had come upon a young Philippine Army lieutenant who had put together a small band of guerrillas, one of the first to start harassing the Japanese. For a while he was their propagandist, making speeches in barrios everywhere, promising the people that the Americans would be back to liberate them—and indeed the very sight of an American was electrifying. Then Konko came down with malaria, which he attempted to treat with a native remedy, dita bark tea, so bitter that as he tried to drink it his throat would constrict, as if his body were telling him it wanted none of it. Konko persisted, getting it down drop by drop, and it checked the malaria, more or less. Then he came down with dysentery. He lost his appetite and became very weak. The rumor of an American general had reached them also, and Lieutenant Andres decided that the best place for his chief propagandist was with General Fertig, where he could get medicine and rest. Fertig was said to be in Jimenez, a town across Panguil Bay, in the province of Misamis Occidental, and Andres arranged for a banca to take Konko over there.

He arrived in Jimenez in the middle of the morning, barefoot and in rags, and as he looked about you could have knocked him over with a feather. There were people everywhere, cars and trucks running on the streets, horses and buggies, a marketplace teeming with shoppers, restaurants, uniformed Filipino soldiers, Americans walking about in good clothes, an American flag flying from the stone fort on the waterfront. To Konko, starved for the familiar, it looked like paradise.

Fertig was not there. He operated from a place kept secret from everyone, but he visited the town once a week. Konko learned this from the remarkable Lady Carmen and her six younger sisters. In almost every province there was one ruling family of Spanish descent, and the widowed Lady Carmen ruled this one. Konko was taken through the iron gates of the Casa Ozamis and up the wide, curved staircase that led to the living quarters of the thick-walled house to meet her. He had envisioned a purse-proud old woman, but dona Carmen was slender and her hair was midnight black and she was beautiful. And who should be there but John Lewis, from the 35 boat.

They told Konko that Fertig used the bottom part of the house as one of his command posts, and sure enough, in a few days he showed up, but not before a Filipino doctor had been summoned to give Konko injections, and a barber to shave him. He was bathed, and treated as gently as a baby. The candlelight, the food, the polished floors, the spacious dining room where silver and bone china gleamed on damask, the civilization of the casa and the elegance of its mistresses was like a dream to Konko, as it had been to Lewis and would be to the others who, one by one, eventually followed the rumor to Misamis and joined Fertig's organization: John Balog, Elwood Offrett, Ben Licodo, Francis Napolillo, Otis Noel, Paul Owen, George Winget, and Charles Beckner. Once their work with the Mindanao guerrilla began, however—with its many perils and hardships and inherent loneliness—the casa and its gracious occupants would become just that, a fantastic dream that as time passed would more and more seem never to have happened.

***

Illif Richardson and Ernest Pierson had made it back to Leyte, where they managed to buy a small sailboat and stock it with food and water. Along with eleven stranded air corps men who also had no intention of surrendering, they set off for Australia, fifteen hundred miles away. They got as far as the east coast of Mindanao, perhaps two hundred miles. There a storm overturned the boat eight miles from shore. They all made it to the beach, though barely, and spent almost a year in the area without money, medicine or clothes, the group gradually drifting apart after one of them died. Richardson made his way back to Leyte and found work with that island's guerrilla commander, Colonel Ruperto Kangleon, helping him establish a civil government and run his 3,000-man army.

***

To be an American guerrilla in the Philippines was an adventure in the true sense of the word and not as that word has come to be employed, where all is pleasant and except perhaps for a few inconveniences nothing bad ever happens. There was the pervading fear, something each man had to learn to control. As a fugitive who would be executed if caught, there was always the thought that the next minute could change your whole life, or end it. There was always a sense of isolation, of being far, very far, from home. The things one missed and yearned for most varied with the individual, but it was almost always a simple pleasure: a slice of buttered bread, a chocolate sundae, fresh strawberries with the taste of the North American climate in them, a crisp autumn day, a hot bath on a cold evening. No matter how much a man came to like the Filipinos as a people, there was the loneliness of not being among your own kind.

Perhaps the greatest fear was getting sick. There were so many diseases you could get in the Philippines, and no medicines to treat any of them. The whole idea of getting sick and not being able to take care of yourself preyed on the mind constantly.

All of this together, over such a long period of time, made for frayed nerves and short tempers. Everyone wore sidearms and it was not uncommon for two men to square off over a trifle. A man would crack his knuckles, a habit since childhood and in normal circumstances all but ignored. But it would work on the tightened nerves of another man until it reached the point where he would pull out his pistol, cock the hammer back and issue an ultimatum: "Crack your knuckles one more time and I'll kill your ass right here," upon which the knuckler would spring to his feet and draw his own weapon. Usually, but not always, other men would jump in and pull them apart.

And there was the nature of guerrilla warfare; it was not for the faint of heart, with its betrayals and summary executions. On Leyte, where Iliff Richardson was working, guerrillas staged a raid on a supply bodega guarded by a few Japanese. The Japanese ran off in the face of superior numbers but they left a sniper behind in a tree, a little boy about ten years old. They had given the boy a rifle and ten pesos and told him to shoot at the strange men who were coming to harm his family. The boy knew the faces of everyone in the barrio and could instantly recognize the guerrillas. He fired three or four times but didn't hit anyone.

The boy's twelve-year-old sister was watching fearfully as the guerrillas ordered him down from the tree. They stood the boy with the back of his head against the tree and smashed his face in with a rifle butt. By their invitation, an American had taken charge of this particular band of guerrillas, and when he heard the commotion he came running up. The boy was lying on the ground and they were holding a tin cup under the boy's chin to catch the blood. The cup was nearly full.

"What's going on here?" the American demanded.

"We make her drink it." The man who spoke pointed to the boy's sister who had been forced to stand there. "It is an example for the people."

The American knelt over the boy, checking for a pulse, but the boy was dead. Tearfully, the boy's sister explained what had happened.

It was imperative that an example be set, but of a different sort, or the residents of this barrio would almost certainly turn against the guerrillas, no longer providing food and shelter, and worse, becoming informants for the Japanese. The population simply could not be alienated in that way.

"Who committed this crime?" the American asked. "This boy was harmless. Who killed him? Who is the murderer?"

The man stepped boldly up to him. The American kicked the man in the stomach and then, as he was bent over, shot him in the head.

And finally there was the life itself, its strangeness and exotic flavor. In a place where nothing worked and where almost nothing was readily available, it was a life of makeshift and make do—how to make fuel for an automobile from the sap of the palm tree, how to make field artillery out of a brass pipe, how to tell time in the jungle at night when you don't have a watch, how to make a bullet out of a curtain rod, how to print money with abaca fiber for paper and berry juice for tinting, how to make an alcohol stove from galvanized pipe, elbows, and copper tubing from a wrecked car.

***

For almost three years this was the world the PT men turned guerrillero inhabited, Bill Konko as Fertig's radio operator, Paul Owen as chief distiller, Elwood Offrett as the manager of a coconut-oil factory, Francis Napolillo as coding officer, John Balog and Charles Beckner in the motor pool, DeWitt Glover as Food Supply Administrator in the civil government set up and run under the noses of the Japanese. John Lewis, Otis Noel, George Winget, and Henry Rooke helped build airfields. Joe Chalker was in command of a small armed launch that was used for transportation. John Tuggle was a liaison officer with the Moros, who presented their own special danger. There were twenty PT men in the Mindanao guerrilla doing all kinds of work, but you might say their greatest achievement was to prove that there is never anything that can't be done, that you can actually do something with nothing. All you need is nerve and courage.

Envoi

There were no welcome home parades for them, no bugles, no drums. The survivors, whether guerrillero or prisoner, returned very late in the war, so much had happened, and on a global scale, to dim the memory of its opening months. Victory was in the air, and the men of Squadron 3 had been part of one of the worst defeats in American history, which people preferred not to think about. So the men were largely forgotten, having disappeared as suddenly and completely as if all had perished. No word of them reached their families for so long a time that many were written off; officially listed as missing, it was believed by grieving parents, brothers, sisters, that they were never going to come home.

But some of them did, 54 men out of the 71 who had been left behind. They came home one or two at time, occasionally in a small group, some of them, the ones from the camps, in shock as it was called then, post-traumatic stress disorder, with its sudden flashbacks and relentless nightmares. Whether guerrillero or prisoner of war, most preferred not to talk about their experiences except in the most general way, sensing, correctly, that no one who hadn't been through what they had been through could bridge the chasm that had opened between them and the ordinary and mundane. As has been said, though, Time is a gentleman, and as the years passed they learned to live with the nightmares. Almost all of them prospered, and indeed, what they had experienced became a special part of their past, having fought the war in a special way, with a different kind of valor, and having survived the brutal aftermath of the surrender with honor. The nation owes these men a debt it can never repay.

Notes

Chapter 1

The aerial view of Corregidor comes from personal observation. While in the Philippines doing research I flew over the island in a light plane. The prewar description of the island and the starkly contrasting scene in March 1942 come from Steve Mellnik's *Philippine Diary, 1939–1945* and from several other officers who served on Corregidor, whose accounts can be found in James H. Belote and William M. Belote's *Corregidor, The Saga of a Fortress*. The scenes with John Bulkeley and the 41 boat at Sisiman Cove and Corregidor are related by Bulkeley in William White's *They Were Expendable* and in Bulkeley's later oral history, housed at the Dwight D. Eisenhower Library in Abilene, Kansas, with additional details coming from Iliff Richardson's account of his experiences in the Philippines, recorded in an unpublished 152-page typescript. The meeting between Bulkeley and MacArthur can be found in White, Bulkeley's oral history, and MacArthur's *Reminiscences*, which also contains an account of the General's departure from Corregidor, also described in White, Bulkeley's oral history, and Sidney Huff's *My Fifteen Years With MacArthur*, both a memoir and an informal biography of his boss. Huff was MacArthur's aide and was unusually close to the General.

Chapter 2

Bulkeley's early life and his experiences at the U.S. Naval Academy are related in detail in William Breuer's biography of Bulkeley, *Sea Wolf*, which he based almost entirely on interviews with his subject. Bulkeley's daughter, Joan Bulkeley Stade, has much to say about him in her book, *Twelve Handkerchiefs*. Additional details and insights into his character can be found in Bulkeley's oral history and among his collected papers in the Eisenhower Library.

Chapter 3

In this and all the chapters that follow in which these men appear, the information about them prior to their naval service comes from surviving family members and to a small extent from their military service records.

Chapter 4

The development of the motor torpedo boat and the story of its acceptance and deployment by the U.S. Navy is discussed in detail in three exhaustive studies: "Motor Torpedo Boats: A Technical Study," by Gordon Adamson and Douglas Van Patten, in *U.S. Naval Institute Proceedings*, July 1940; "The Motor Torpedo Boat—Past, Present and Future History, Development, Employment and Tactics," by W. S. Humphrey and W. C. Sprecht; and "An Administrative History of PTs in World War II," by Frank Tredinnick and Harrison Bennett. Charles Edison's dealings with Henry Sutphen and Franklin Roosevelt is explored in John Venable's *Out of the Shadow: The Story of Charles Edison* and in Kenneth Davis's *FDR: Into the Storm.* Bulkeley's oral history and the interviews in *Sea Wolf* provide additional details.

Chapter 5

When it comes to Douglas MacArthur, there appears to be no middle ground. What has been written about him by those who knew him or in some way had come in contact with him is either adulatory or venomous, though the accounts of his severest critics are often tinged with spite. All of the following were consulted and from them I tried to find the man, elusive but certainly human:

Robert Bullard's *Personalities and Reminiscences of the War*, Robert Considine's *MacArthur the Magnificent*, William Ganoe's *MacArthur Close-Up*, John Gunther's *The Riddle of MacArthur*, James Harbord's *The American Army in France, 1917–1919* and his *Leaves from a War Diary*, John Hersey's *Men on Bataan*, Sidney Huff's *My Fifteen Years with General MacArthur*, Frazier Hunt's *The Untold Story of Douglas MacArthur*, Allison Ind's *Bataan: The Judgment Seat*, Clark Lee and William Henschel's *Douglas MacArthur*, George Kenney's *The MacArthur I Know*, Francis Sayre's *Glad Adventure*, Manuel Quezon's *The Good Fight*, Carlos Romulo's *I Saw the Fall of the Philippines*, Courtney Whitney's *MacArthur: His Rendezvous With History*, Charles Willougby and John Chamberlain, *MacArthur, 1941–1951.* Here D. Clayton James's three-volume biography, *The Years of MacArthur*, is an exception in that it is a secondary source, but it contains numerous quotes from primary material and in that way proved to be invaluable.

The General's biographer quoted in this chapter is William Manchester. The passage describing Claire Booth Luce's profile of MacArthur in *Life* includes a direct quote from the profile.

Chapter 6

Ron 3's activities after the squadron's arrival in the Philippines and before the outbreak of war are described in White, Bulkeley's oral history and the interviews in *Sea Wolf*, "Narrative of Rear Admiral F. W. Rockwell," and in the Richardson manuscript. This remarkable account, written by Iliff Richardson while he was still in the Philippines and on the run, survives as a tattered, weather-stained collection of typed pages at the National Museum of the Pacific War in Fredericksburg, Texas, and contains a wealth of firsthand observations and detail about the squadron and many of the men in it. An account of the meeting between John Bulkeley and Douglas MacArthur can be found in Bulkeley's oral history and MacArthur's *Reminiscences*, but the observations about their respective characters are my own and are based on the sources previously mentioned.

Chapter 7

The sources for this chapter are the same as those cited for Chapter 6 but also include Walter D. Edmonds's *They Fought With What They Had*, which contains a detailed account of the attack on Clark Field based on interviews with the participants that were conducted while their memories were still fresh. Also consulted were the firsthand accounts contained in William Bartsch's *Doomed at the Start* and William White's *Queens Die Proudly*.

Chapter 8

The account of the bombing of Cavite and the actions of the PT boats is based on White's *They Were Expendable*, the Richardson manuscript, the 16th Naval District war diary, Narrative of Rear Admiral F. W. Rockwell, MTB Squadron action report of December 10, 1942, and comments made by Admiral Rockwell outside of his official narrative that appeared in a *New York Times* article on December 15, 1941, "Admiral at Cavite Narrowly Escapes Bomb; Filipino at

His Side in Shelter Ditch is Killed." Rockwell had his headquarters at Cavite and was there during the bombing and its aftermath, when he personally directed the rescue work and the futile efforts to contain the fires.

Chapter 9

The scenes of the sinking of the *Corregidor* and the subsequent rescue work are based on the Richardson manuscript, the accounts given by Bulkeley and several other PT men in White's *They Were Expendable*, Bulkeley's oral history, "Sinking of the S.S. *Corregidor*" in PT Boats Inc. *Knights of the Sea*, and "Narrative by William F. Konko, World War Two Interviews."

Chapter 10

The most detailed, informative, and scholarly history of the war in the Philippines as it was fought between December and May 1942 is Louis Morton's *The Fall of the Philippines*, based on a wealth of primary documents. For the view of MacArthur and the scene on the *Don Esteban* the main sources are MacArthur's *Reminiscences*, Sidney Huff's memoir, and Clark Lee's *They Call It Pacific*, a journalist's firsthand account of his time in the Philippines.

Chapter 11

The Richardson manuscript, White, Bulkeley's oral history, and Henry Brantingham's memoir *Fire and Ice* all describe the incident. There is also Brantingham's detailed account in "Report of Circumstances of Grounding on a Coral Reef off Luzon during Night Action," his official report.

Chapter 12

George Cox and Tony Akers give detailed accounts of their adventures in White's *They Were Expendable*. Additional details come from "Narrative by Ensign D. L. Glover, Chief E. H. Offrett & Chief F. J. Napolillo: Philippine Experiences, World War II Interviews" in the National Archives.

This account by three members of the squadron rivals the Richardson manuscript in detail and insight. For the fall of Manila and the Santo Tomas internment camp, two memoirs were especially valuable: Margaret Sams's *Forbidden Family* and Shelley Smith Mydans's *Open City*.

Chapter 13

For the account of the fighting, Morton's *Fall of the Philippines*, Donald Young's *The Battle of Bataan*, and John Whitman's *The Last Ditch*, all based on extensively quoted firsthand sources, provided much of the detail. The scenes involving MacArthur are based on his *Reminiscences*, Sidney Huff's memoir, and the MacArthur papers at the MacArthur Memorial Bureau of Archives in Norfolk, Virginia, which contain radiograms, cables, correspondence, memoranda, operation orders, plans, and reports, all donated by the General and his key aides. Squadron 3's travails were recorded in detail by Iliff Richardson with additional information coming from Brantingham's memoir and the accounts of Bulkeley, Kelly, and some of the other officers in White's *They Were Expendable*, and the Glover, Offret & Napolillo narrative.

Chapter 14

The encounter between Rockwell and Bulkeley that opens the chapter is based on Rockwell's "Narrative of Naval Activities in Luzon Area, December 1, 1941 to March 9, 1942," as well as his "Supplement of Narrative for December 1 to March 9, 1942" (in four volumes), along with White, Breuer, Smith, and Bulkeley's oral history.

The sources detailing the separate fates of PT 34 and PT 31 are numerous and more often than not contradictory, and judicious decisions had to be made in presenting the account. White, Breuer, and Bulkeley's oral history were helpful, as well as the Richardson manuscript, Brantingham's memoir, and the Glover, Offrett, & Napolillo narrative.

Chapter 15

The story of DeLong and his men is based on DeLong's official report, "CO PT-31, Report of Circumstances of Loss of this Boat," January 23, 1942 (in which the young boat captain went into great detail, as if attempting to justify his actions, which were in no way derogatory and in many ways commendable), and an interview of James Culp recorded after the war and quoted in George Smith's *MacArthur's Escape*.

Contributing to the story were comments made later by DeLong, Culp, and some of the other men to Richardson and Brantingham and recorded in the Richardson manuscript and Brantingham's memoir, and a postwar interview with DeLong quoted in Smith.

Chapter 16

The scene with Bulkeley and Rockwell is based on Rockwell's "Narrative of Naval Activities" and the Supplement mentioned above. The newspaper headlines are taken directly from those editions. Here and in future chapters the reports of Japanese losses (or the lack of them) are based on "Japanese Naval and Merchant Shipping Losses During World War II by All Causes," published in Washington D.C. by the Government Printing Office in 1947, the result of an extensive study of Japanese records captured after the war. The account of the fighting on land is based on Morton and Young. The poem is from Henry Lee's *Nothing But Praise*, a small book of his poems and letters, passionate and deeply moving.

Chapter 17

The Richardson manuscript records the incident in great detail, including the emotions of those involved, in which Richardson always seems to have the most interest. Additional details come from White, Bulkeley, the Glover, Offrett, & Napolillo narrative, and the official report in the 16th Naval District war diary.

Chapter 18

The account of the fighting on Bataan is based on Morton, Young, and Jonathan Wainwright's *General Wainwright's Story.* The material on General Homma comes from interviews of Japanese officers conducted by historian John Toland for his book *But Not in Shame*. Bulkeley, Brantingham and Richardson all have something to say about the USS *Canopus*. The account of PT 32's night action was recorded by Schumacher in his "Report of Attack of PT 32 on Enemy Cruiser-Type Surface Ship off Subic Bay," February 3, 1943. Richardson also contributes details from what was told to him by Schumacher, DeLong and some of the men on the 32. Actual Japanese losses are recorded in the previously mentioned "Japanese Naval and Merchant Shipping Losses."

Chapter 19

Much of what transpired between MacArthur and Washington can be found among the cables and radiograms in the MacArthur archives in Norfolk, Virginia. James's *The Years of MacArthur* contains much firsthand information, including the account presented here by Malcolm Champlin. The deteriorating condition of Squadron 3 is recorded in the 16th Naval District war diary and commented on in detail by Richardson and Brantingham in their accounts and to a lesser extent by Bulkeley and Kelly in White's *They Were Expendable*. Juanita Redmond's memoir, *I Served on Bataan*, was useful. Bulkeley's plan for the China trip can be found in White and in Clark Lee's *They Call It Pacific*.

Chapter 20

Marshall's about-face and Roosevelt's agreement that MacArthur should be brought out is well documented in a series of radiograms and memos that passed between the three men. As for whether or not he would come: Hugh Johnson, a West Point classmate of MacArthur's, wrote in his column in the *Toledo Blade* (February 26, 1942) that the General would never obey an order to leave his men. Elaborating on that, J. Monroe Johnson, who had served with MacArthur in France, said that he would ignore any such order unless it came directly from the president. In his diary, we can see Henry Stimson, who worked closely with both Marshall and Roosevelt, worrying about that. FDR's dilemma, and his ultimate decision, can be found in Robert Sherwood's *Roosevelt and Hopkins, An Intimate History*. Sherwood's account was drawn from the cabled messages that passed between Roosevelt, Churchill, and Prime Minister Curtin of Australia. Churchill also touches on the episode in his book, *Their Finest Hour*. MacArthur's reaction to Roosevelt's order was recorded by Clark Lee in his book, *They Call It Pacific*, and also appears in the memoirs of both Sidney Huff and Paul Rogers, and in MacArthur's *Reminiscences*. Letters urging the recall of MacArthur from Corregidor can be found in Box 40 and Box 42 under "Correspondence concerning MacArthur" in the Franklin D. Roosevelt Library. The most reliable source for the staff meeting, during which MacArthur was talked out of disobeying Roosevelt's order, is John Beck's interview with General Richard Marshall, one of MacArthur's two closest advisors in 1942 (the other being Richard Sutherland). For details of MacArthur's arrangements to leave there are the cables and radiograms between George Marshall and MacArthur in the Military Records Division of the National Archives. Carlos Romulo's insight into MacArthur's emotional state can be found in his book, *I Saw the Fall of the Philippines*. The decision to use PT boats for the escape is treated in Sidney Huff's memoir, Charles Willoughby's book, *MacArthur, 1941–1951*, Bulkeley's oral history, White's *They Were Expendable*, John Beck's interview with General Marshall, Romulo's book, and MacArthur's *Reminiscences*, which also contains his rationale in choosing the people who would go with him.

Chapter 21

The planning for the run to Mindanao is documented in two official reports: "Summary of Operations Motor Torpedo Boat Squadron Three" and "Commandant Sixteenth Naval District to CO MTNRON Three, Operation Order, March 10, 1942," both on file with the Department of the Navy, with added details from Sidney's Huff's memoir. The scenes in Sisiman Cove are based on Bulkeley's oral history, Richardson's manuscript, an interview with Robert Kelly conducted by the historian John Beck, Brantingham's *Fire and Ice*, and White's *They Were Expendable*—though it must be noted that these accounts often conflict with each other. The meeting between MacArthur and Wainwright can be found in their memoirs, though neither man remembers it in quite the same way. The account of the final departure comes from White, Bulkeley's oral history, the Richardson manuscript, Huff's memoirs, and a memoir by Paul Rogers, *The Good Years*. Rogers was the only enlisted man among the passengers, chosen by Richard Sutherland because of his superior typing skills. The other accounts differ from Rogers (and from each other), but Rogers is the most detailed and makes the most sense.

Chapters 22 to 24

The run to Mindanao was recounted by five of the naval officers in often conflicting versions, and judicious decisions had to be made as to which version of a particular incident was the most accurate. As if to make things harder for anyone trying to tell the story, both Bulkeley and Robert Kelly, in interviews long afterwards, contradict their own earlier accounts, and both their earlier and later accounts often clash with Iliff Richardson's version, which he began writing not long after arriving on Mindanao. These can be found in White's *They Were Expendable*, Bulkeley's oral history, interviews with Kelly and Bulkeley conducted by historians John Beck and William Breuer, Jack Ryan's interview with Bulkeley ("MacArthur's Closest Call") in the May 27, 1952 issue of *Family Weekly*, and the Richardson manuscript. The accounts of Sidney Huff, LeGrande Diller, Charles Willoughby, Hugh Casey, and Paul Rogers, all passengers, are more consistent. MacArthur offers his version in his *Reminiscences*. Henry Brantingham's *Fire and Ice*, written long afterwards, contains additional details but at times only adds to the confusion. The official report of the escape can be found in "Narrative of Rear Admiral F. W. Rockwell, 1 August 1942." PT men William Konko, John Tuggle, DeWitt Glover, Elwood Offret, and Francis Napolillo all comment on the episode in their narratives, "World War II Interviews," housed in the National Archives.

Chapter 25

All the scenes in this chapter are based on the accounts given by Bulkeley, Kelly, Anthony Akers, and George Cox in White's *They Were Expendable*, the narratives of William Konko, John Tuggle, DeWitt Glover, Elwood Offrett, and Francis Napolillo, the Richardson manuscript, and Brantingham's *Fire and Ice.*

Chapter 26

Bulkeley's oral history and the account he gave to William White in *They Were Expendable* as well as the interviews in *Sea Wolf* provide much of the detail relating to Bulkeley's meeting with MacArthur and his encounter with Quezon. In his various accounts Bulkeley contradicts himself at times but the essence of these two encounters is made perfectly clear, especially in the dialogue that Bulkeley himself provides. Anthony Akers comments on the role of the 35 boat in White's *They Were Expendable.* Manuel Quezon's *The Good Fight* provides additional details.

Chapter 27

Much of what occurs in this chapter comes from the Richardson manuscript, including the shooting incident in Cagayan. During this time Richardson was at the center of events, experiencing firsthand the damage to the 34 and the repairs that had to be undertaken. Bulkeley and Kelly in White's *They Were Expendable* contribute details, as do PT men William Konko, DeWitt Glover, John Tuggle, and Francis Napolillo in their narratives.

Chapter 28

The encounter with the cruiser is described by Richardson in two different accounts: his typed manuscript and the book *American Guerrilla in the Philippines*, written in 1945, and between them he provides a wealth of detail as well as a vivid rendering of emotions, his own and those of several of the men. Kelly also has much to say about the action in White's *They Were Expendable* and in a later interview by the historian William Breuer. The role of the 41 boat in the attack is described by Bulkeley in White and in his oral history, and John Tuggle, who was aboard the 41, also talks about it in his narrative. Adding to the account is Bulkeley's "Report of Night Action with Enemy Surface Ship off Cebu Island by PTs 41 and 34," April 12, 1942.

Chapter 29

This chapter is an extension of the encounter with the cruiser, involving as it does the 34 boat as it returns to Cebu from the night action, and the sources, except for Bulkeley and Tuggle, are the same as for the previous chapter.

Chapter 30

The Richardson manuscript, *American Guerrilla in the Philippines*, Kelly's account in *They Were Expendable*, and Henry Brantingham's memoir *Fire and Ice* provide most of the details for the scenes found here. In his narrative Francis Napolillo, who was also stranded for a time on Leyte, also contributes.

Chapter 31

Bulkeley vividly describes his emotions as he leaves Mindanao in White, his oral history, and in an interview conducted many years later by William Breuer, in which it is clear that the anguish he felt then was not diminished by the passage of time. Kelly relates in detail his arrival on the island and his flight out in *They Were Expendable* and in a later interview with Breuer. The fate of the 32 boat and Schumacher's decision to scuttle her is described in his report, "U.S.S. PT 32—Report of Destruction of," March 15, 1942. Bulkeley's encounter with Schumacher comes from accounts by both men: Bulkeley's "Announces Destruction of PT 32 at Tagauayan Island, P.I. on 13 March 1942 and Requests Investigation of Circumstances," his angry report to the Commander of Allied Naval Forces in the Southwest Pacific, and Schumacher's interview with historian John Beck in 1969, in which Schumacher disputes much of what Bulkeley says.

Chapter 32

Juanita Redmond's *I Served on Bataan* describes the last-minute evacuation of fifty people from Corregidor. She was among the nurses rescued by the two PBY Catalina seaplanes and her account also provides details of what happened to the passengers once they reached Mindanao. DeLong's account was told to William Konko and others upon DeLong's arrival at Lake Lanao. The scenes at the lake, from the arrival of the PBYs to their departure, are from the narratives of William Konko, DeWitt Glover, Francis Napolillo, and John Tuggle.

Chapter 33

The scenes described here are based on the narratives of Konko, DeWitt, Napolillo, and Glover, with the addition of Elwood Offrett's narrative.

Chapter 34

Louis Morton's *The Fall of the Philippines* and John Beck's *MacArthur and Wainwright* both contain vivid firsthand accounts of the fighting on Corregidor and the subsequent surrender. Also useful was Wainwright's *General Wainwright's Story*. The speech at Camp O'Donnell is mentioned in the accounts of a number of prisoners who survived captivity, and a version of it can be found in Donald Knox's Death March, a graphic and ultimately heartbreaking account of the prison camps and the hell ships told in the words of the survivors. The list of prisoners from Squadron 3, both the survivors and those who perished, comes from "POW List for MTB RON 3," the most authoritative source, which can be found online. The Fourth of July parade was witnessed by a large number of unsurrendered Americans who were hiding in the hills, including Chief Elwood Offrett and Wendell Fertig, whose account of it appears in John Keats's *They Fought Alone*.

Chapter 35

The initial wanderings of the fugitive PT sailors and the scenes of guerrilla life on Mindanao are taken from the narratives of William Konko, DeWitt Glover, Francis Napolillo, Elwood Offrett and John Tuggle, all of whom played a major role in Wendell Fertig's organization and describe it in detail. Keats's *They Fought Alone* tells the story of the Mindanao guerrilla, based on the author's extensive interviews of Fertig and Fertig's unpublished 600-page account. Iliff Richardson recounts his days as a guerrilla in *American Guerrilla in the Philippines*.

Sources

Adamson, Gordon and Douglas Van Patten. "Motor Torpedo Boats: A Technical Study. *U.S. Naval Institute Proceedings*. July, 1940.

"Admiral at Cavite Narrowly Escapes Bomb, Filipino in Ditch Next To Him Is Killed." *New York Times*. December 15, 1941.

Bartsch, William. *Doomed at the Start*. Texas A&M University Press, 1992.

Beck, John Jacob. *MacArthur and Wainwright*. Albuquerque, NM: University of New Mexico Press, 1974.

Belote, James H. and William M. Belote. *Corregidor: Saga of a Fortress*. New York: Harper and Row, 1967.

Braly, William C. *The Hard Way Home*. Washington, D.C. Infantry Journal Press, 1947.

Brantingham, Henry. *Fire and Ice*. San Diego, CA: ProMotion Publishing, 1995.

Brantingham, Henry. "Report of Circumstances of Grounding on a Coral Reef off Luzon during Night Action." December 30, 1941.

Brereton, Lewis H. *The Brereton Diaries*. New York: William Morrow and Company, 1946.

Brett, George H. "The MacArthur I Knew." *True*. New York: Fawcett Publications, October, 1947.

Breuer, William. *Sea Wolf*. Novato, CA: Presidio Press, 1998.

Bulkeley, John D. "Announces Destruction of PT 32 at Tagauyan Island, P.I. 13 March 1942 and Requests Investigation of Circumstances." April 23, 1942.

Bulkeley, John D. Personal Papers. Abilene, KS: Dwight D. Eisenhower Library, 1970.

Bulkeley, John D. "Report of Night Action with Enemy Surface Ships off Cebu Island by PTs 41 and 34." April 12, 1942.

Bulkeley, John D. "Report of Operations of PT 41 Night of 24 January 1942." January 26, 1942.

Bulkeley, John D. "Report of Trip to Dumaguete and Lift of President Quezon and Party to Oroquita by PT 41." April 15, 1942.

Bulkeley, John D. "Summary of Operations Motor Torpedo Boat Squadron Three from 7 December 1941 to 10 April 1942." May 21, 1942.

Bulkeley, John D. and Jack Ryan. "MacArthur's Closest Call." *Family Weekly*. May 27, 1962.

Bulkley, Robert J. *At Close Quarters: PT Boats in the United States Navy*. Washington, D.C. United States Government Printing Office, 1962.

Bullard, Robert L. *Personalities and Reminiscences of the War*. Garden City, New York, 1925.

Casey, Huge J. Engineer Memoirs. Washington, D.C.: U.S. Government Printing Office, 1947.

Casey, Huge J. *Engineers of the Southwest Pacific, 1941–1945*. Vol. 1: *Engineers in Theater Operations*. Washington, D.C.: U.S. Government Printing Office, 1947.

Chandler, Alfred (ed.). *The Papers of Dwight David Eisenhower*. Vol. 1: *The War Years*. Baltimore: The Johns Hopkins Press, 1970.

Churchill, Winston S. *Their Finest Hour*. Vol. 2. Boston: Houghton Mifflin Company, 1949.

Considine, Robert. *MacArthur the Magnificent*. Philadelphia: J.B. Lippincott Co., 1942.

Davies, Lawrence E. "Bulkeley Back, Tells of Sinkings." *New York Times*. May 8, 1942.

DeLong, Edward. "Report of Circumstances of Loss of this Boat," January 23, 1942.
Diller, LeGrande. Oral History, in Philippine Diary Project. Wordpress.com.
Edmonds, Walter D. *They Fought With What They Had.* Boston: Little, Brown & Co., 1951.
Eisenhower, Dwight D. *Crusade in Europe.* Garden City, New York: Doubleday, 1948.
Ferrell, Robert H. *The Eisenhower Diaries.* New York: W. W. Norton & Co., 1981.
Ganoe, William A. *MacArthur Close Up.* New York: Generic Publishers, 1962.
Grew, Joseph. *Ten Years in Japan.* New York: Simon & Schuster, 1944.
Gunther, John. *The Riddle of MacArthur.* New York: Harper & Row, 1950.
Haggerty, Edward. *Guerrilla Padre in Mindanao.* New York: Longmans Green, 1946.
Harbord, James. *The American Army in France, 1917–1919.* Boston: Little, Brown & Co., 1936.
Harbord, James. *Leaves from a War Diary.* New York: Kessinger Publishing, 2010.
Hersey, John. *Men on Bataan.* New York: Alfred A. Knopf, 1942.
Hewlett, Frank. "A PT Expendable Shows Up on Leyte." *New York Times.* October 28, 1944.
Huff, Sidney. *My Fifteen Years With General MacArthur.* New York: Paperback Library, 1964.
Humphrey, W. S. and W. C. Sprecht. "The Motor Torpedo Boat—Past, Present and Future History, Development, Employment and Tactics." Box 13, Motor Torpedo Boat Materials, Naval Historical Center. Washington, D.C. Paper delivered in 1943.
Hunt, Frazier. *MacArthur and the War Against Japan.* New York: Charles Scribner's Sons, 1944.
Hunt, Frazier. *The Untold Story of Douglas MacArtthur.* New York: Charles Scibner's Sons, 1952.
"IJN Kuma: Tabular Record of Movement," in Japanese Imperial Navy Page, www.combined fleet.com/kuma_t.htm.
"IJN Minelayer Yaeyama: Tabular Record of Movement," in Imperial Japanese Navy Page, www.combinedfleet.com/Yaeyama_t.htm.
Ind, Allison. *Bataan: The Judgment Seat.* New York: Macmillan Co., 1944.
James, D. Clayton. *The Years of MacArthur.* Vol. 1. Boston: Houghton Mifflin Co., 1970.
"Japanese Destroyers: Tabular Movement Records," in Imperial Japanese Navy Page, www.combinedfleet.com/lancers.htm.
Joint Army-Navy Assessment Committee. *Japanese Naval and Merchant Shipping Losses during World War II by All Causes.* Washington, D.C.: U.S. Government Printing Office, 1947.
Keats, John. *They Fought Alone.* Philadelphia: J.B. Lippincott Co., 1963.
Kelly, Robert. "Report of Attack on Japanese Cruiser off Cebu Island and of Subsequent Loss of PT 34 to Japanese Air Attack while Attempting to Reach Cebu Harbor," n.d.
Kenney, George. *The MacArthur I Know.* New York: Duell, Sloan and Pearce, 1951.
Knox, Donald. *Death March.* New York: Harcourt Brace, 1981.
Lee, Clark. *They Call It Pacific.* New York: Viking Press, 1943.
Lee, Clark and Richard Henschel. *Douglas MacArthur.* New York: Henry Holt & Co., 1952.
Lee, Henry G. *Nothing But Praise.* Culver City, California: Murray and Gee, 1948.
MacArthur, Douglas. Record Groups, in the MacArthur Memorial Bureau of Archives in Norfolk, Virginia.
MacArthur, Douglas. *Reminiscences.* New York: McGraw-Hill, 1964.
MacArthur, Douglas. "Report on National Defense in the Philippines." Manila, 1936.
Manchester, William. *American Caesar.* New York: Little, Brown & Co., 1978.
"Medal of Honor Given Bulkeley." *New York Times.* August 5, 1942.
Mellnick, Steve. *Philippine Diary 1939–1945.* New York: Van Nostrand Reinhold Co., 1969.
Miller, Edward S. *War Plan Orange: The U.S. Strategy to Defeat Japan.* Annapolis, MD.: Naval Institute Press, 1991.
Miller, Ernest B. *Bataan Uncensored.* Long Prairie, Minn.: The Hart Publications, 1949.
Morton, Lewis. *The Fall of the Philippines.* Washington, D.C.: U.S. Government Printing Office, 1953.

"Mosquito Boat Skippers to be Pine for Action." *Chicago Tribune*. September 4, 1942.

"Motor Torpedo Boats: Tactical Orders and Doctrine." Headquarters of the Commander in Chief, United States Fleet. Washington D.C.: U.S. Government Printing Office, 1942.

Muster roll. Motor Torpedo Boat Squadron Three. October, 1941.

Mydans, Shelley. *The Open City*. New York: Doubleday, Doran & Co., 1945.

"Narrative by Ensign D. L. Glover, Chief E. H. Offrett & Chief F. J. Napolillo. Philippine Experiences." World War II Interviews. College Park, MD.: National Archives. Interviews conducted in 1945.

"Narrative by Lieutenant Iliff D. Richardson. Guerrilla Experiences in the Philippine Islands." World War II Interviews. College Park, MD.: National Archives. Interviews conducted in 1945.

"Narrative by William F. Konko, Warrant Electrician, USN. Philippine Guerrillas. World War II Interviews. College Park, MD.: National Archives. Interviews conducted in 1945.

"Navy Hero Opens Relief Fund Drive." *New York Times*. May 15, 1942.

"New PT Boat Leaves the Ways." *New York Times*. May 17, 1942.

"New Yorker Leads Daring Raid on Foe." *New York Times*. January 21, 1942.

Office of Public Relations, U.S. Navy. *Navy Department Communiques 1-300 and Pertinent Press Releases*. Washington, D.C.: U.S. Government Printing Office, 1943.

"POW List for Motor Torpedo Boat Squadron 3." www.west-point.org/family/japanese-pow/MTB-3.htm.

PT Boats, Inc. "Sinking of the S.S. *Corregidor*" in *Knights of the Sea*. Dallas, TX.: Taylor Publishing Co., 1982.

Quezon, Manuel L. *The Good Fight*. New York: D. Appleton-Century Co., 1946.

Rockwell, Rear Admiral F. W. "Narrative of Naval Activities in Luzon Area, December 1, 1941 to March 9, 1942." August 1, 1942.

Rockwell, Rear Admiral F. W. "Operation Order, 10 March 1942." Naval History Division.

Rockwell, Rear Admiral F. W. "Supplement of Narrative for December 1, 1941 to March 9, 1942." (Four Volumes.)

Rogers, Paul. "Correspondence Concerning MacArthur." Franklin D. Roosevelt Library, Hyde Park, New York.

Rogers, Paul. *The Good Years*. New York: Henry Holt & Co., 1956.

Romulo, Carlos P. *I Saw the Fall of the Philippines*. New York: Doubleday, Doran & Co., 1943.

Sackett, Captain Earl, Commanding Officer, USS *Canopus*. "The History of the USS *Canopus*." Washington, D.C.: Office of Naval History, 1946.

Sams, Margaret. *Forbidden Family*. New York: The MacMillan Co., 1946.

Sayre, Francis B. *Glad Adventure*. New York: The Macmillan Co., 1957.

Sayre, Francis B. "War Days on Corregidor." *Life*. April 20, 1942.

Schumacher, Vincent. "U.S.S. PT 32—Report of Destruction of." March 15, 1943.

Sherwood, Robert E. *Roosevelt and Hopkins: An Intimate History*. New York: Harper & Brothers, 1948.

Smith, George. *MacArthur's Escape*. Duluth, MINN. Zenith Press, 2005.

Stade, Joan Bulkeley. *Twelve Handkerchiefs*. Tuscan, AZ.: Patrice Press, 2001.

Stimson, Henry L. Papers and Diary. Washington D.C.: National Archives.

Stimson, Henry L. with McGeorge Bundy. *On Active Service in Peace and War*. New York: Harper & Brothers, 1948.

Toland, John. *But Not in Shame*. New York: Random House, 1961.

"Torpedo Boats Can Knock Out Japs: Bulkeley." *Chicago Tribune*, May 9, 1942.

Tredinnick, Frank and Harrison Bennett. "An Administrative History of PTs in World War II." Washington, D.C.: Office of Naval History, 1946.

John L. Tuggle Collection. Veterans History Project, American Folklife Center, Library of Congress, Washington, D.C.

Undated Manuscript. Iliff Richardson Collection. Nimitz Education and Research Center, National Museum of the Pacific War, Fredericksburg, Texas.

Venable, John. *Out of the Shadow: The Story of Charles Edison*. New York: Harper & Row, 1971.

Wainwright, Jonathan M. *General Wainwright's Story*. New York: Doubleday & Co., 1946.

War Diary, Sixteenth Naval District, December 1, 1941 to May 8, 1942.

Weinstein, Alfred. *Barbed Wire Surgeon*. New York: The Macmillan Co., 1948.

White, W. L. *Queens Die Proudly*. New York: Harcourt Brace & Co., 1943.

White, W. L. *They Were Expendable*. New York: Harcourt Brace & Co., 1942.

Whitman, John. *Bataan: The Last Ditch*. New York: Hippocrene Press, 1990.

Whitney, Courtney. *MacArthur: His Rendezvous With History*. New York: Alfred A. Knopf, 1964.

Willoughby, Charles A. and John Chamberlain. *MacArthur: 1941–1951*. New York: McGraw-Hill Book Co., 1954.

Young, Donald. *The Battle of Bataan*. Jefferson, N.C.: McFarland & Co., 2009.